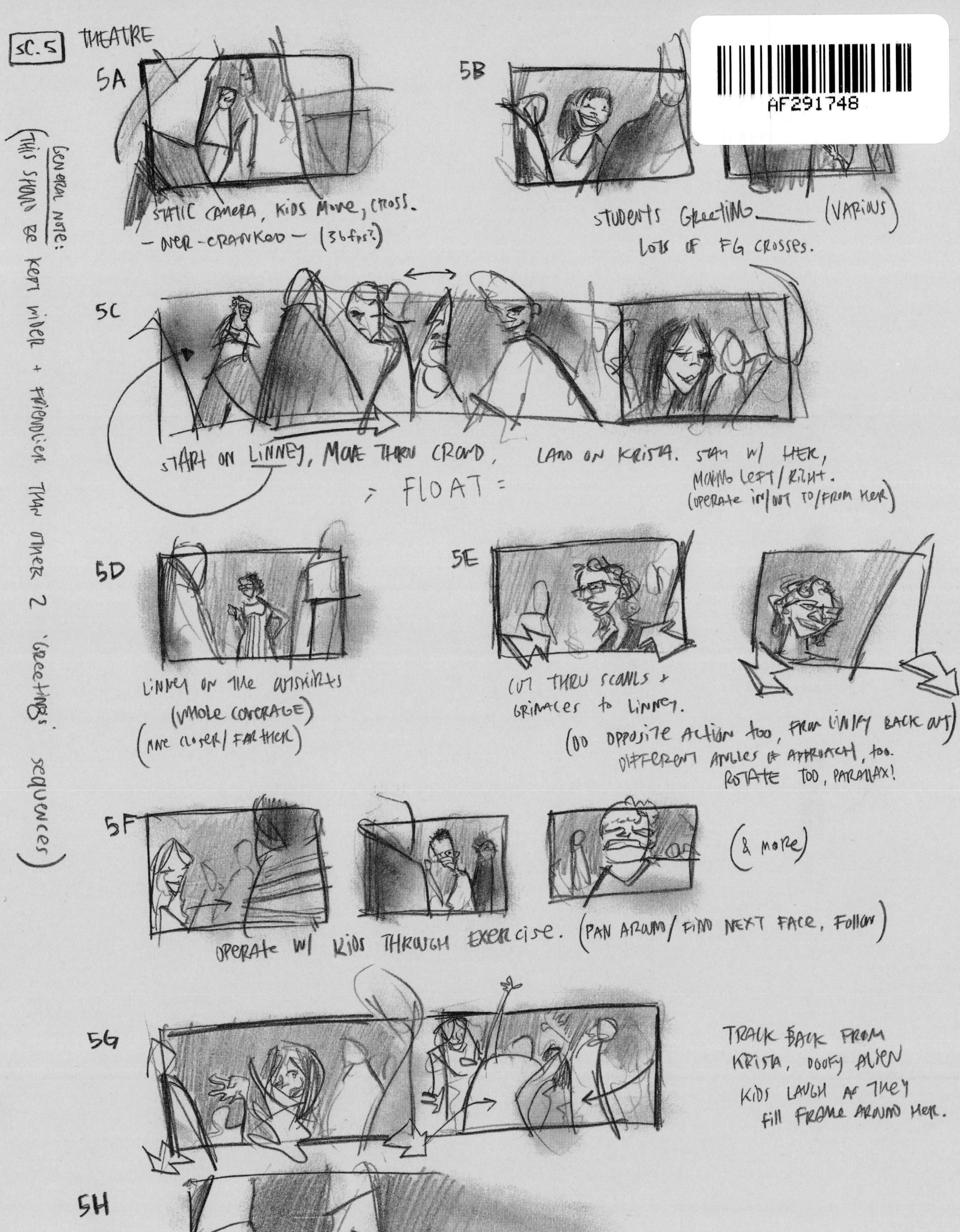
AF291748
SC.5   THEATRE
GENERAL NOTE: (THIS SHOULD BE KEPT WIDER + FRIENDLIER THAN OTHER 2 'GREETING' SEQUENCES)
5A
STATIC CAMERA, KIDS MOVE, CROSS.
- OVER-CRANKED - (36 fps?)
5B
STUDENTS GREETING___ (VARIOUS)
LOTS OF FG CROSSES.
5C
START ON LINNEY, MOVE THRU CROWD,   LAND ON KRISTA. STAY W/ HER,
MOVING LEFT/RIGHT.
(OPERATE IN/OUT TO/FROM HER)
= FLOAT =
5D
LINNEY ON THE OUTSKIRTS
(WHOLE COVERAGE)
(MOVE CLOSER/FARTHER)
5E
CUT THRU SCOWLS +
GRIMACES TO LINNEY.
(DO OPPOSITE ACTION TOO, FROM LINNEY BACK OUT)
DIFFERENT ANGLES & APPROACH, TOO.
ROTATE TOO, PARALLAX!
5F
OPERATE W/ KIDS THROUGH EXERCISE. (PAN AROUND/ FIND NEXT FACE, FOLLOW)
(& MORE)
5G
TRACK BACK FROM
KRISTA, DOOFY ALIEN
KIDS LAUGH AS THEY
FILL FRAME AROUND HER.
5H
over cranked
PAN AWAY FROM BODIES, TO BLACK CURTAINS

OUR
STRANGE
NEW
LAND

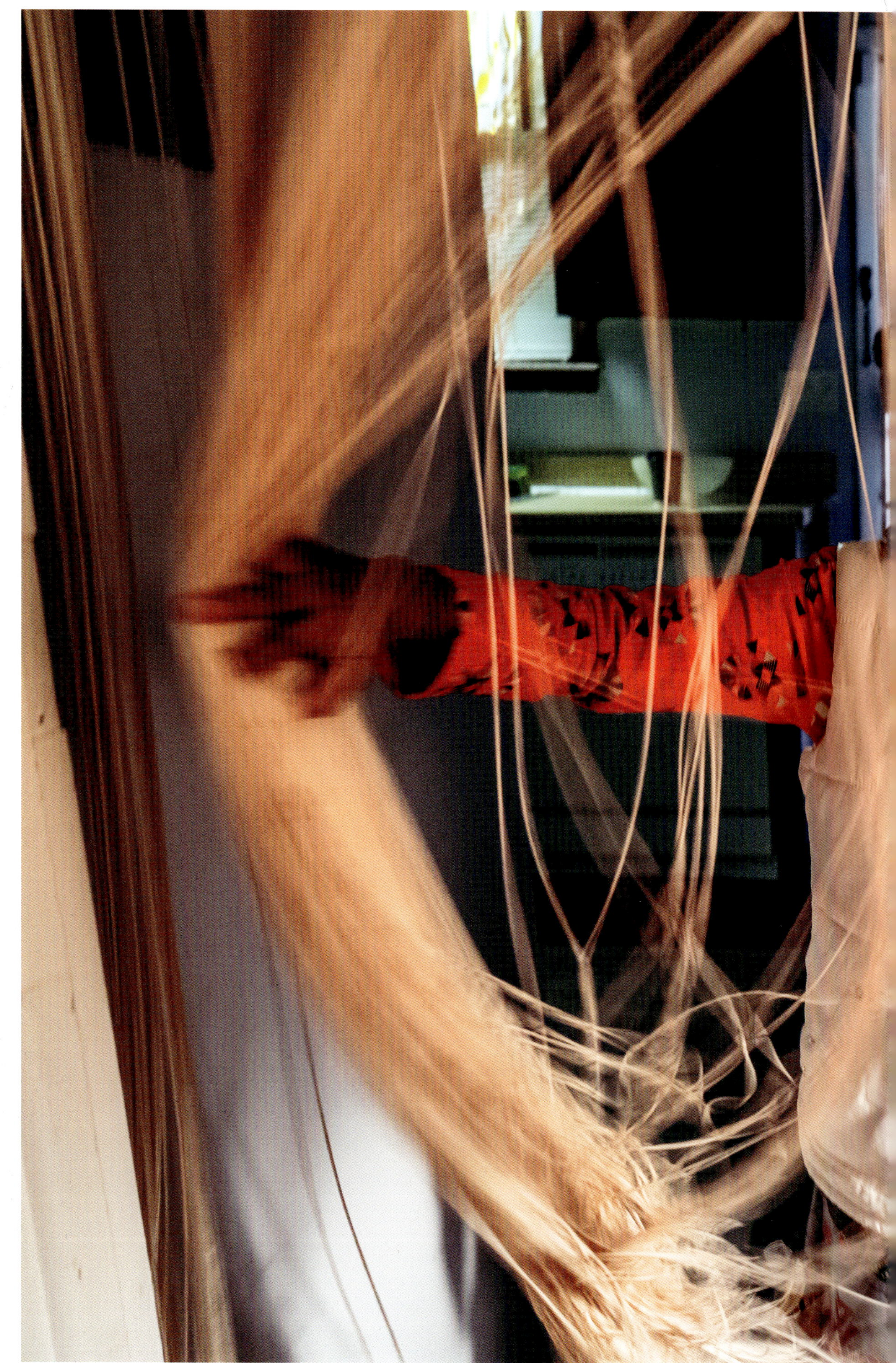

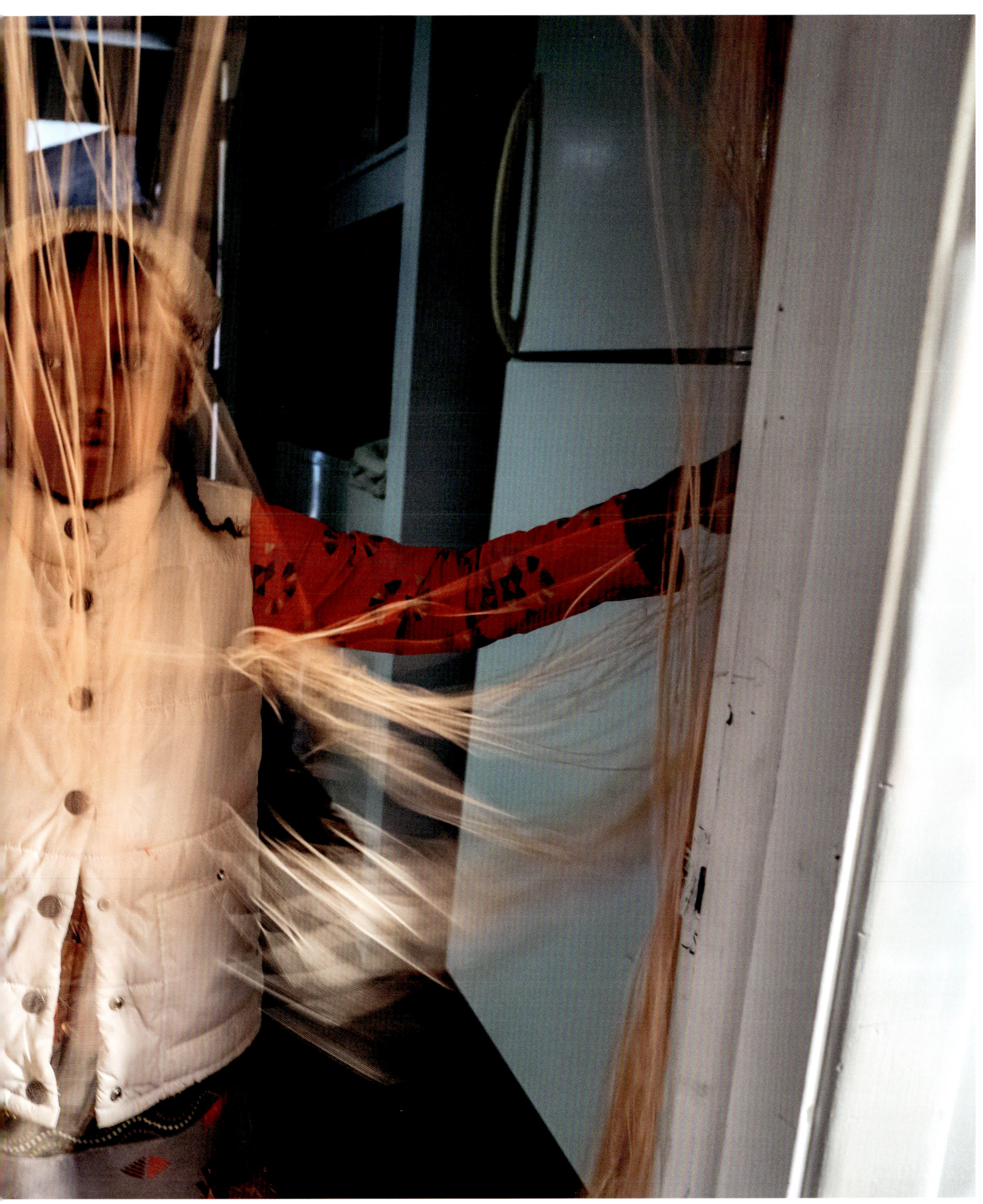

OUR STRANGE NEW LAND

NARRATIVE MOVIE SETS
IN THE AMERICAN SOUTH

PHOTOGRAPHS by ALEX HARRIS

EDITED by ALEX HARRIS & MARGARET SARTOR

ESSAY by RONI NICOLE HENDERSON-DAY

YOFFY PRESS, ATLANTA, GA

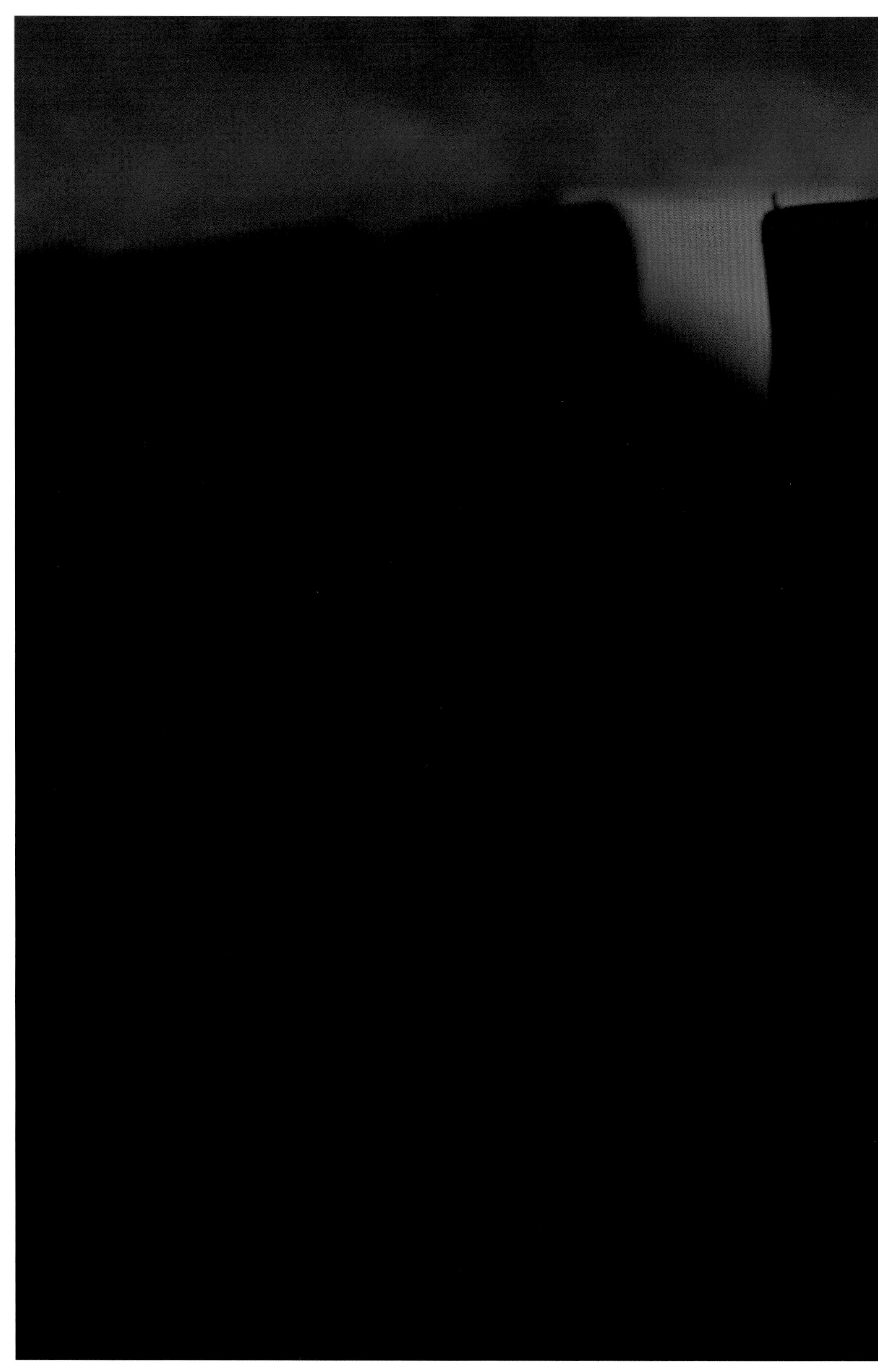

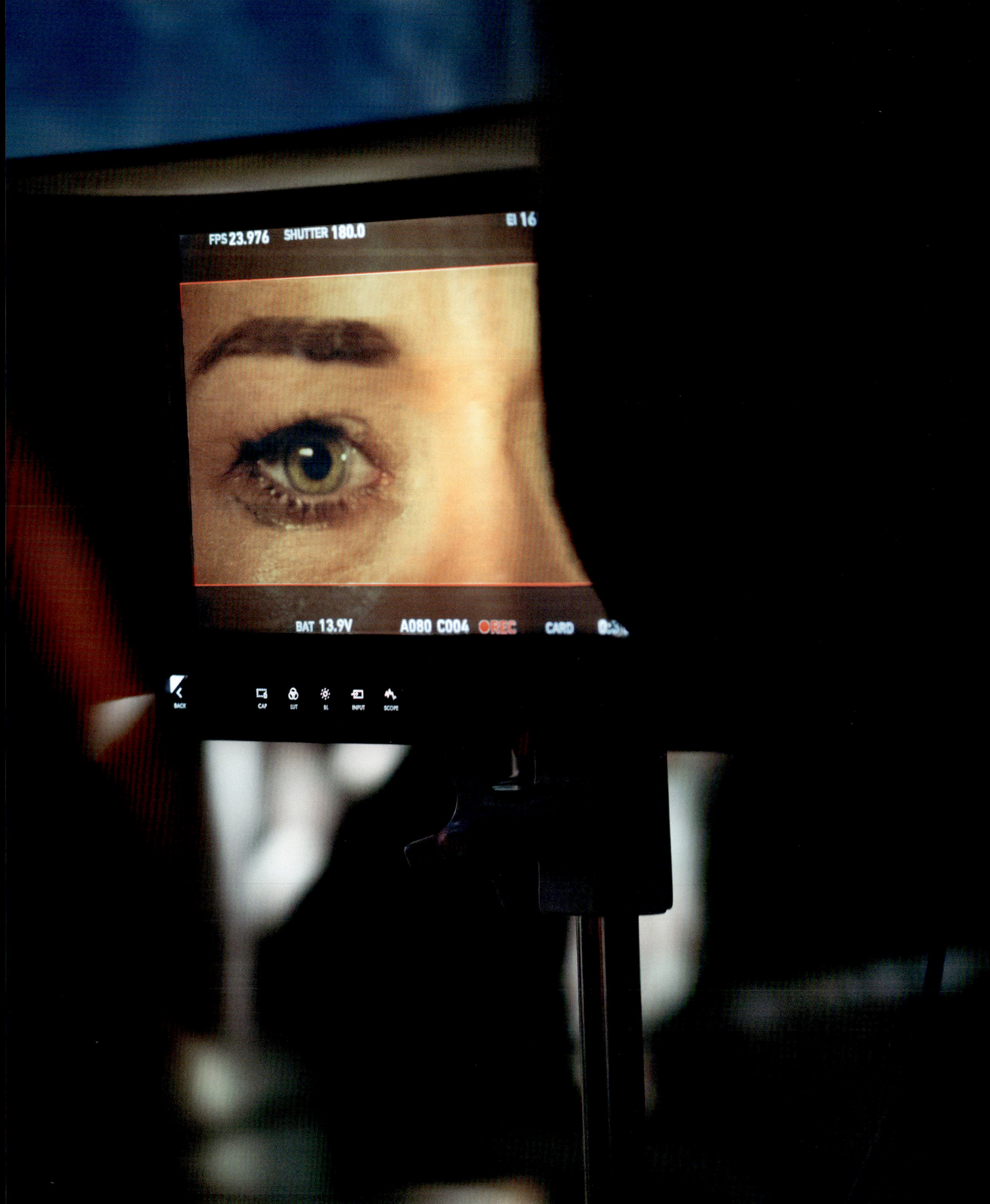

FPS 23.976   SHUTTER 180.0
EI 16
BAT 13.9V   A080 C004   REC   CARD
BACK
CAP
LUT
BL
INPUT
SCOPE

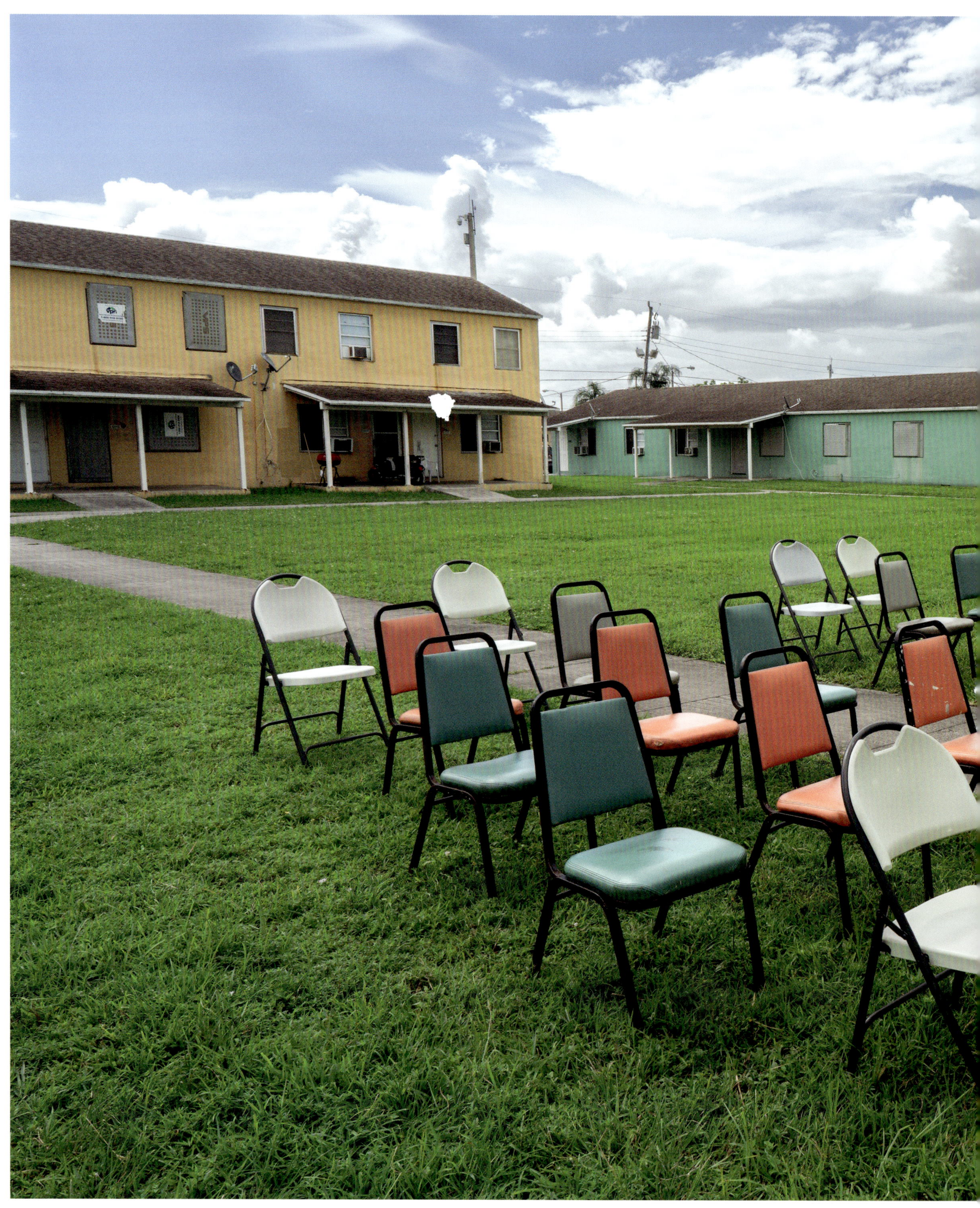

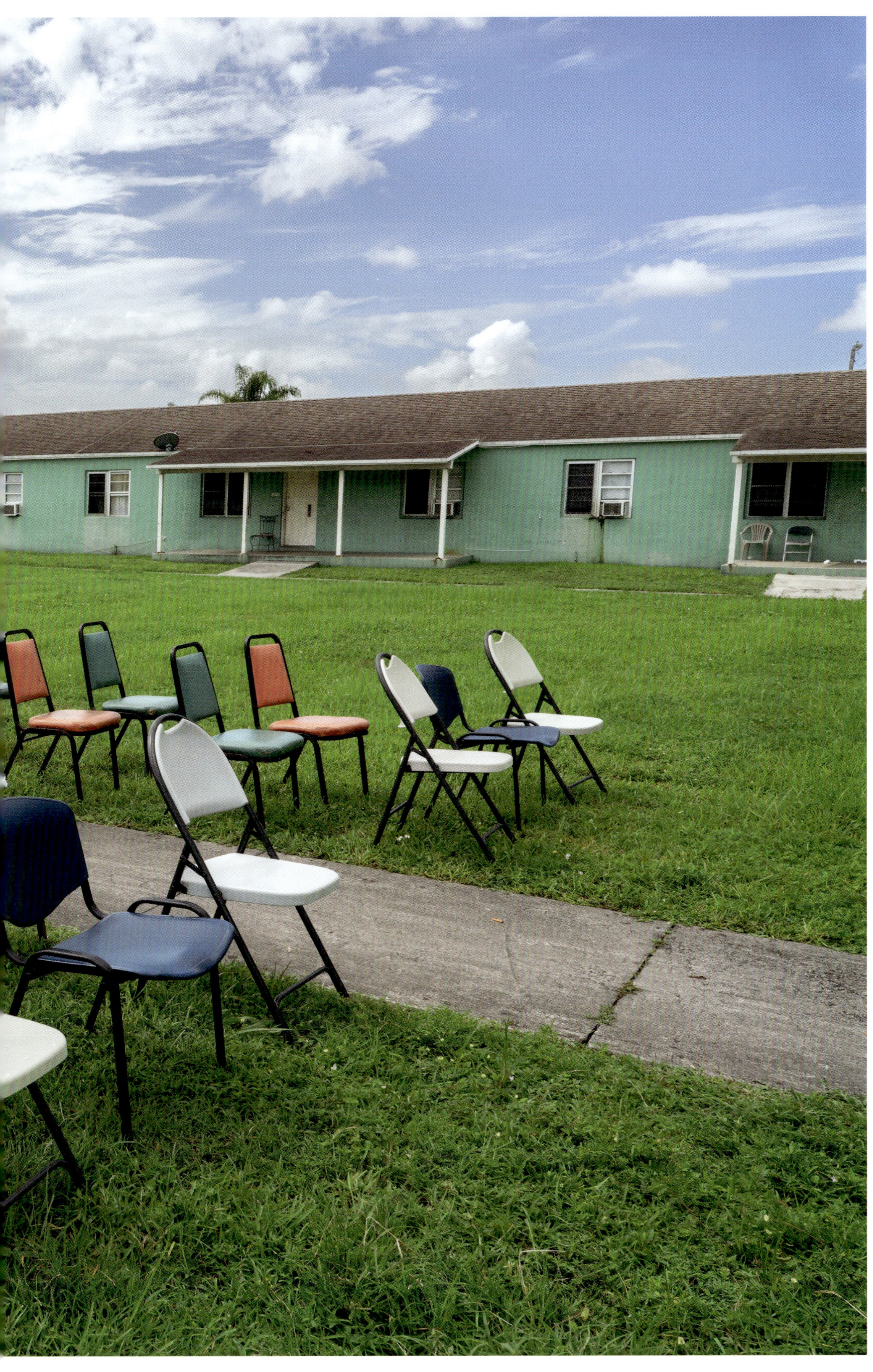

For Will and Eliza,
our movie companions

Every feeling waits upon its gesture. Then when it does come, how unpredictable it turns out to be, after all.

—Eudora Welty

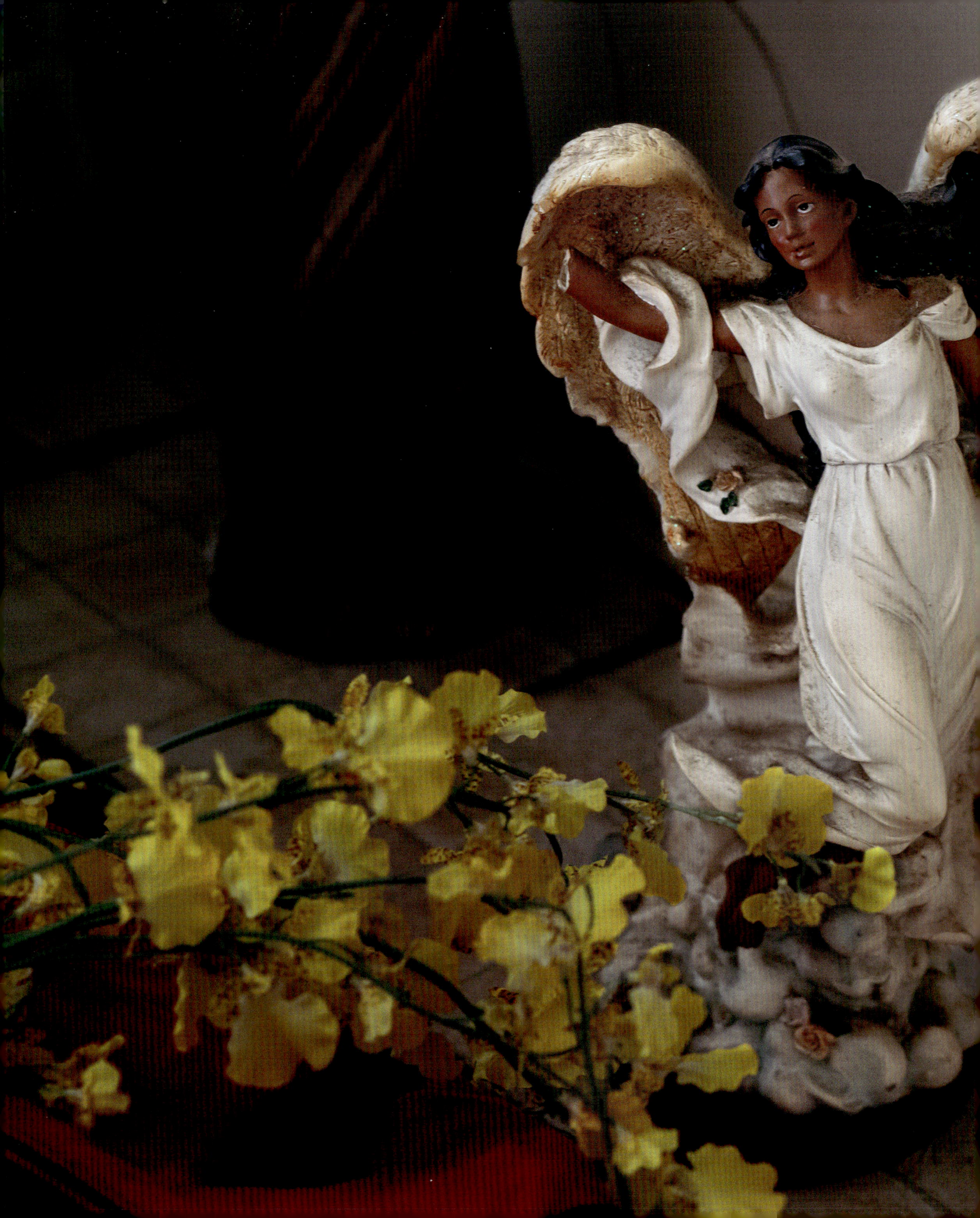

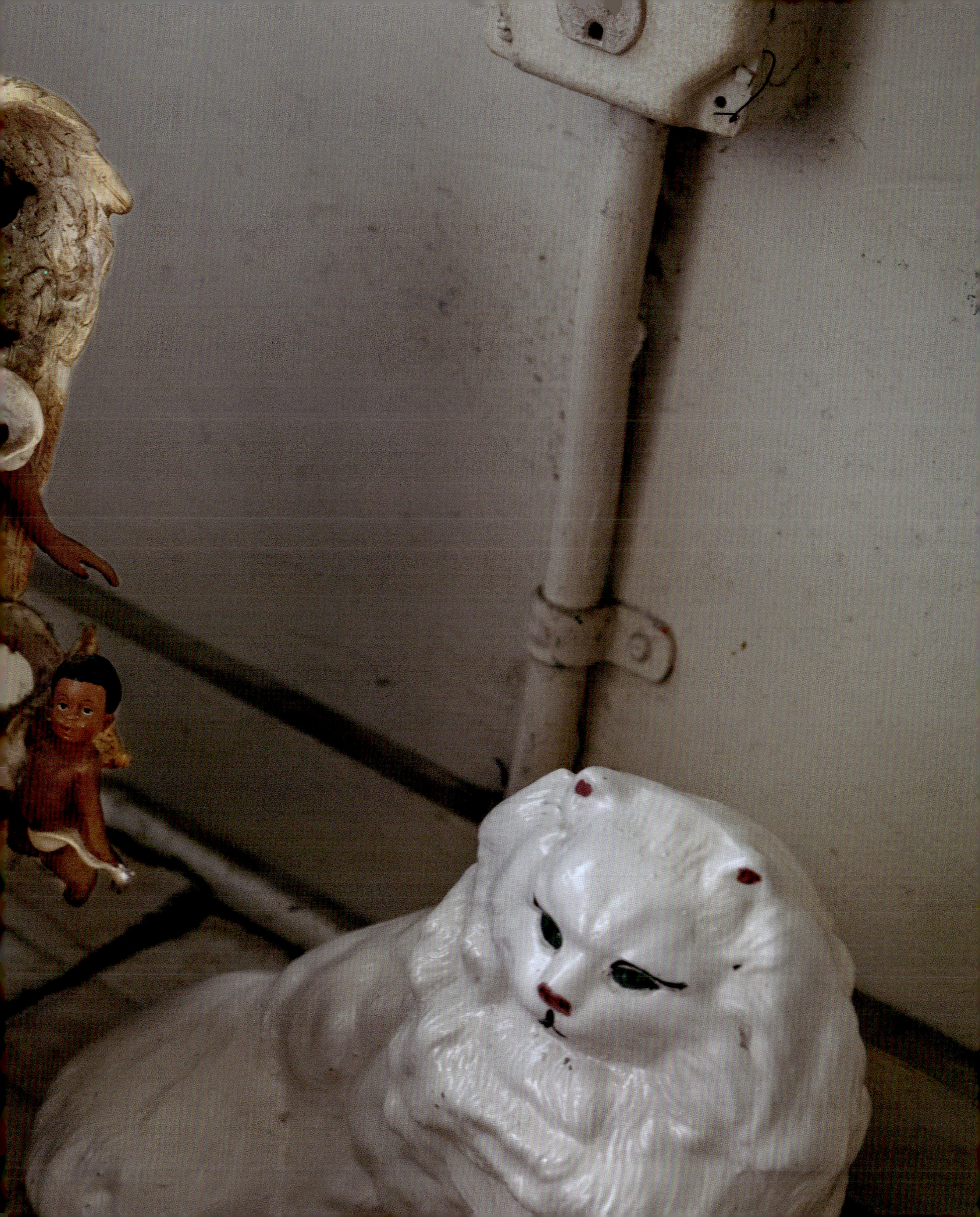

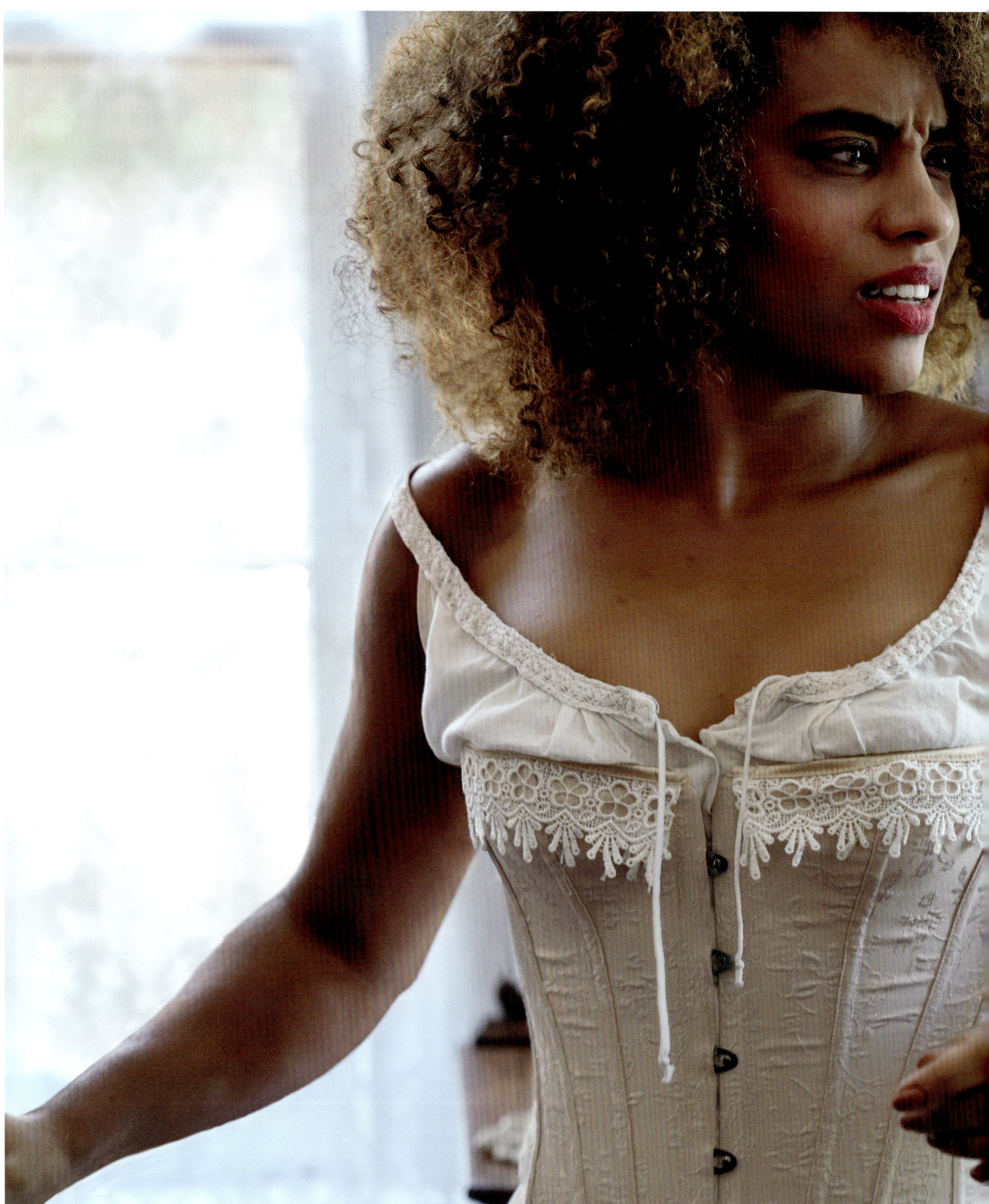

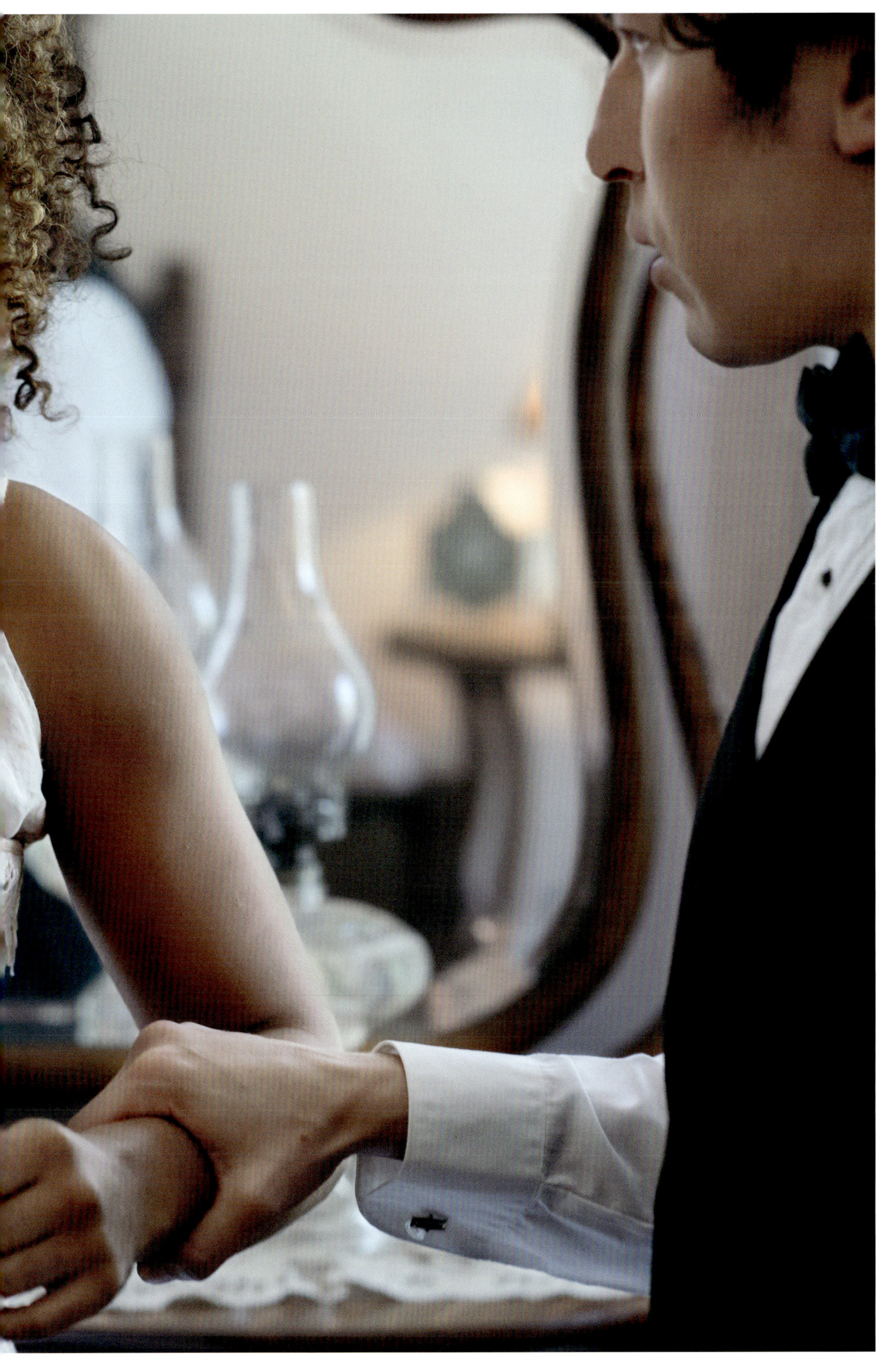

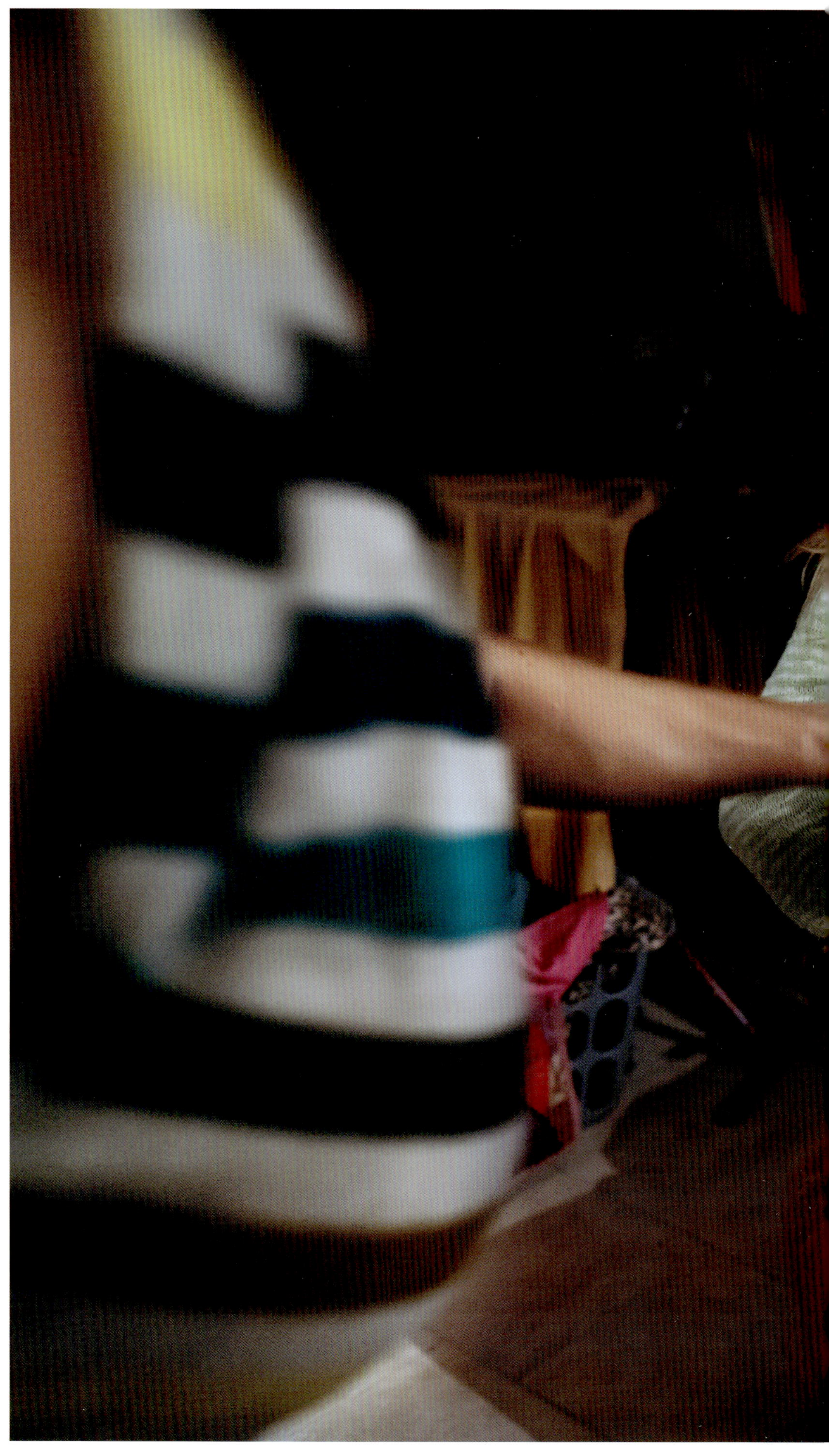

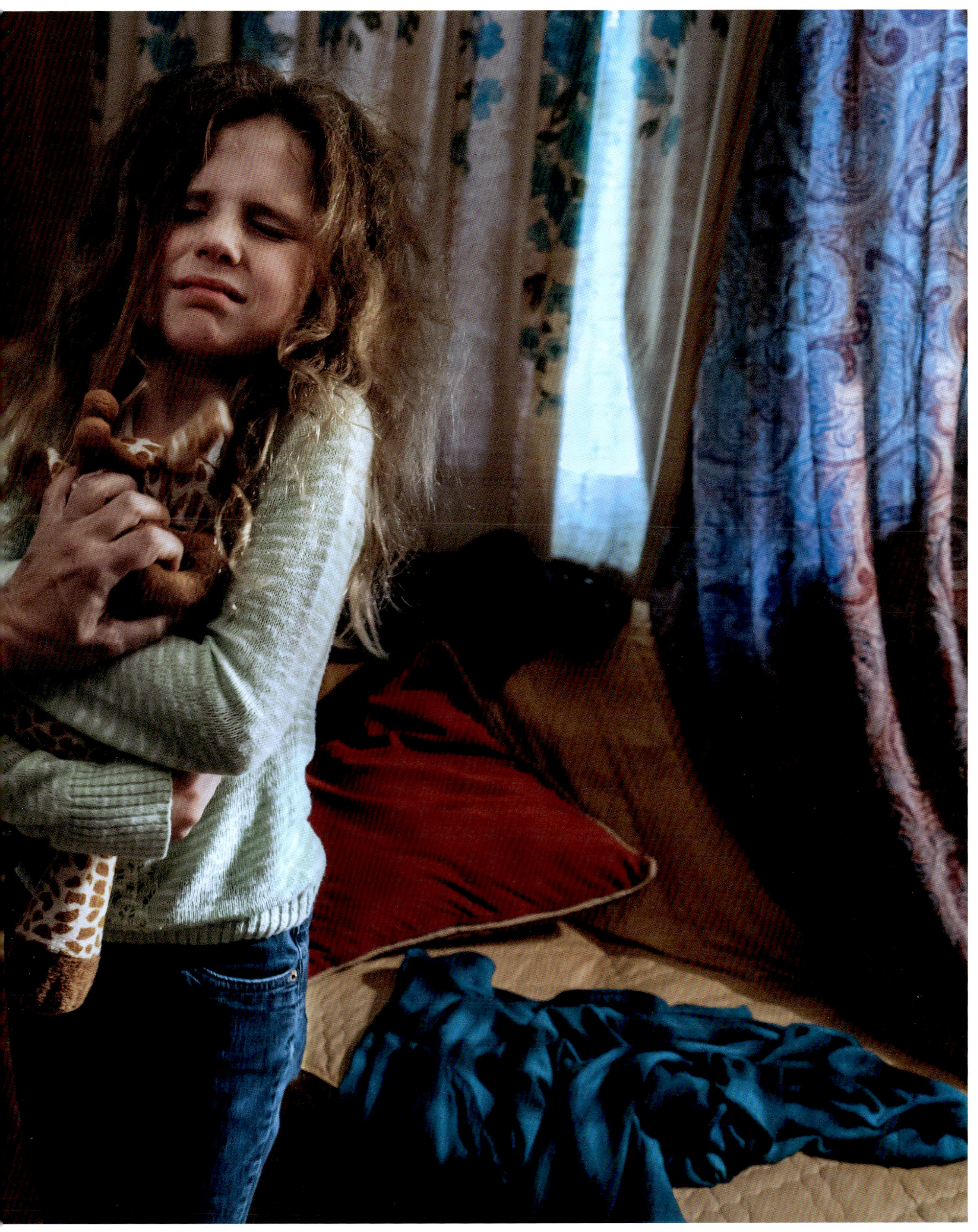

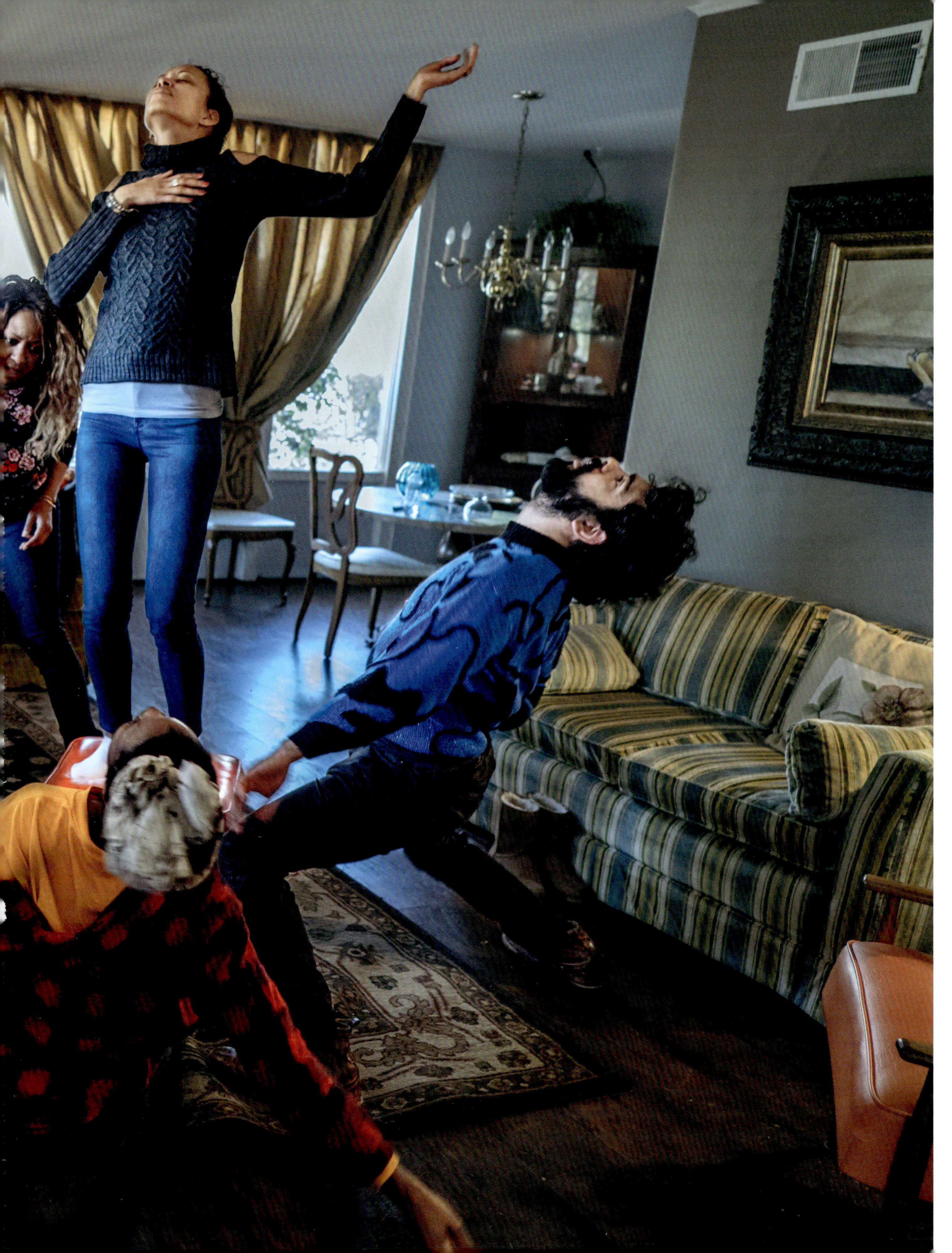

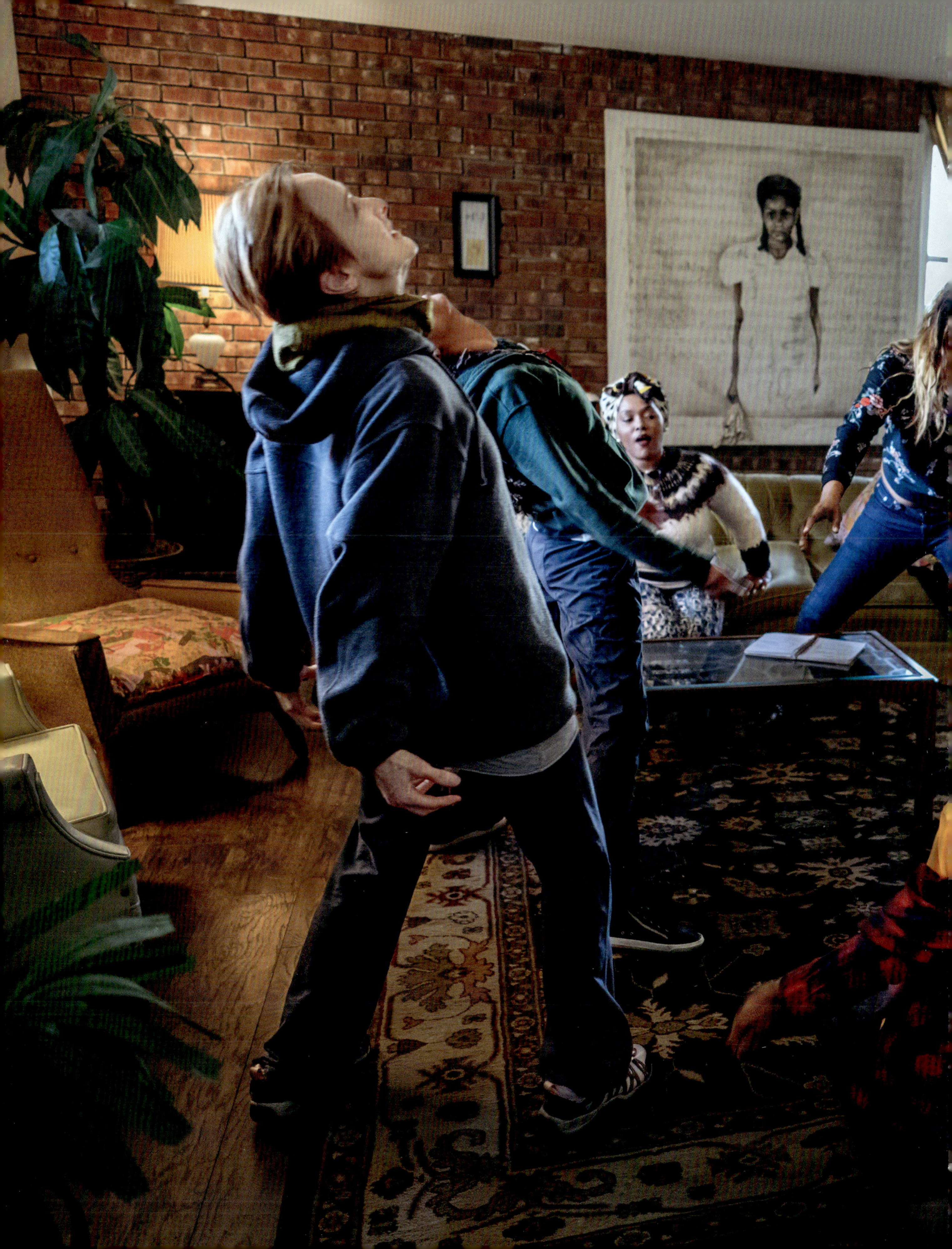

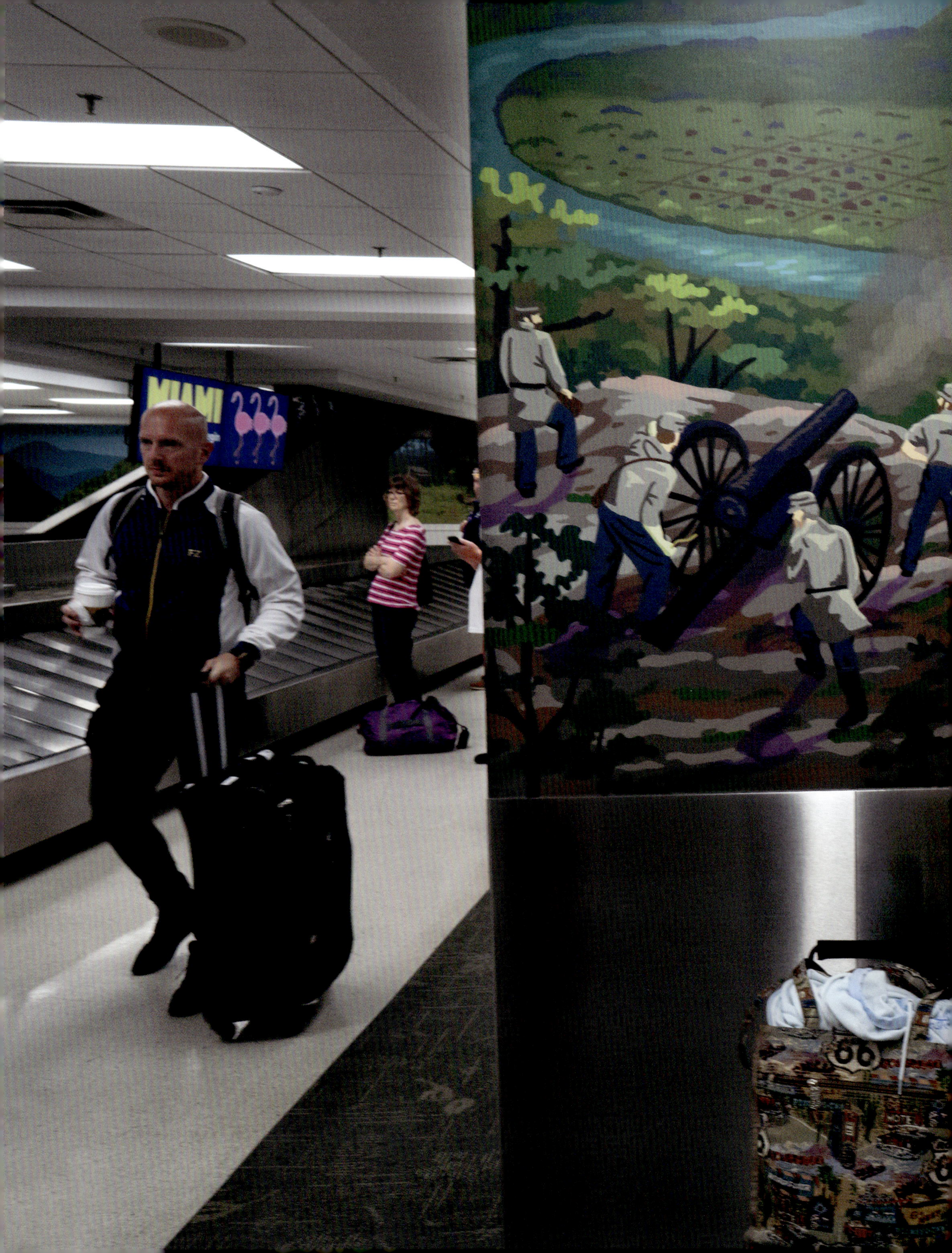

MIAMI

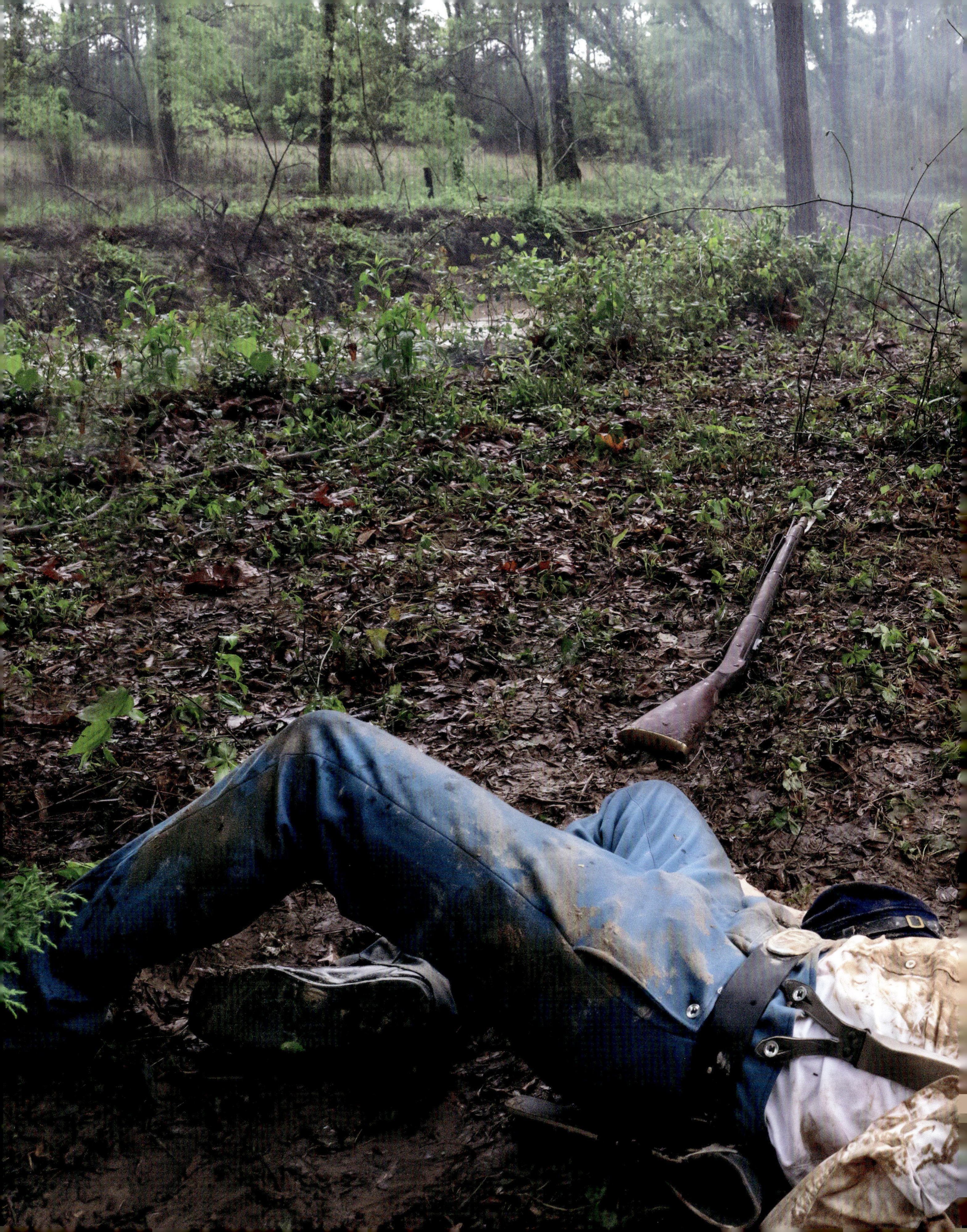

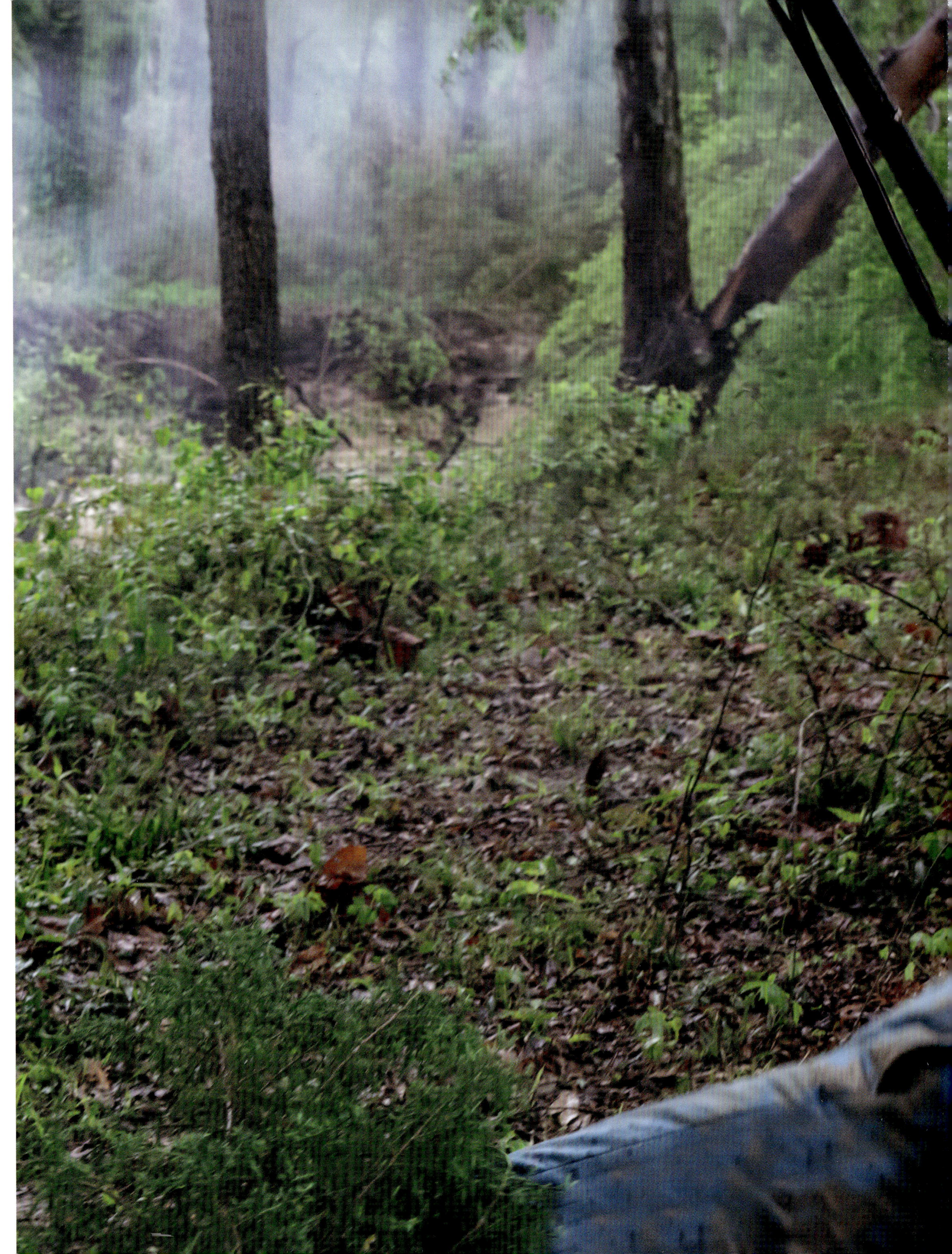

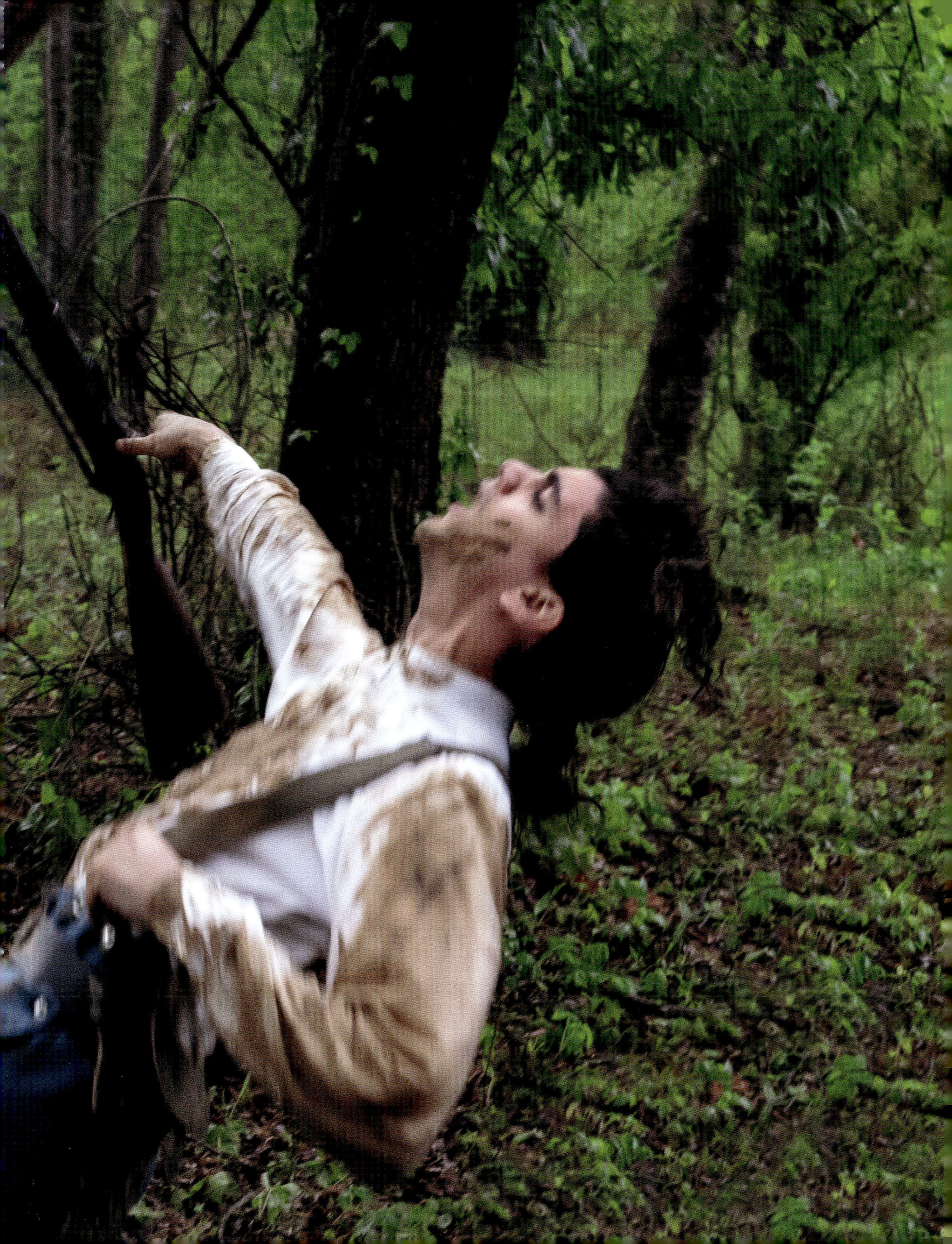

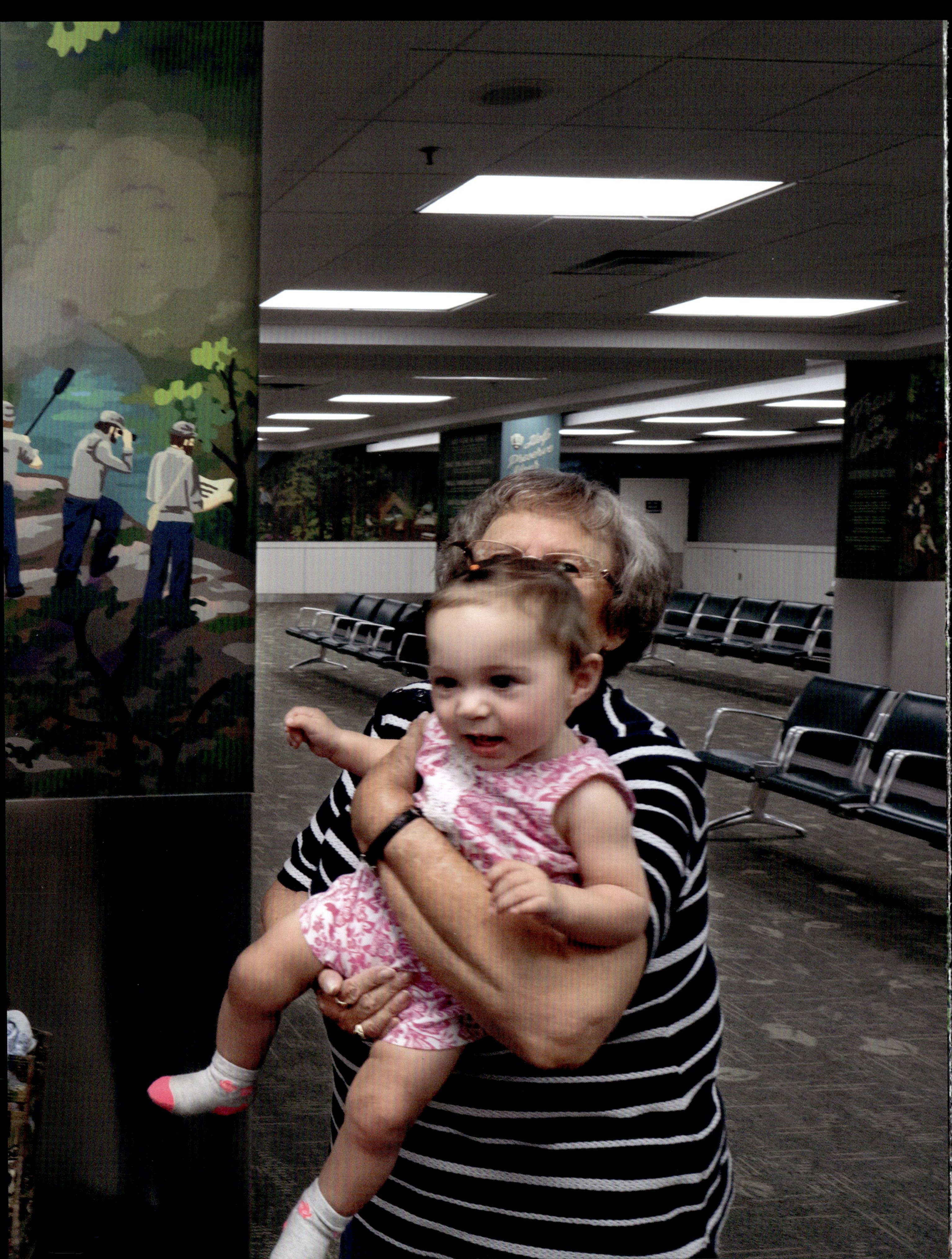

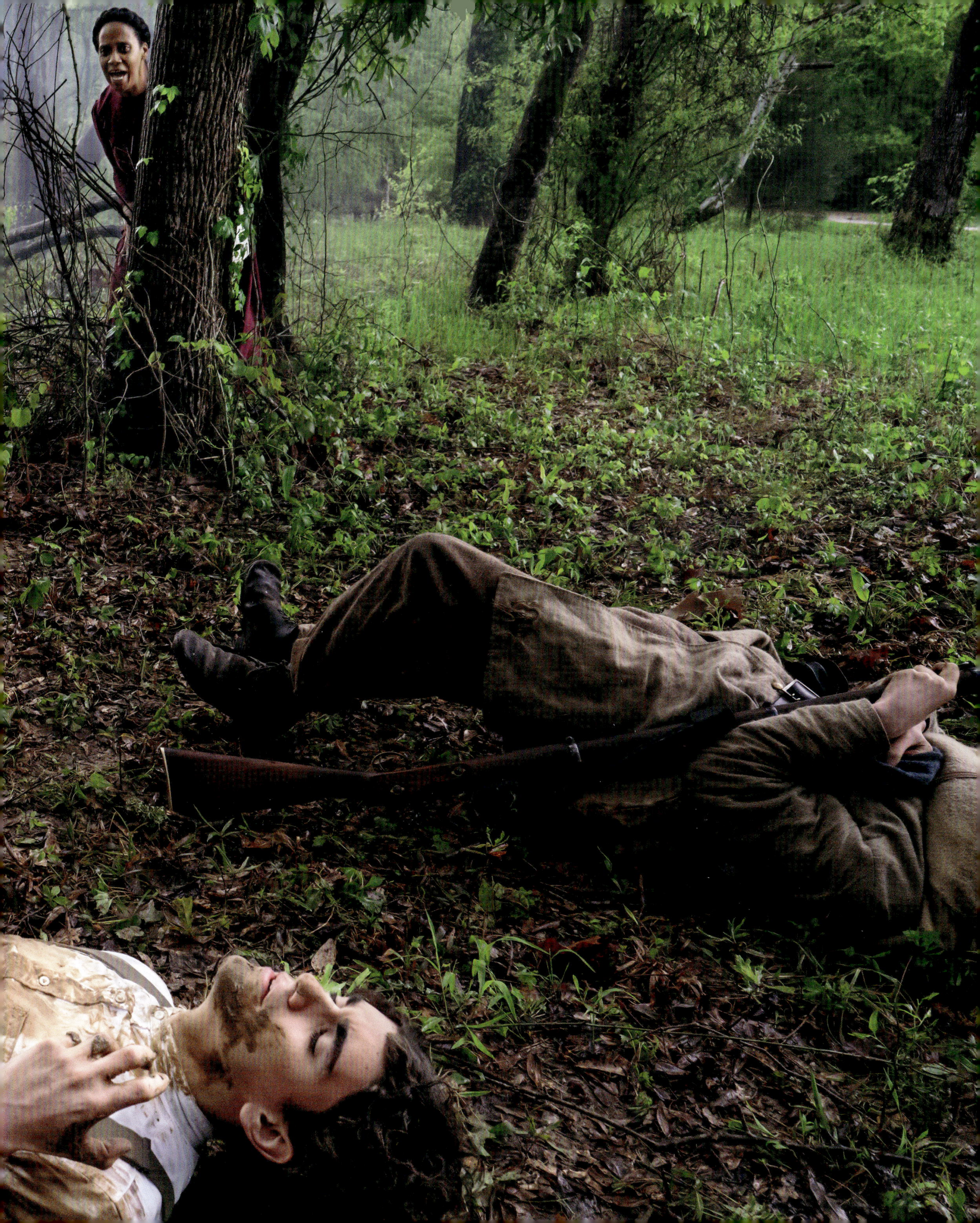

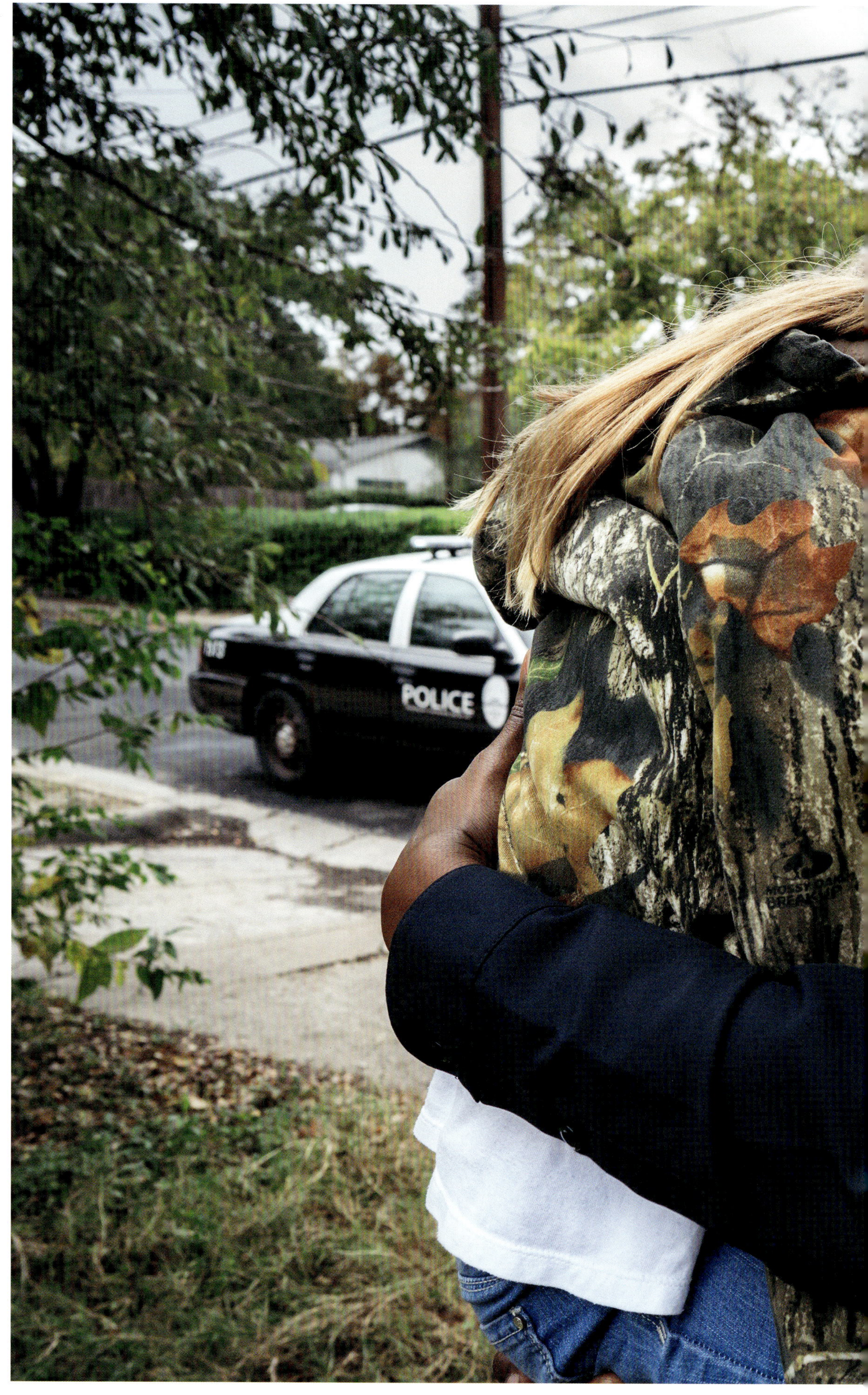

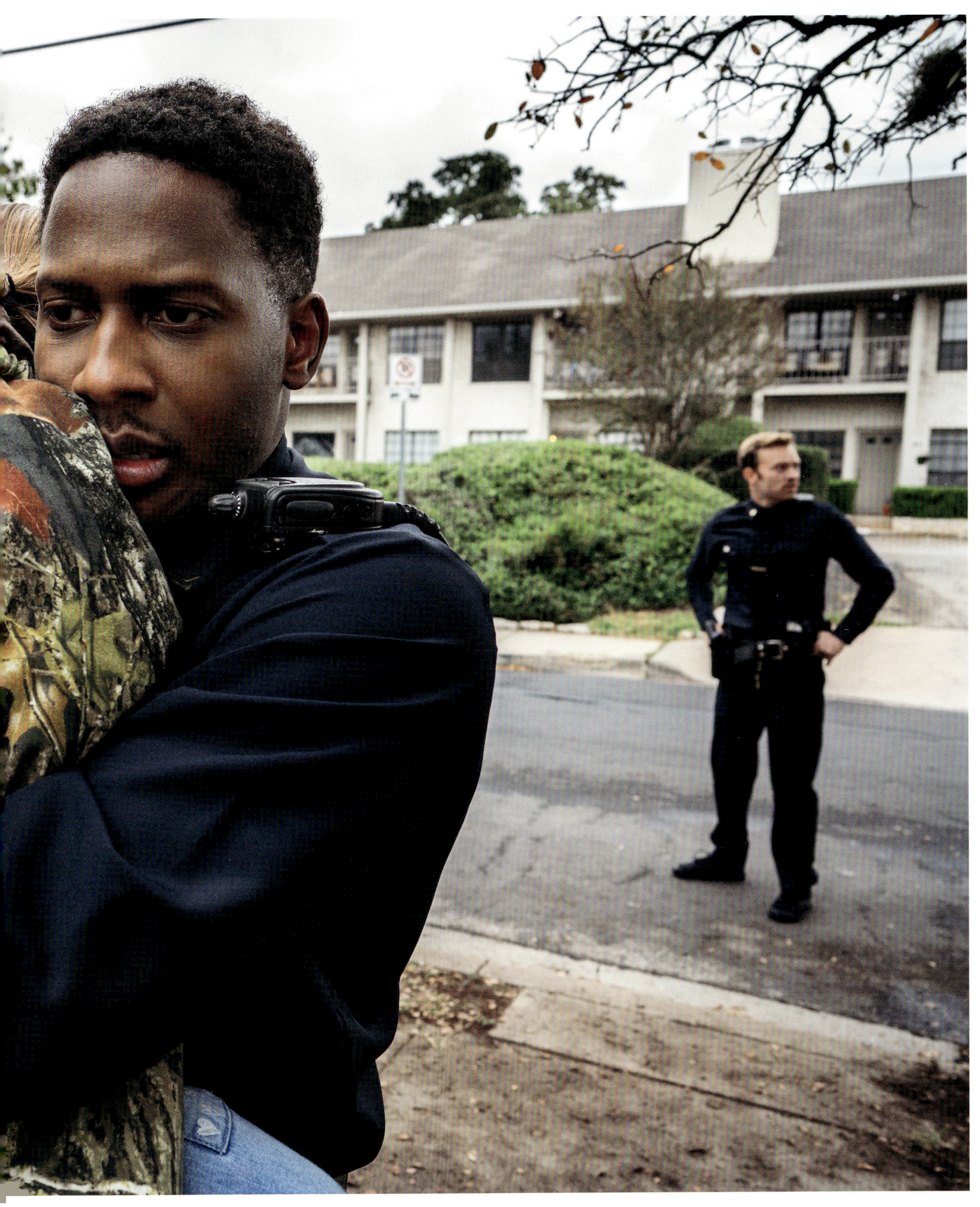

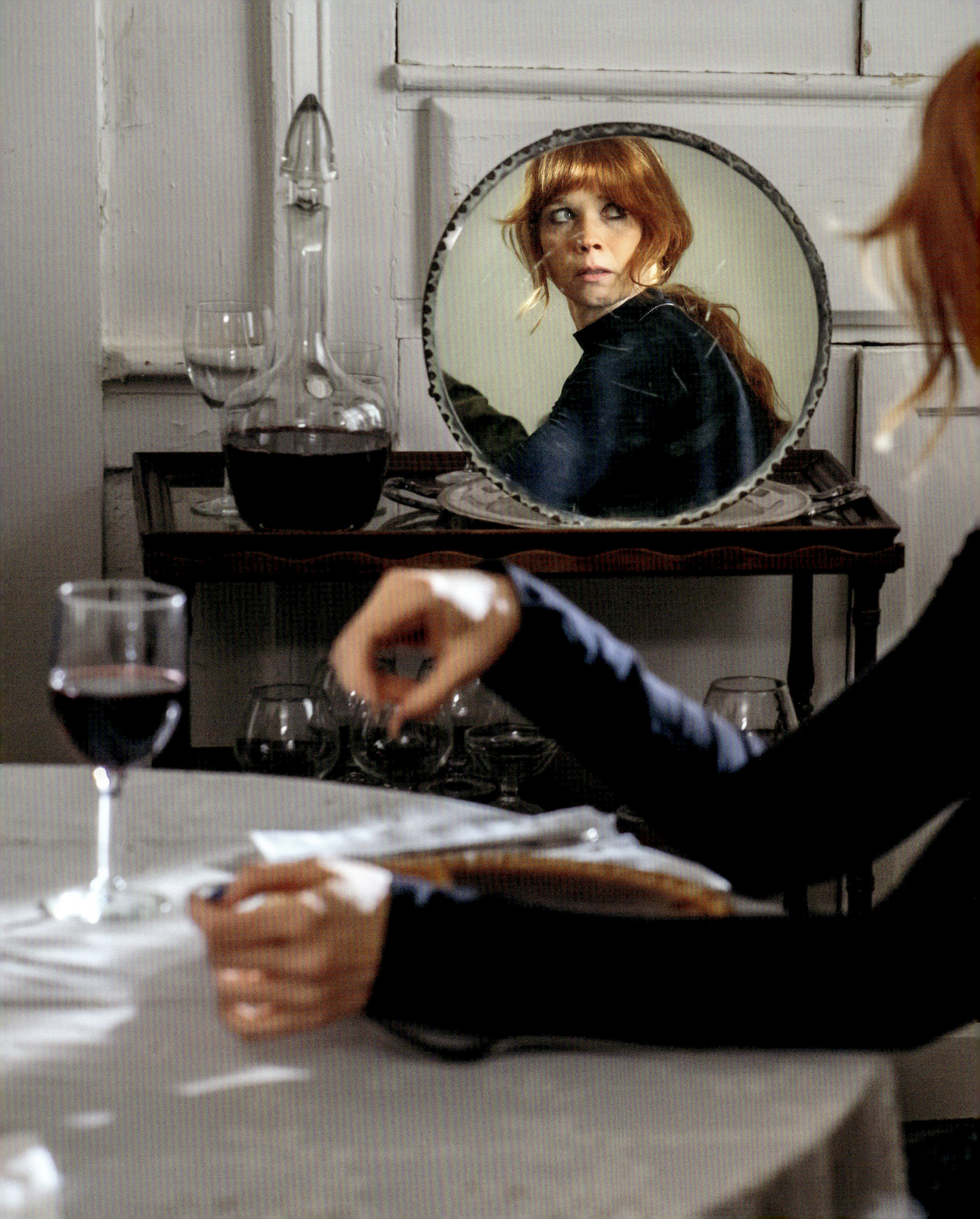

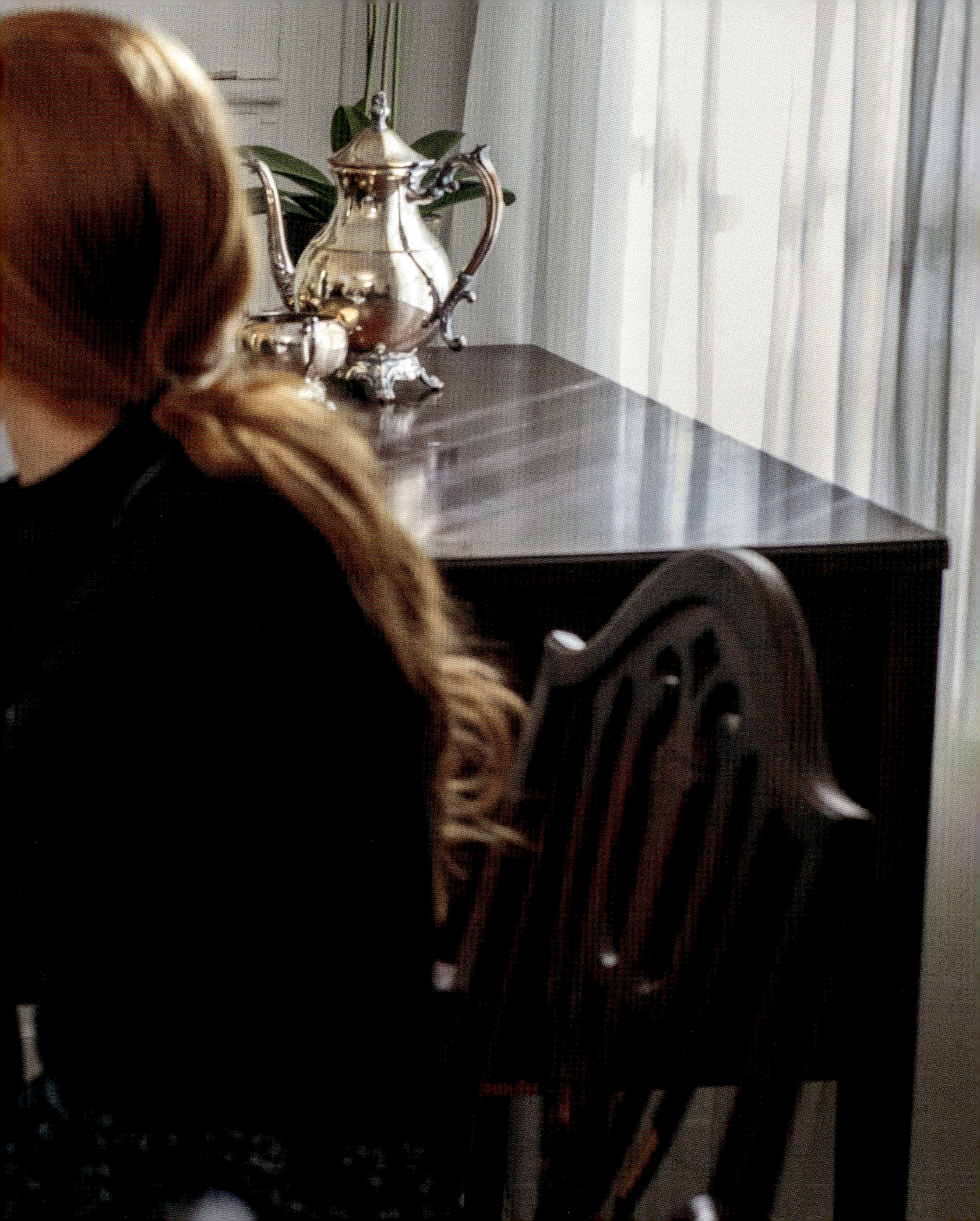

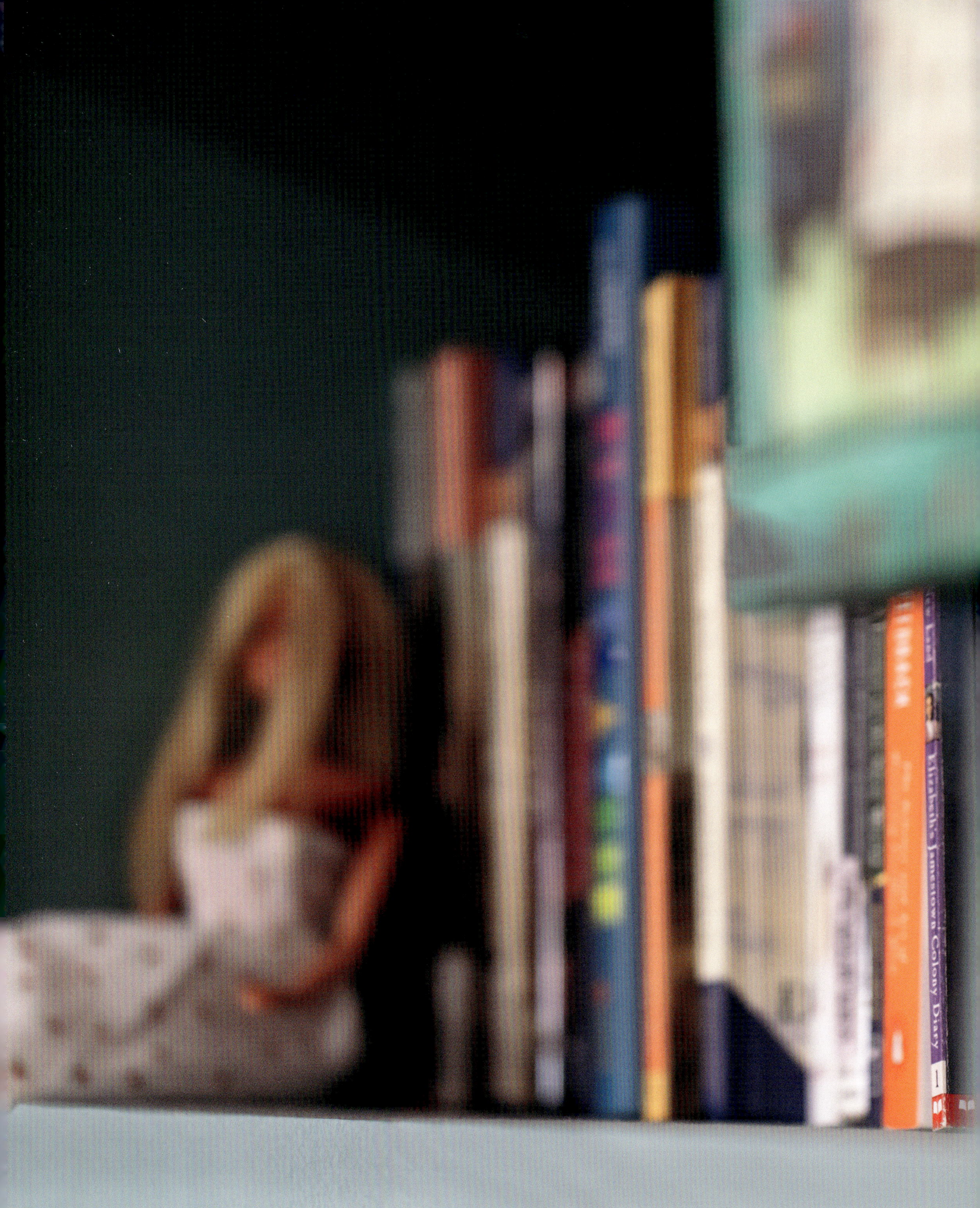

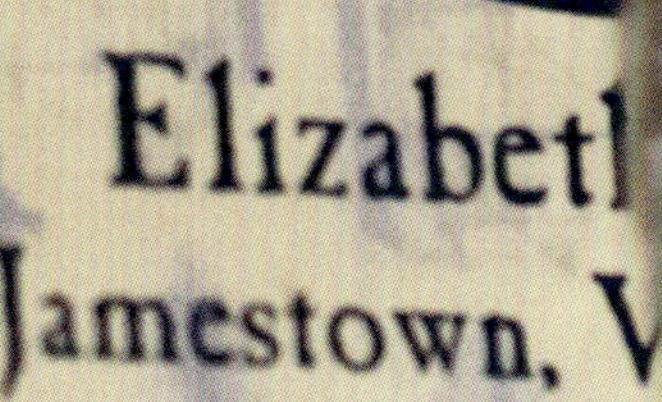
A Dear America BOOK
MY AMERICA
Our Strange New Land
Elizabeth
Jamestown, V

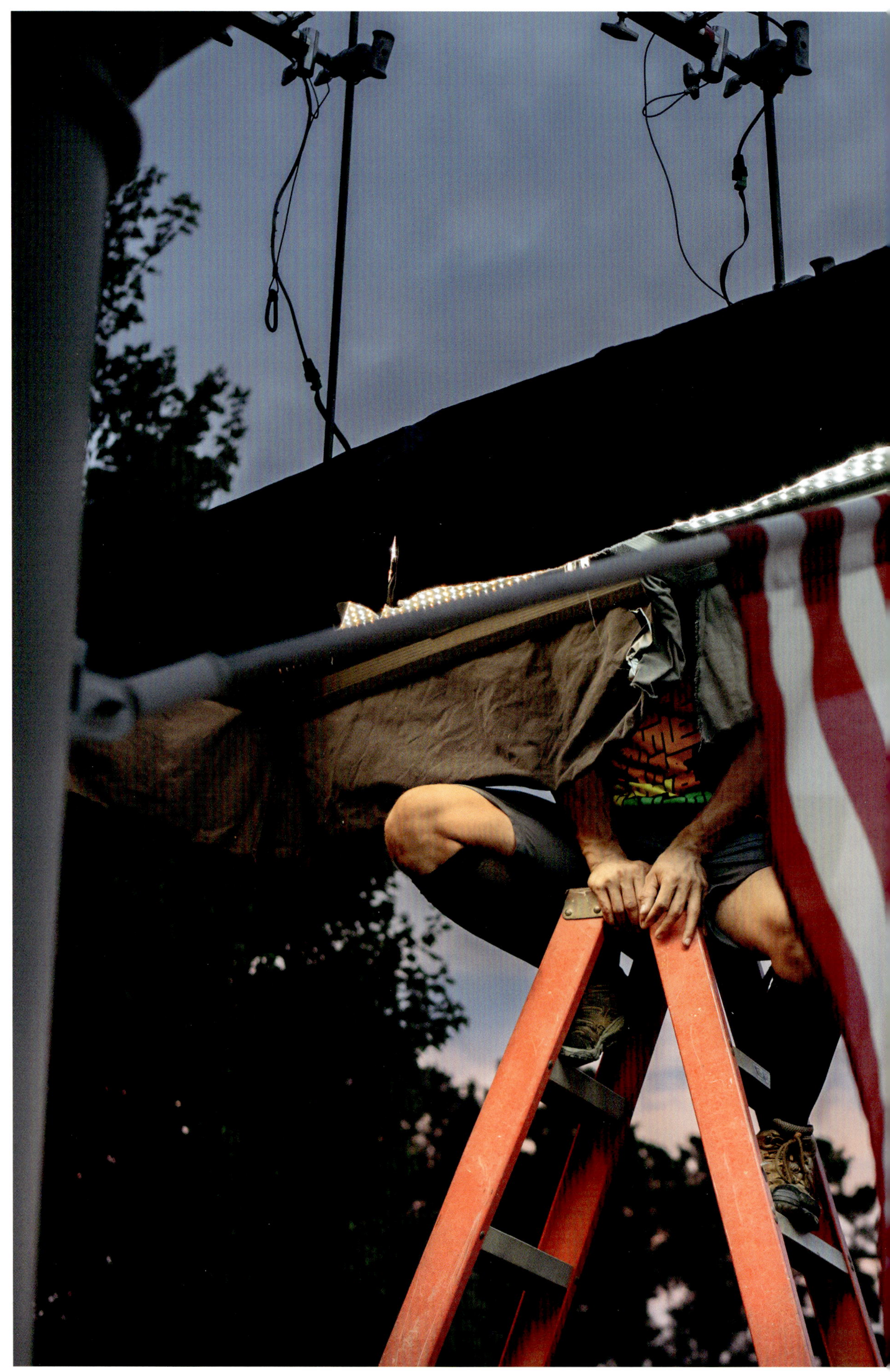

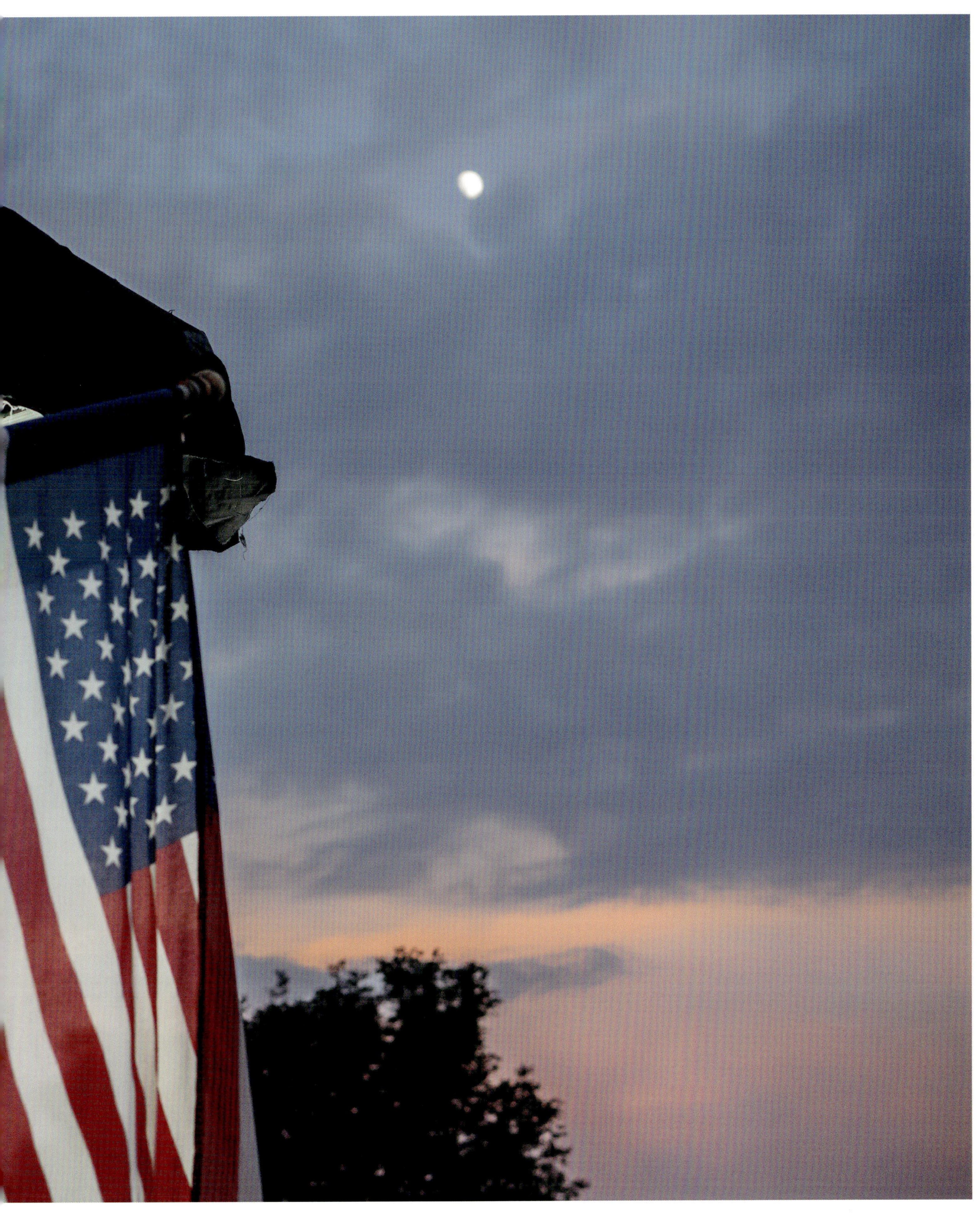

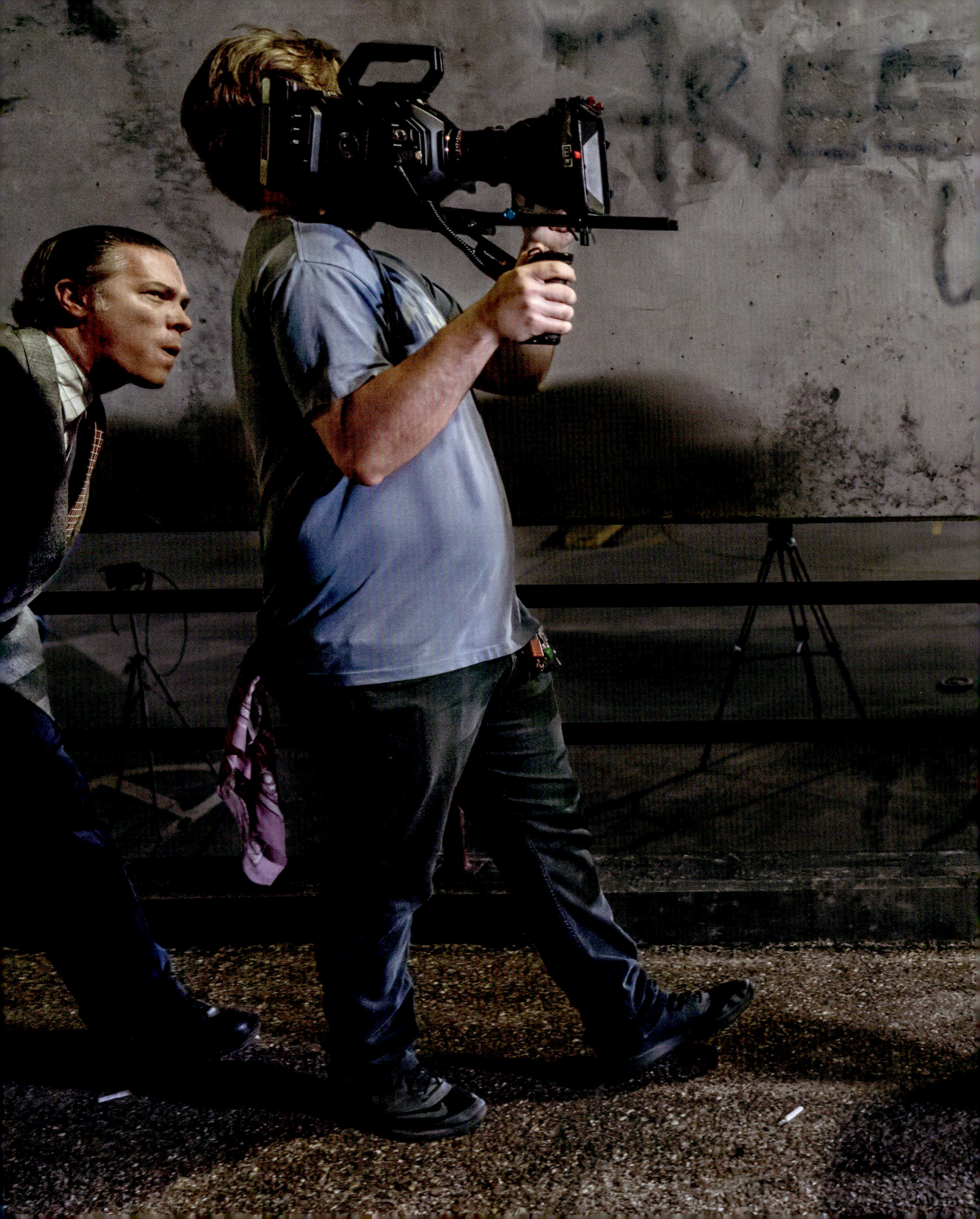

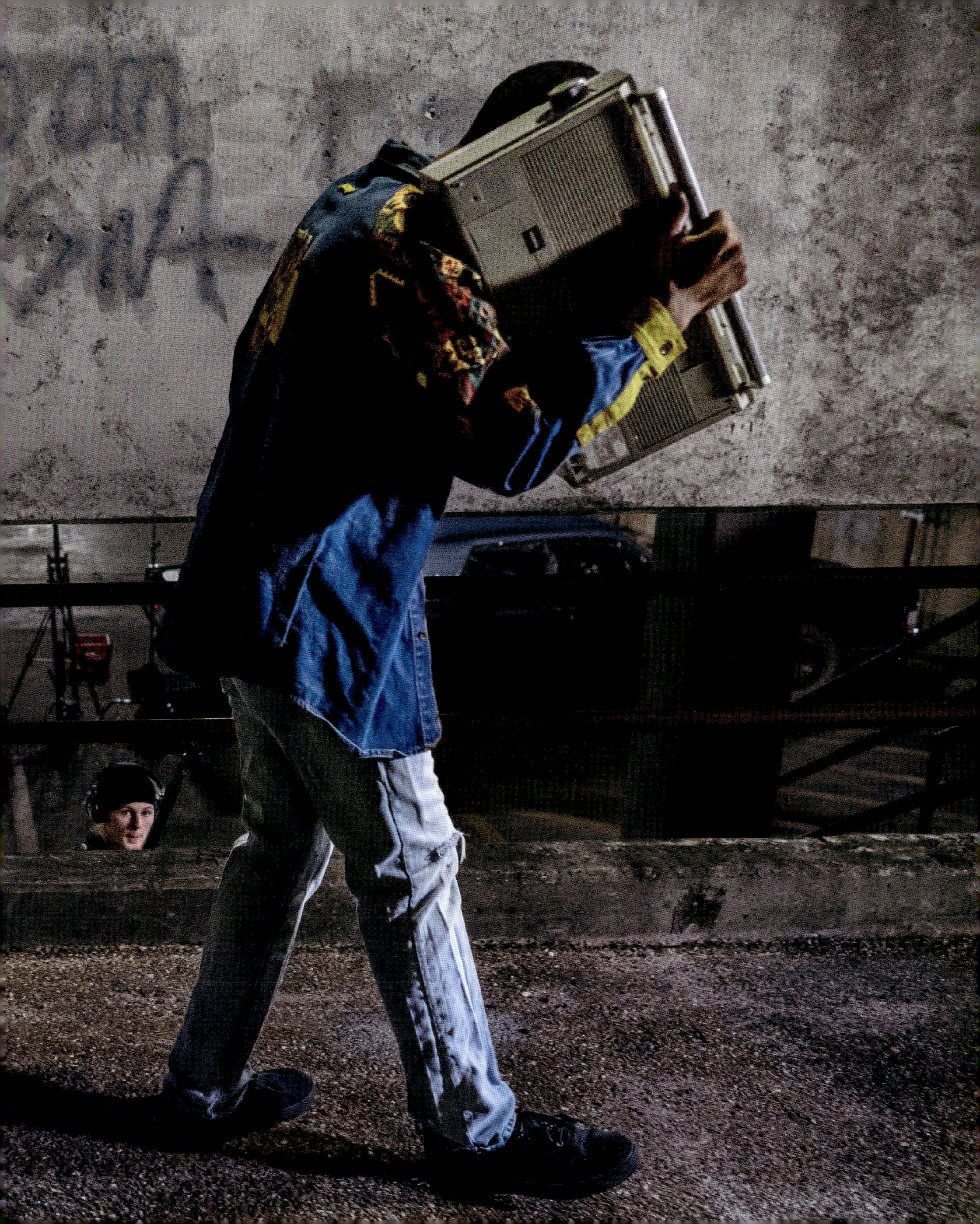

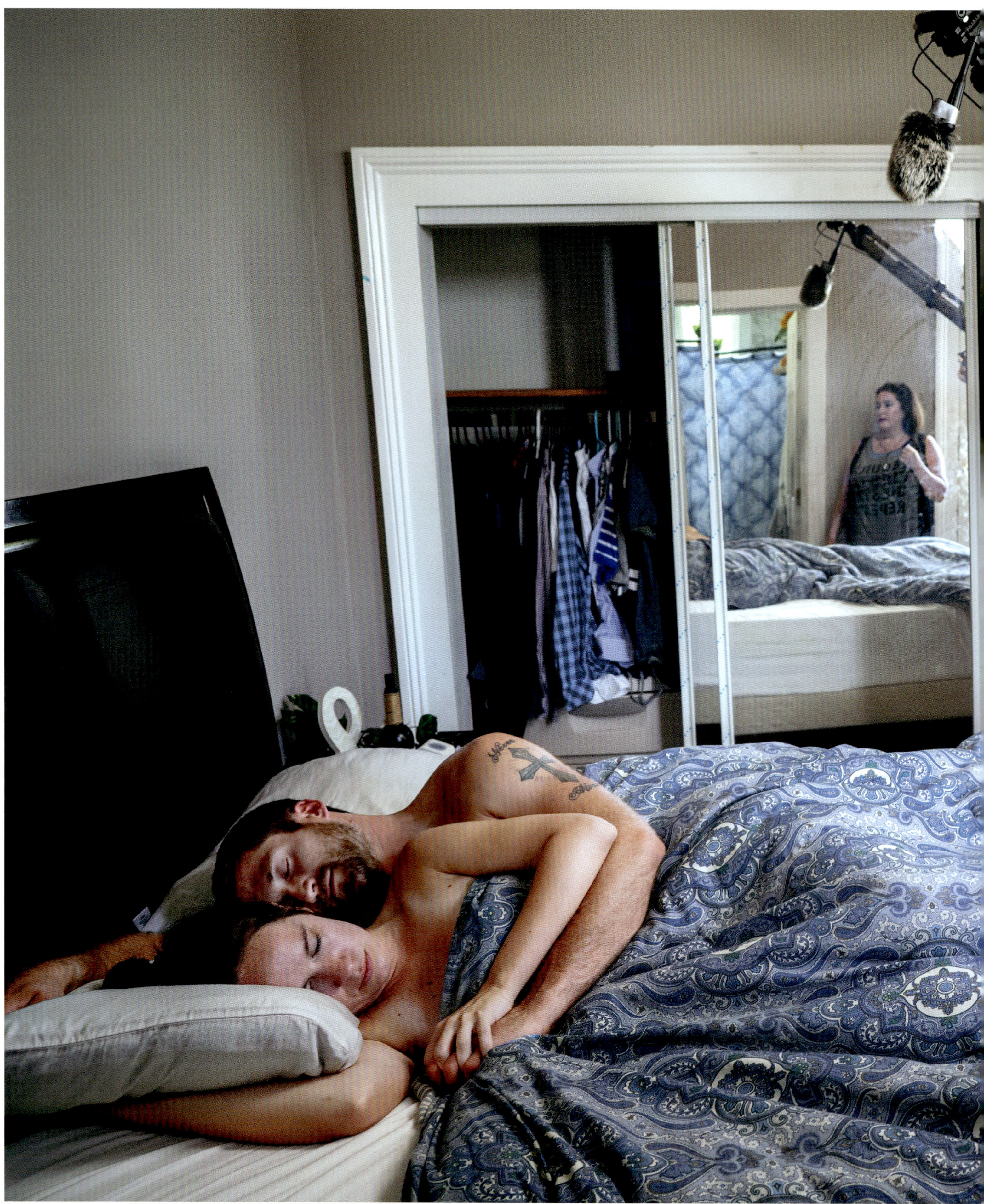

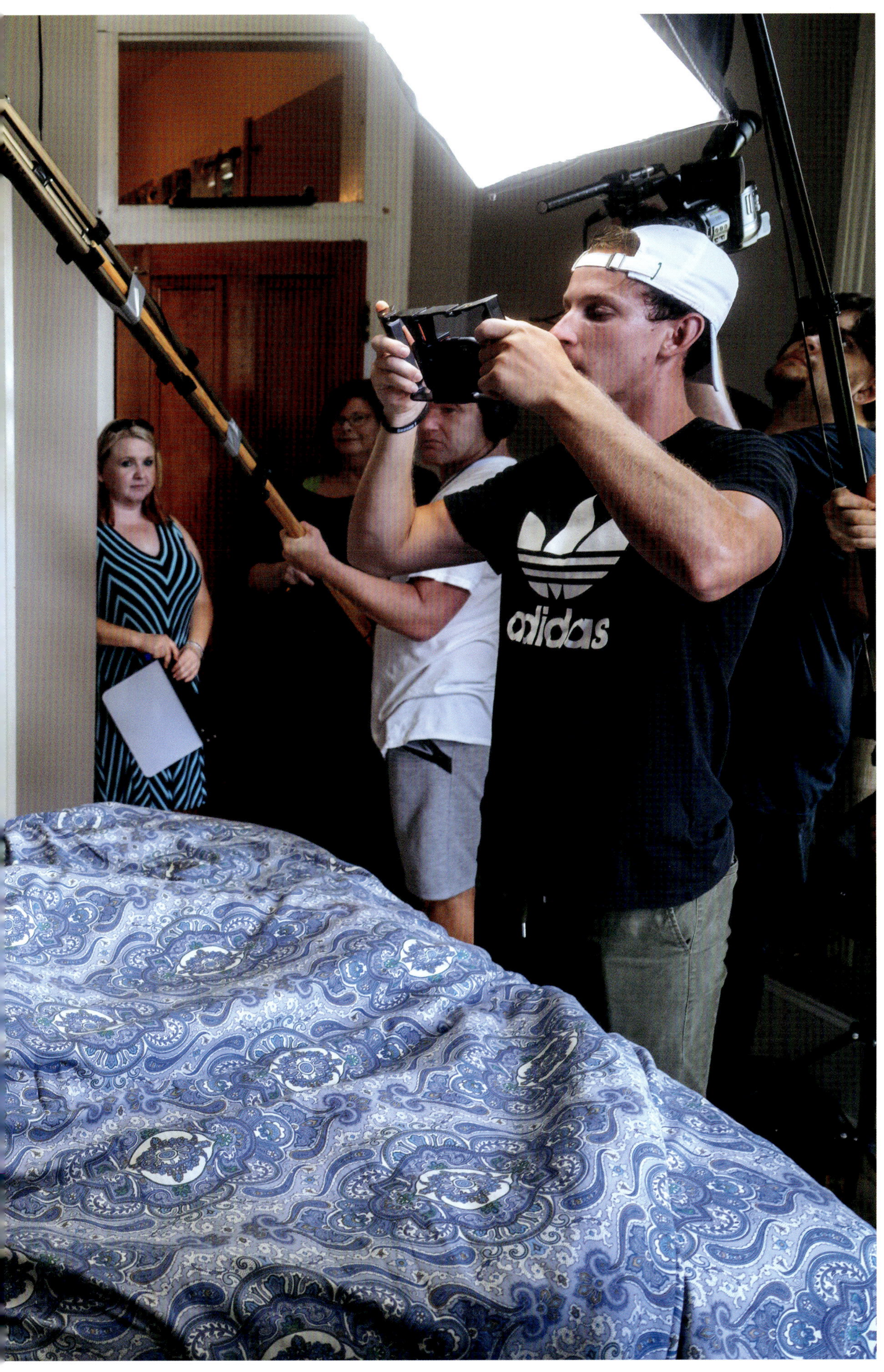

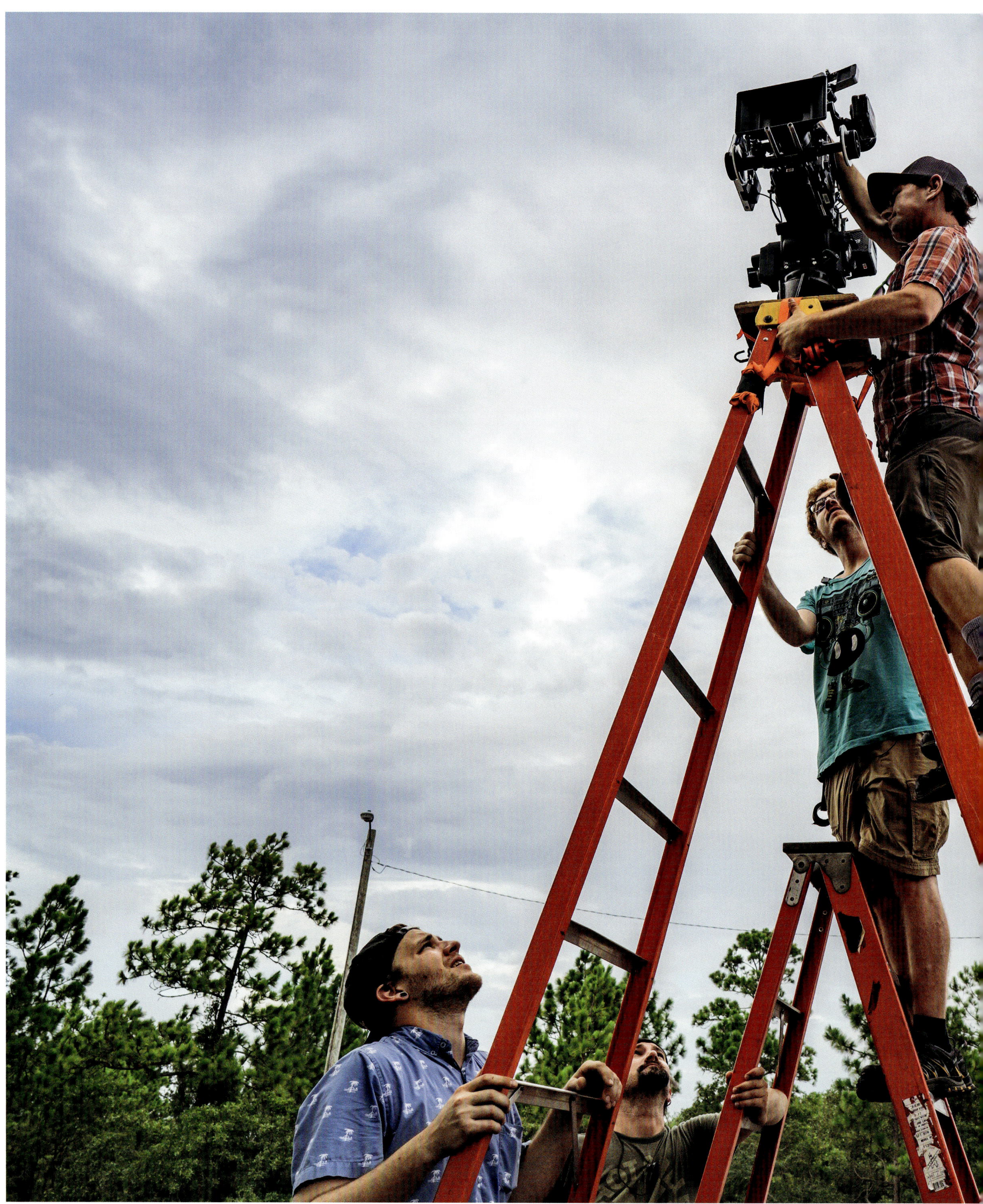

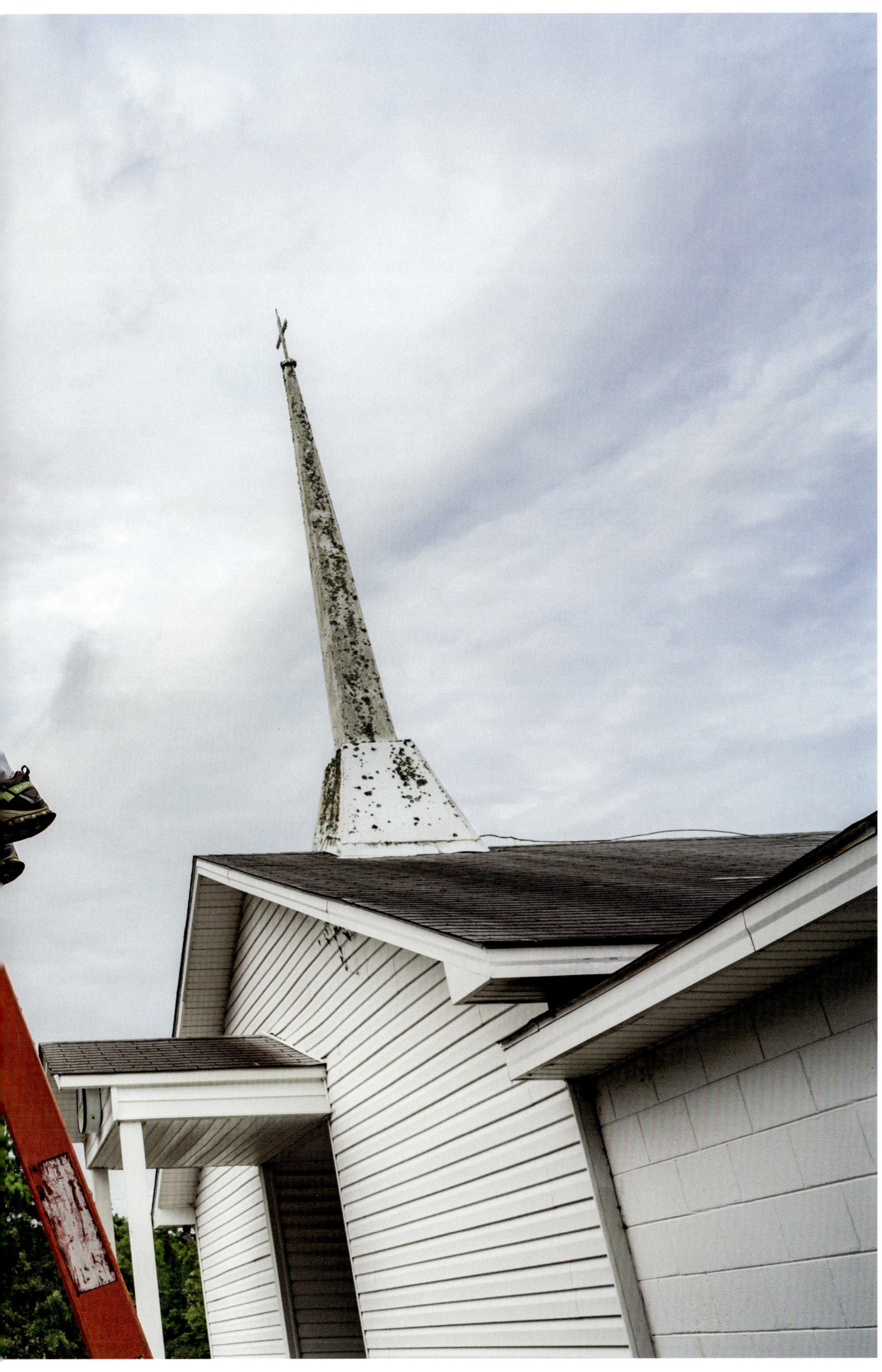

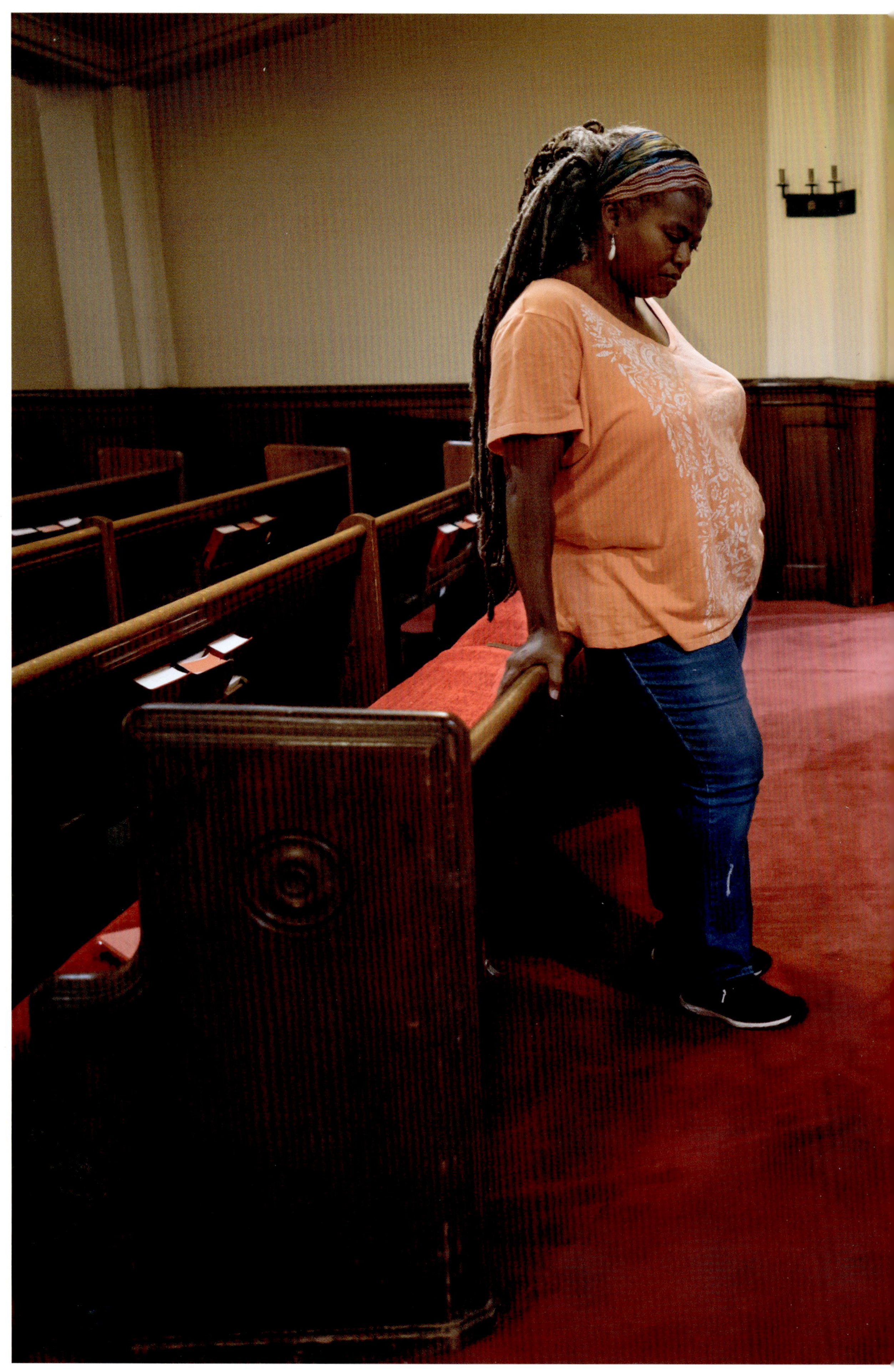

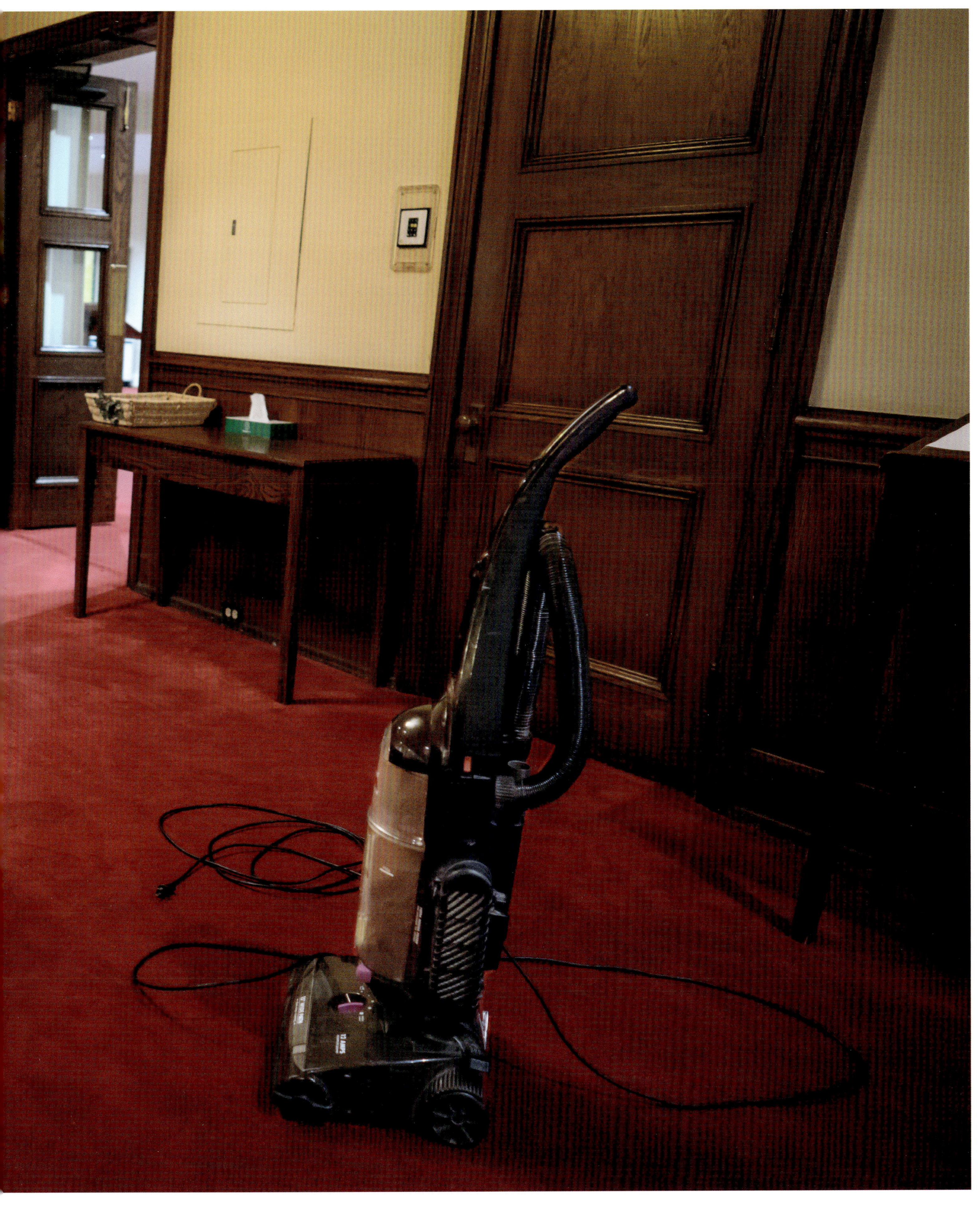

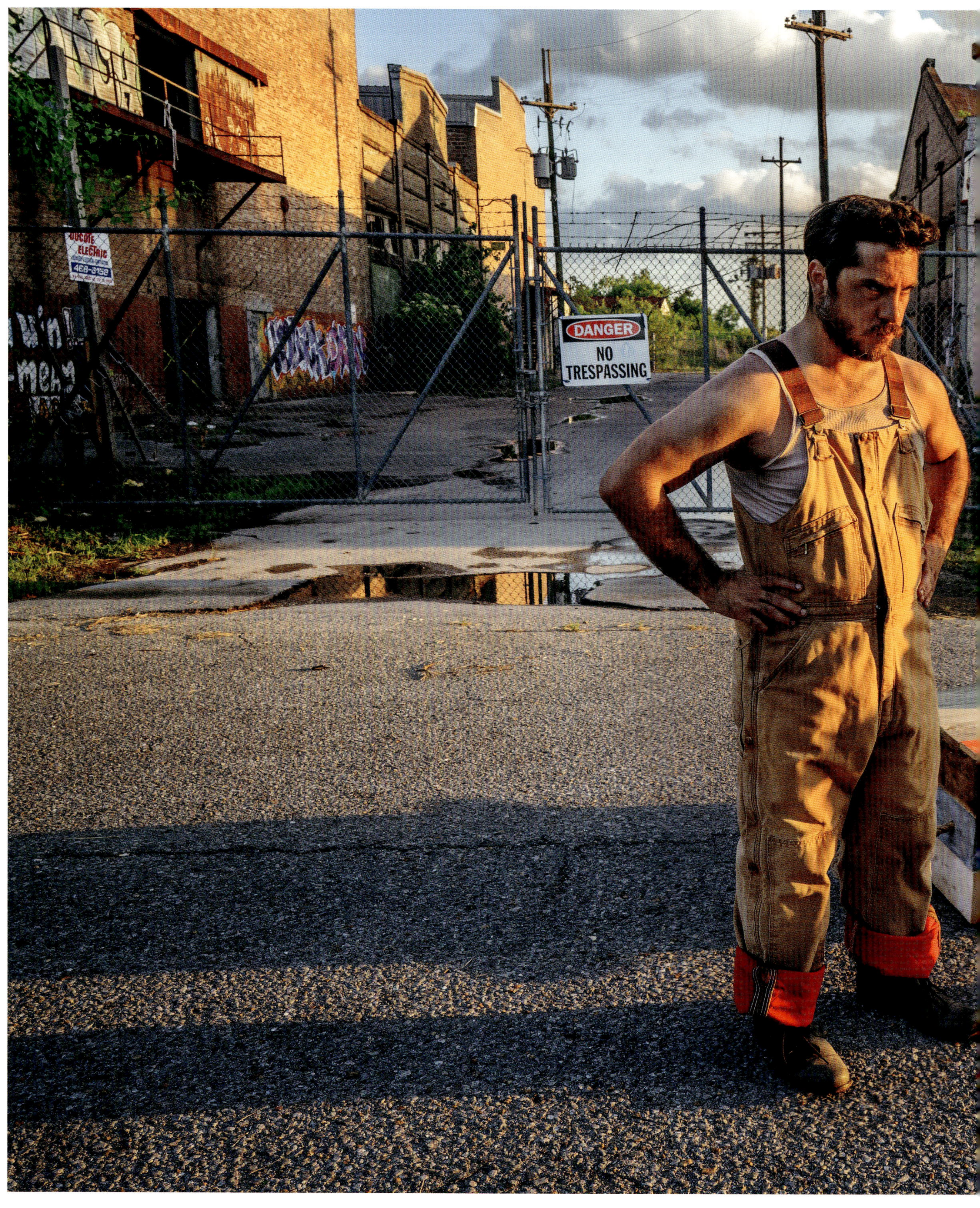
DANGER
NO
TRESPASSING
DUCOTE
ELECTRIC
468-3158

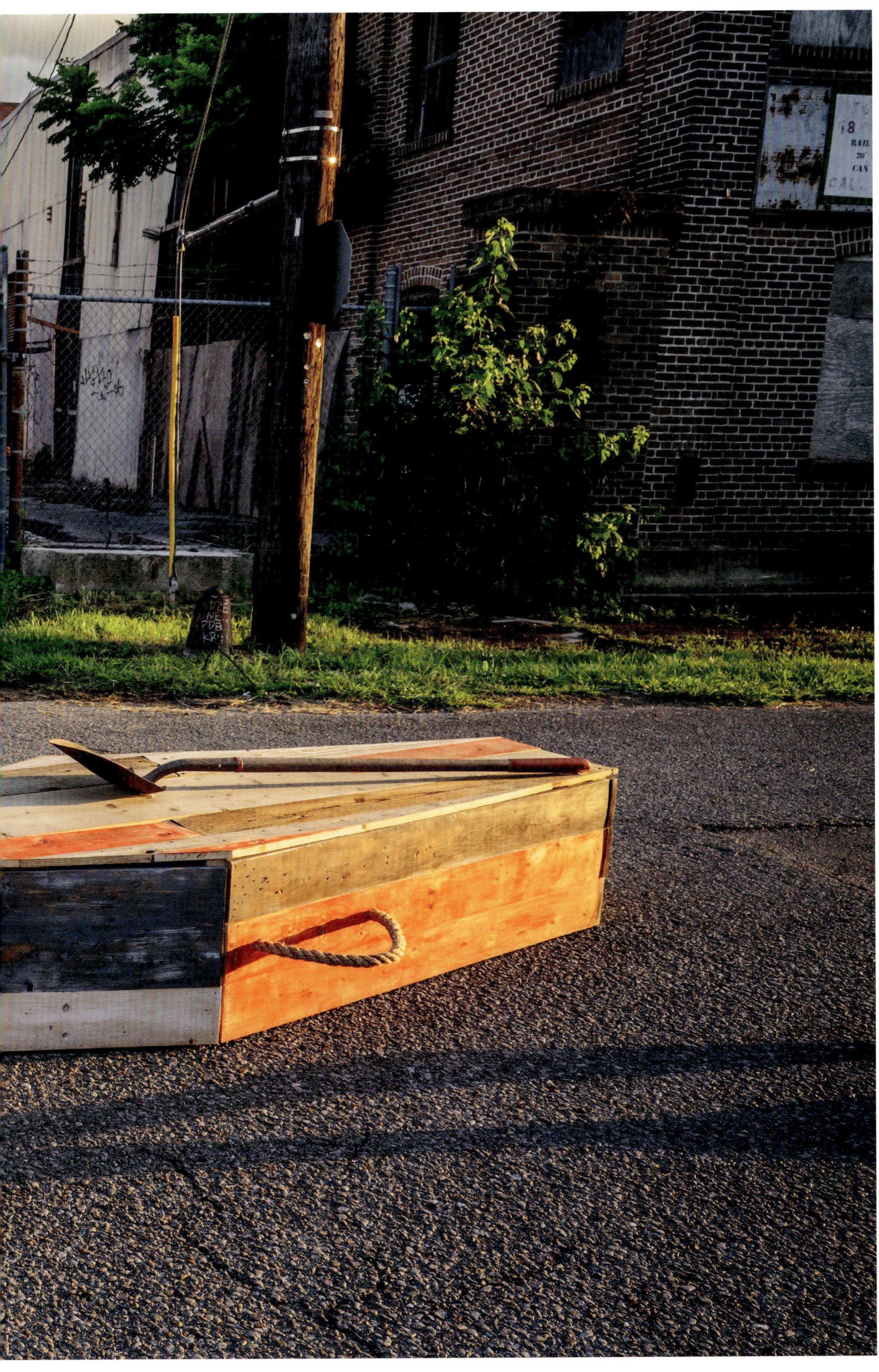

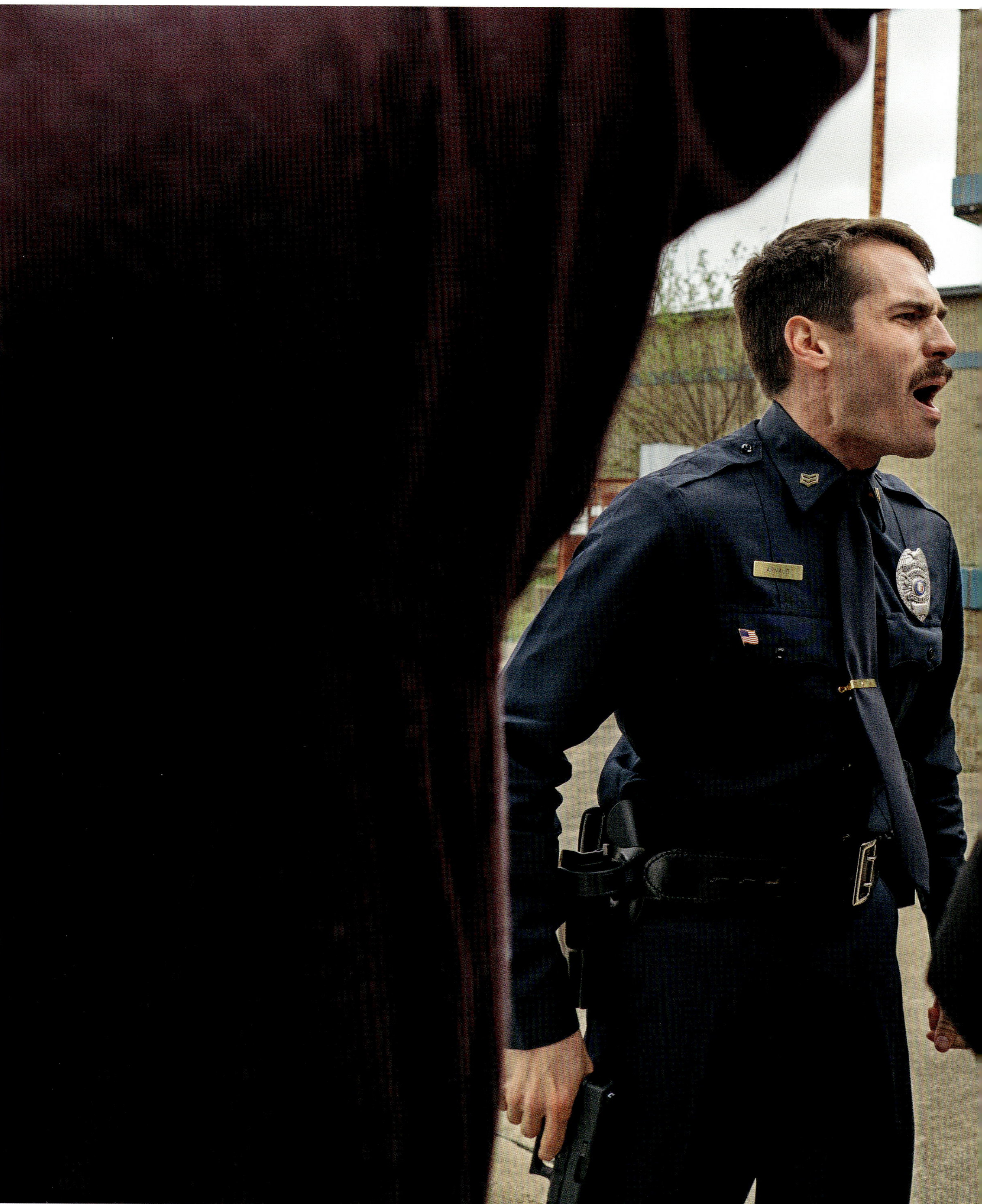

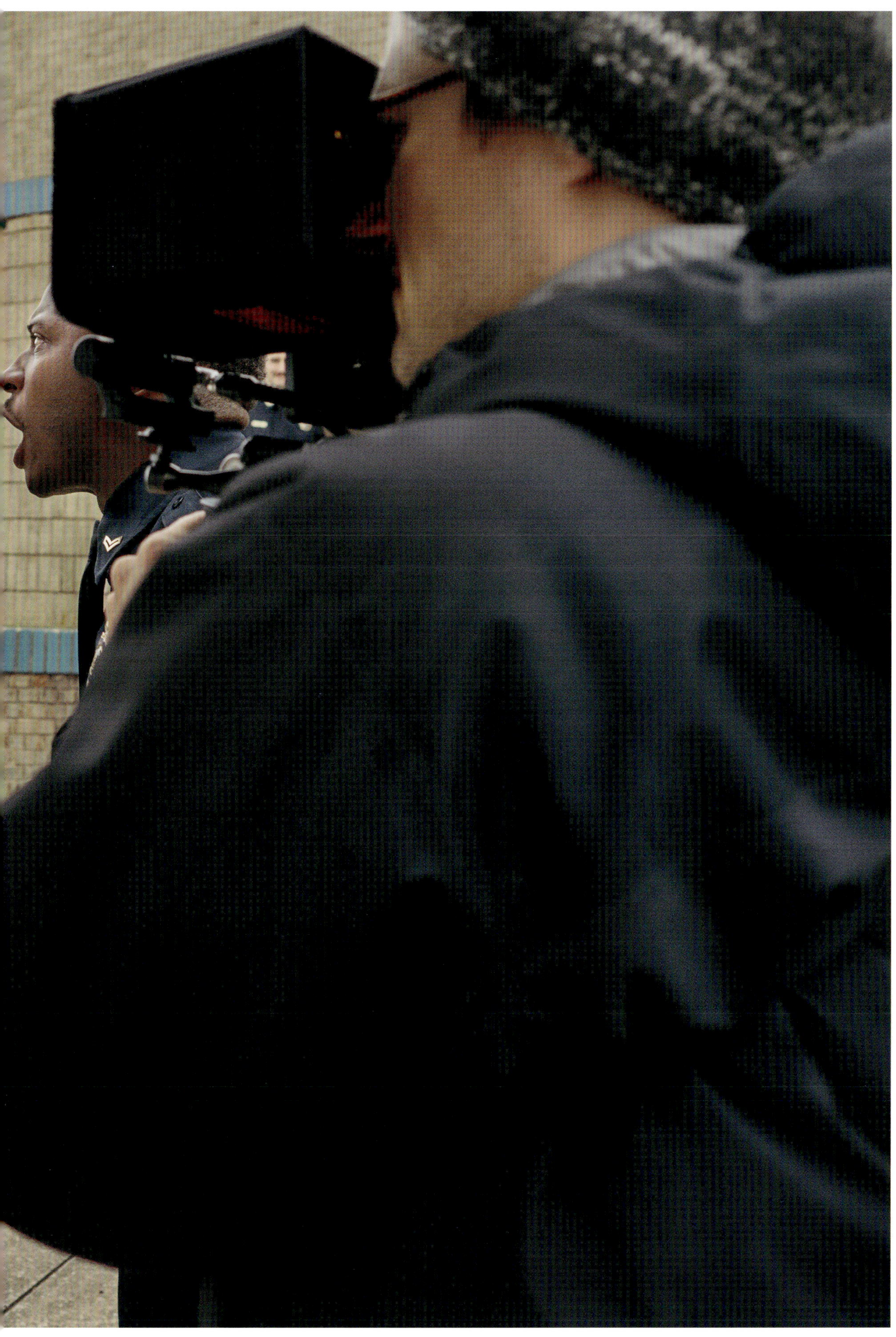

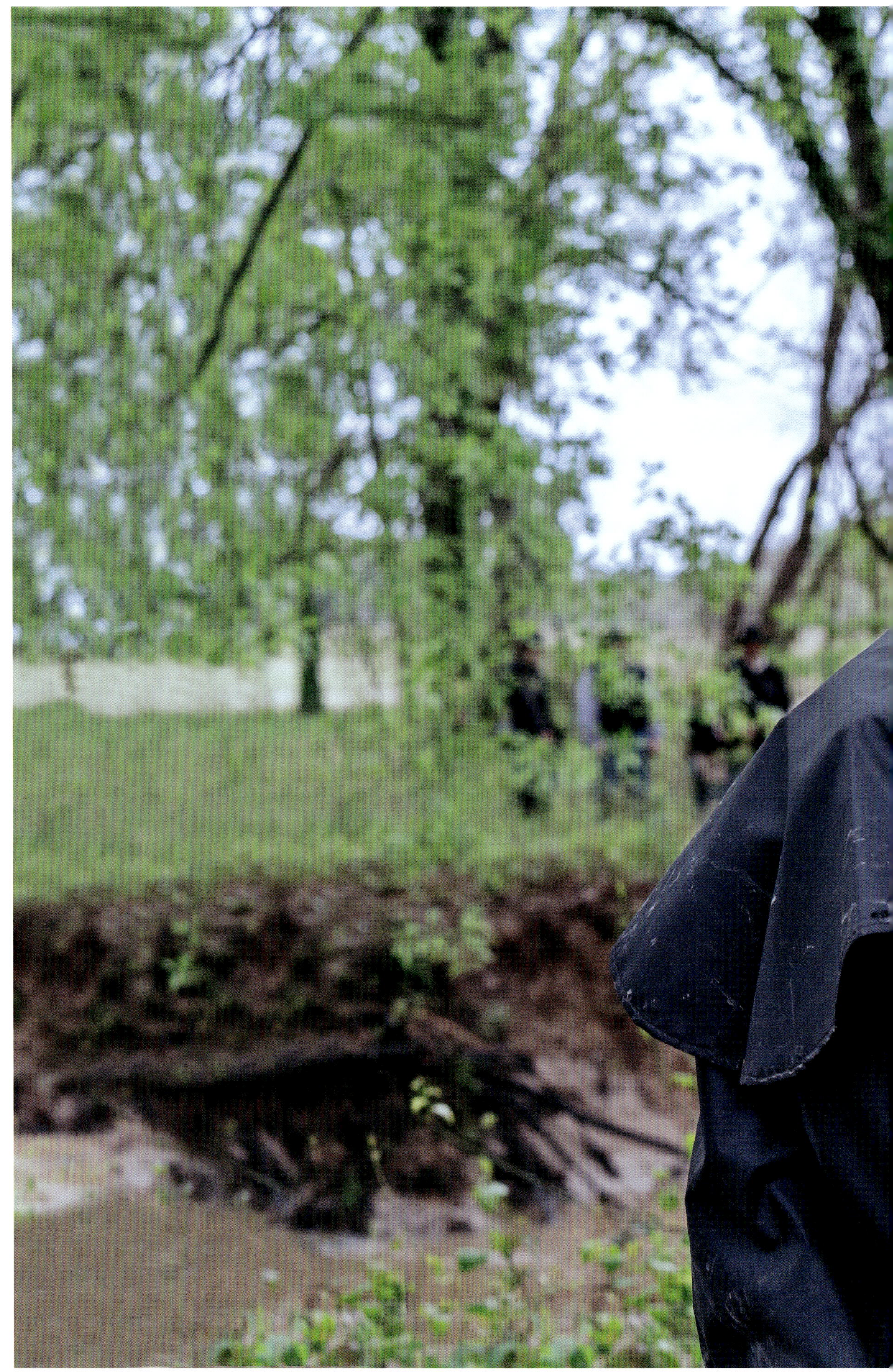

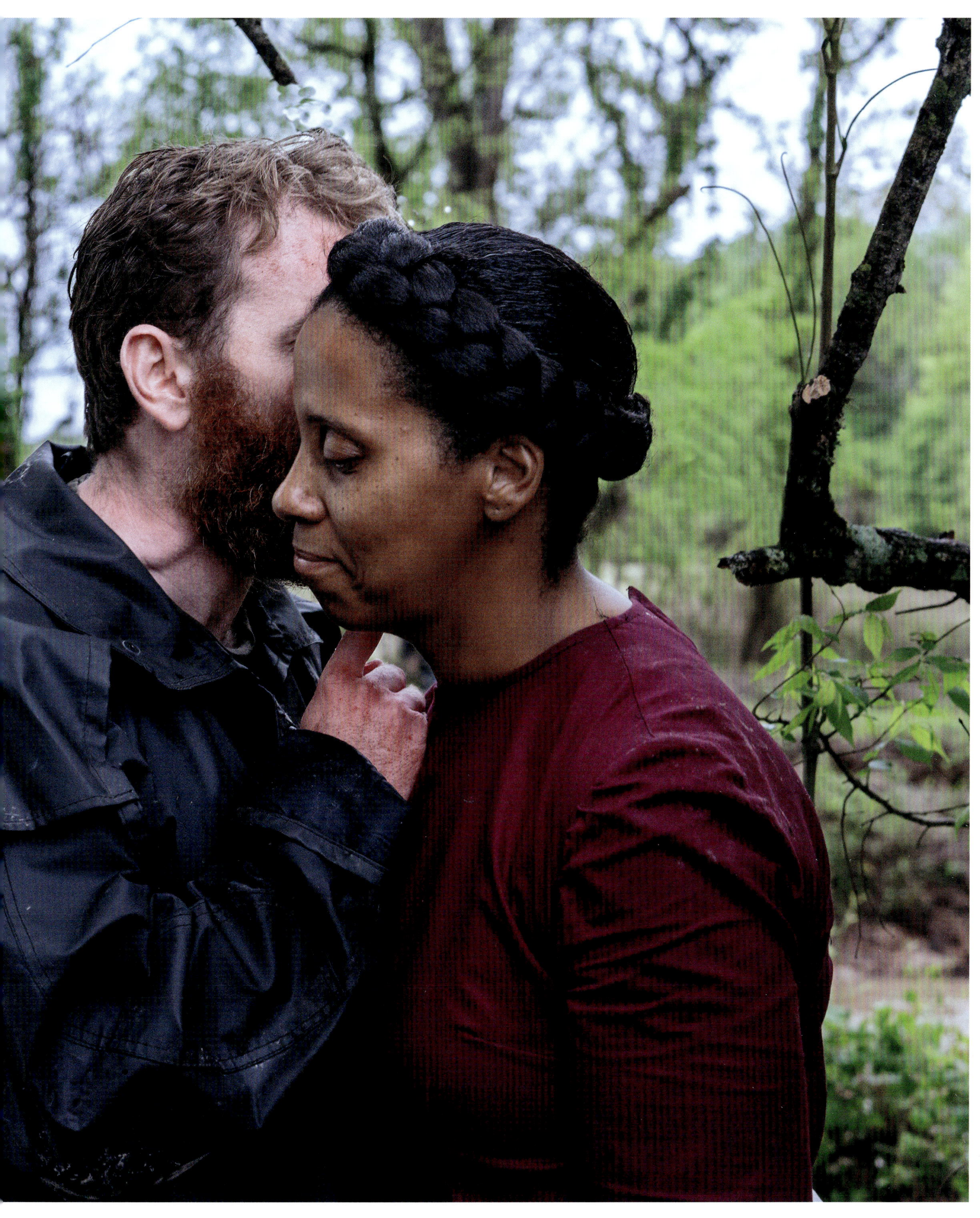

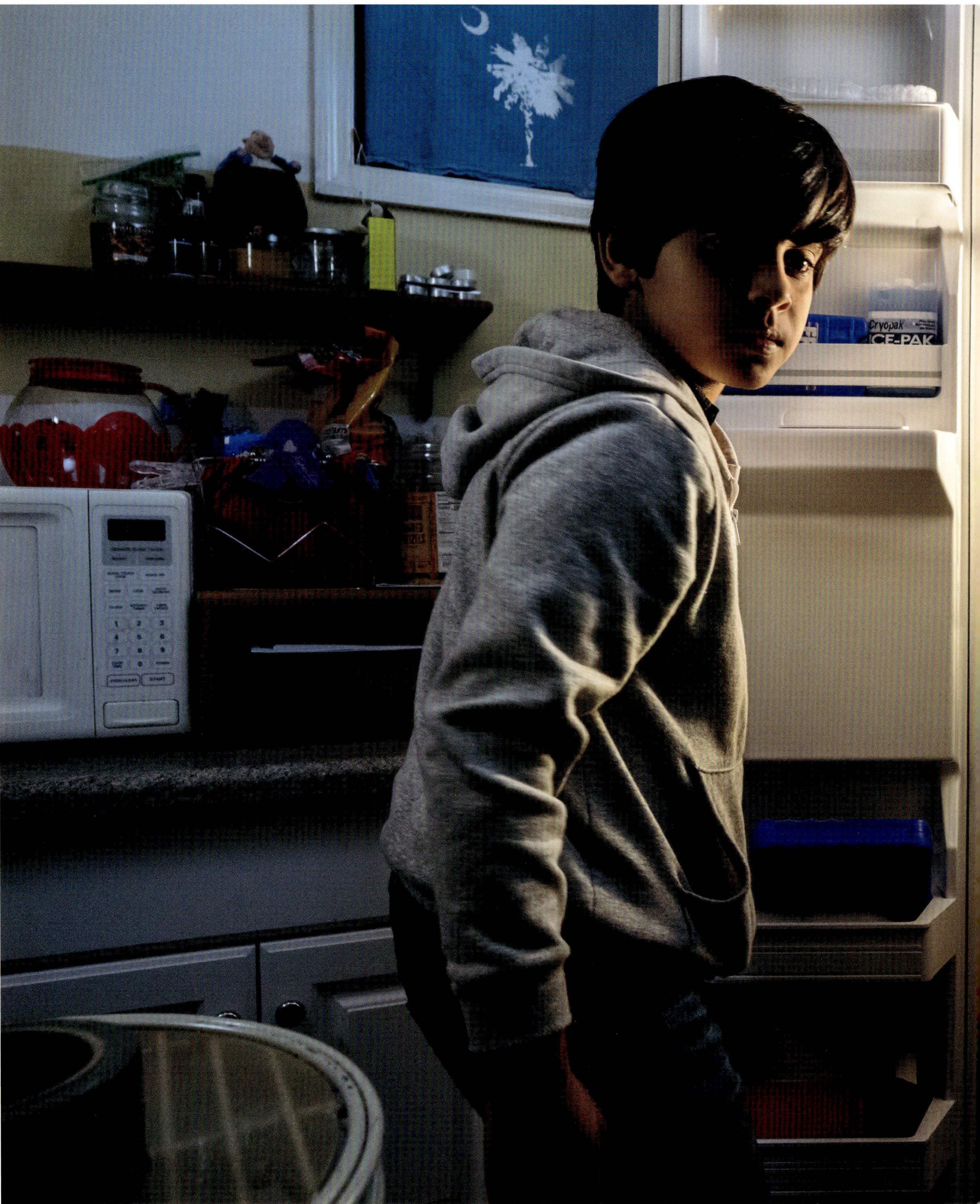

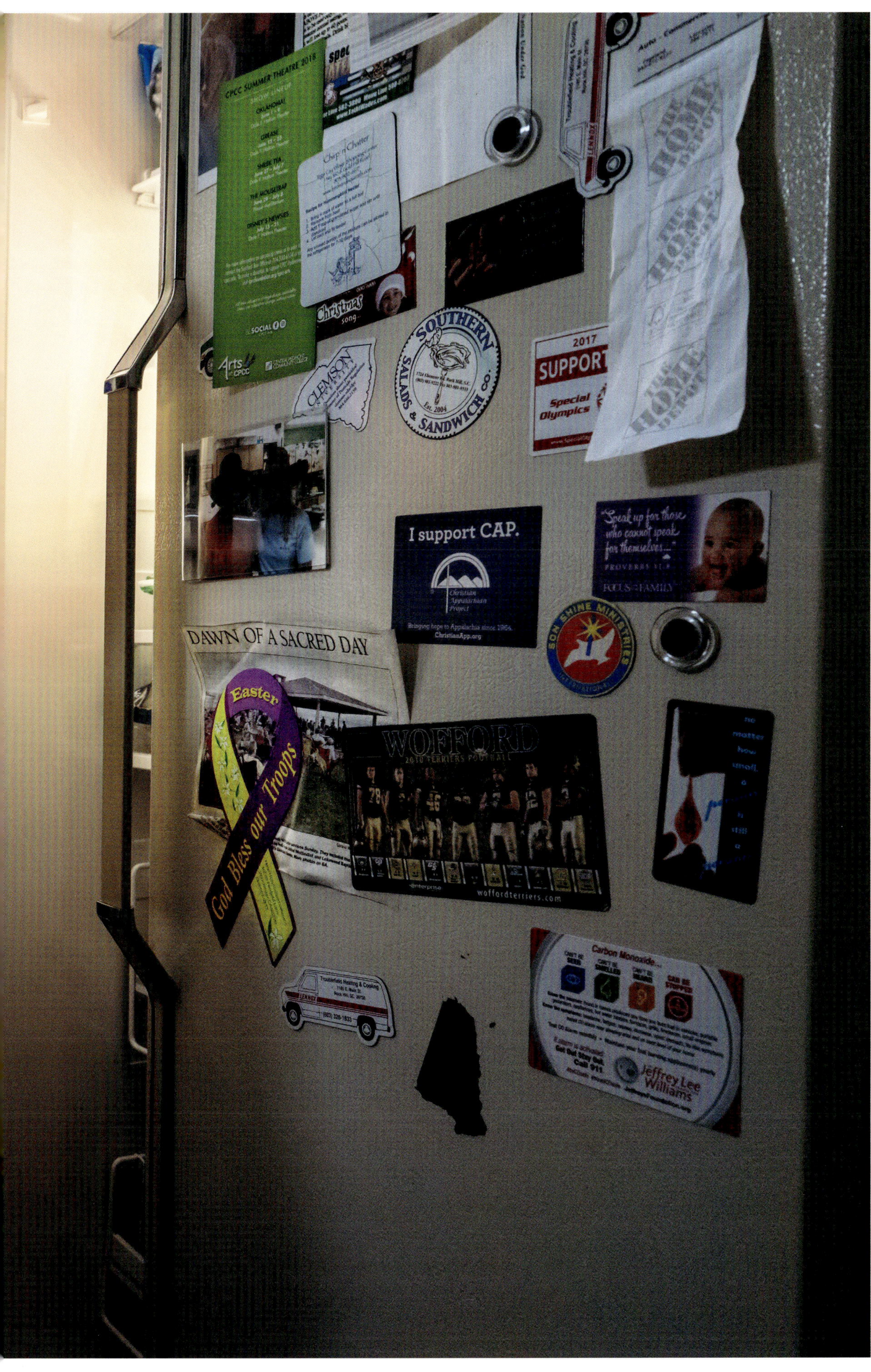

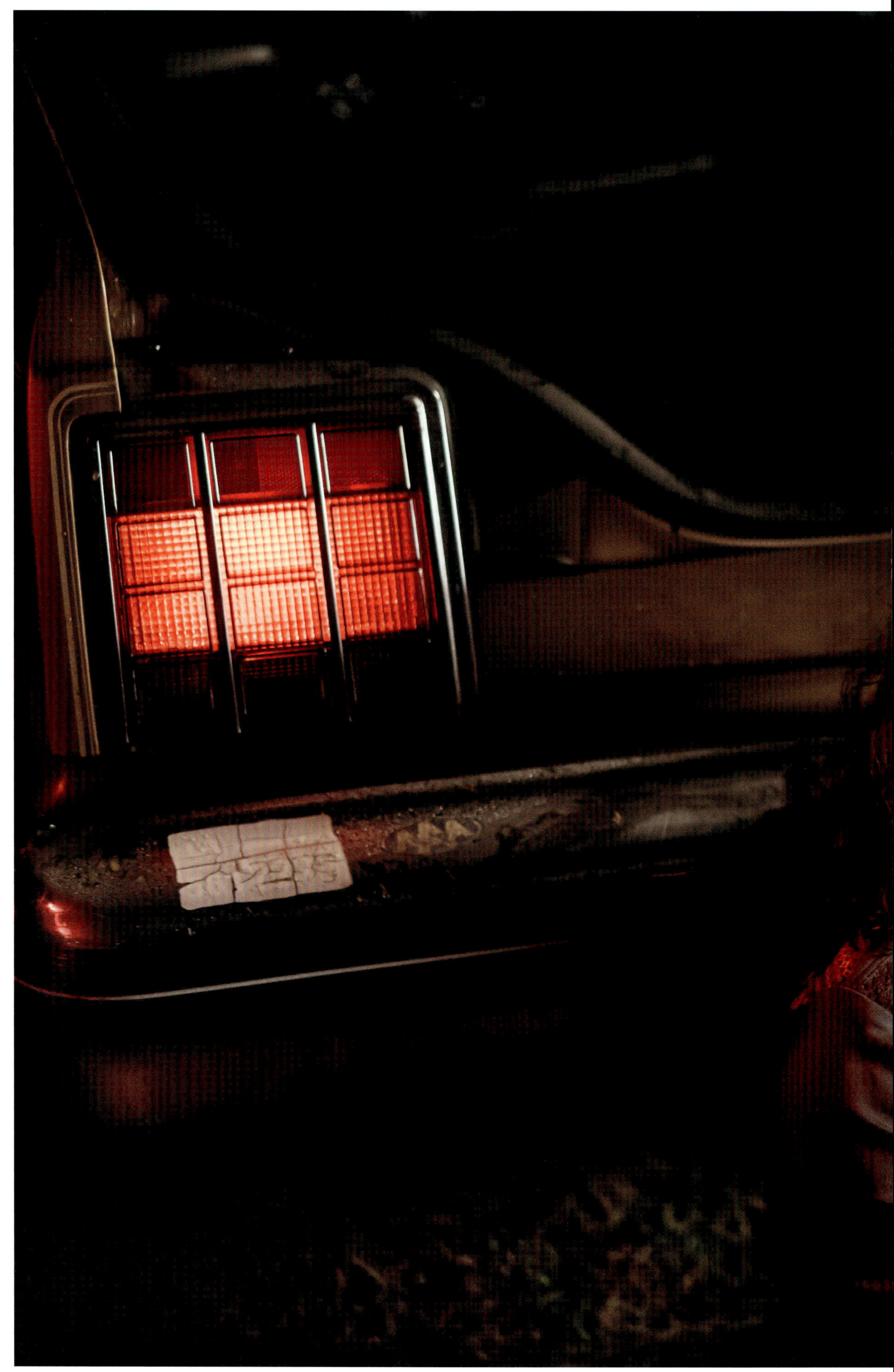

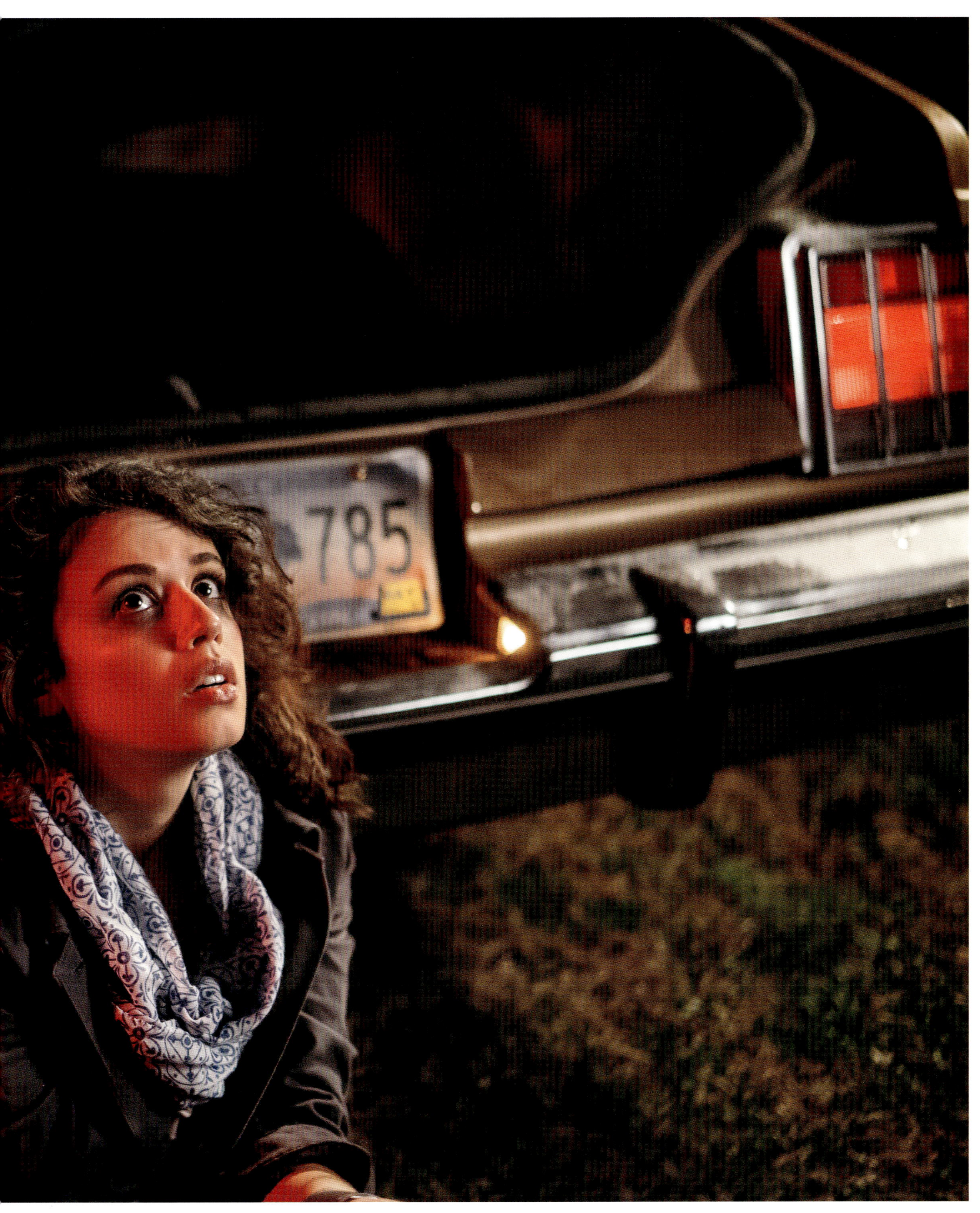

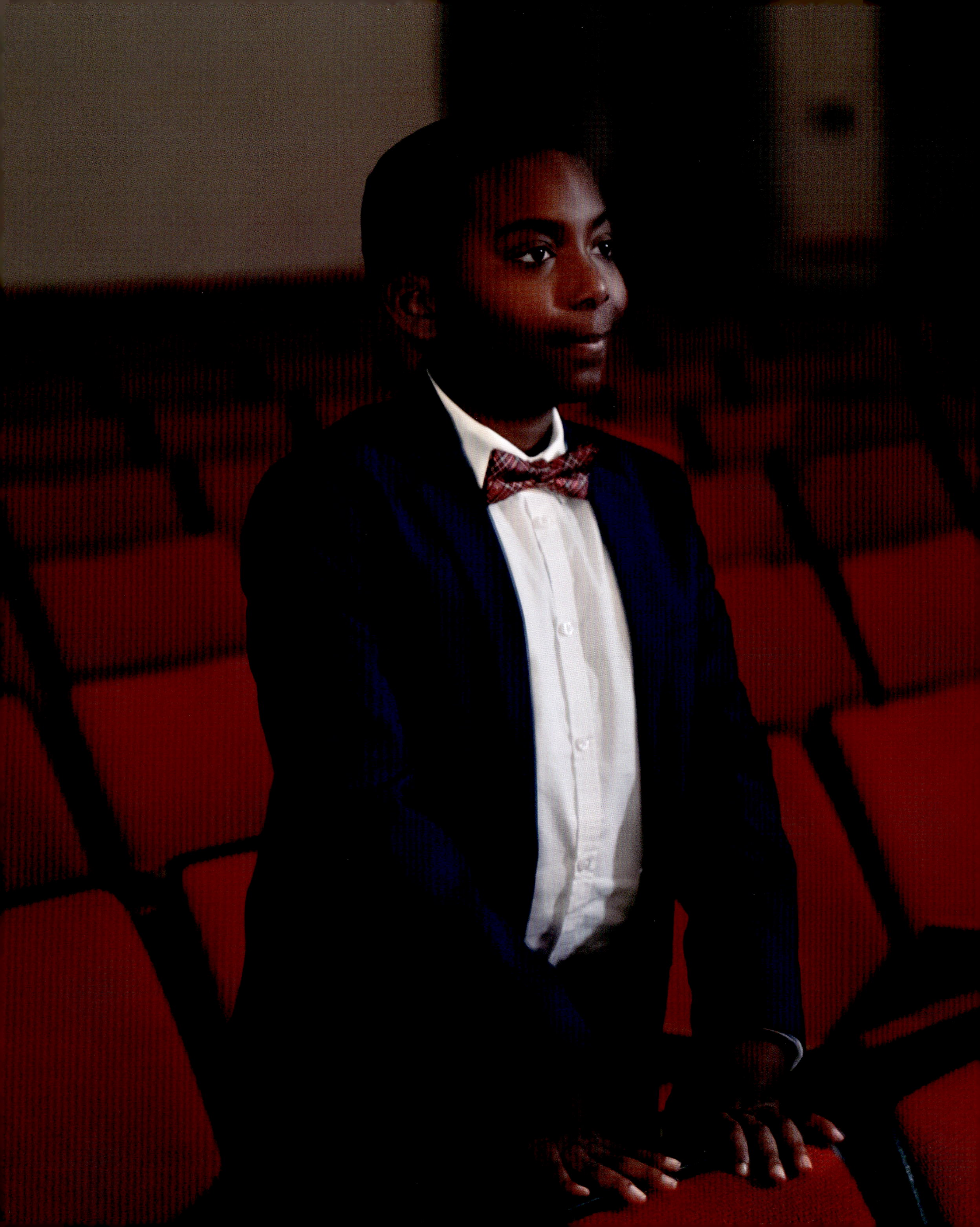

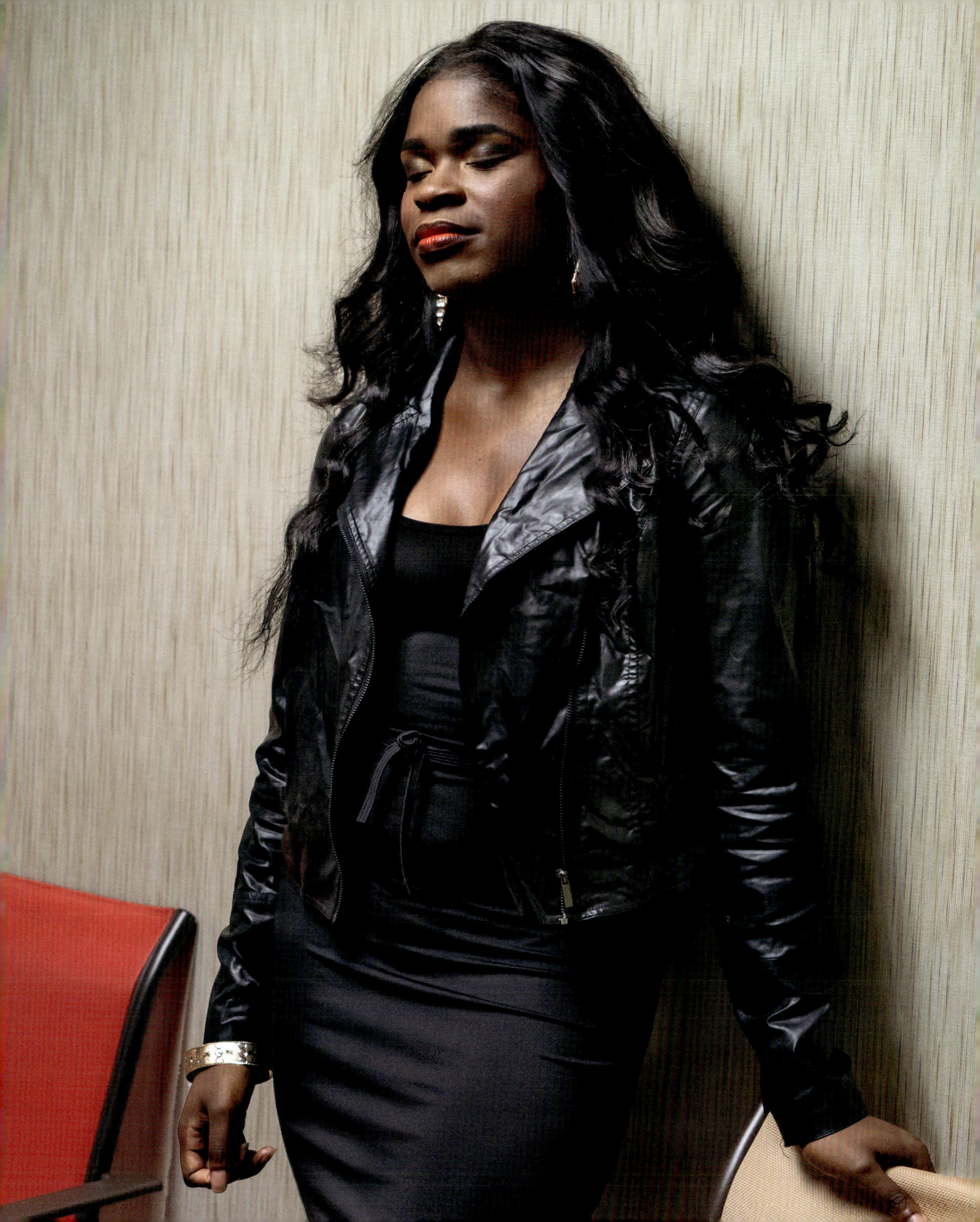

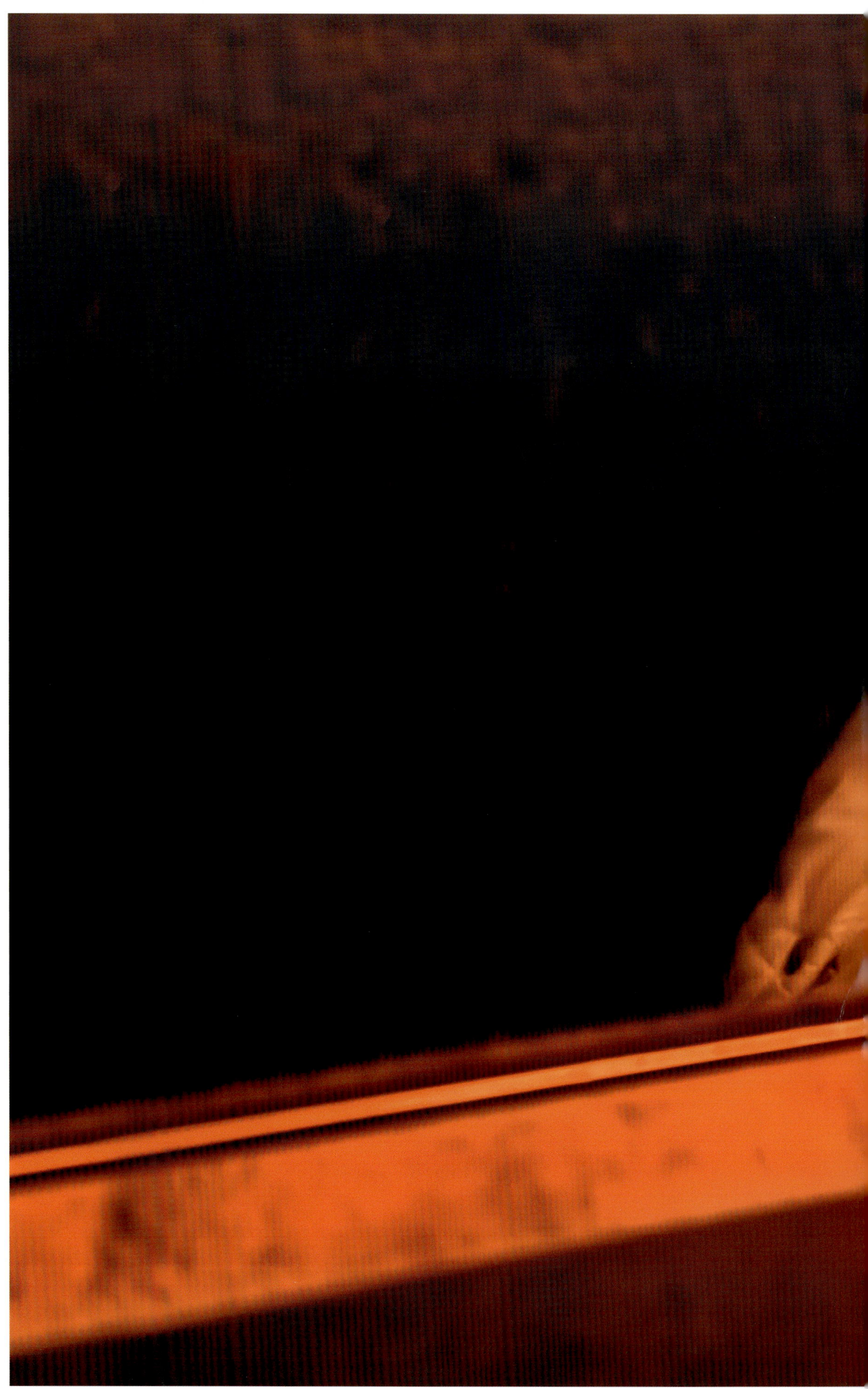

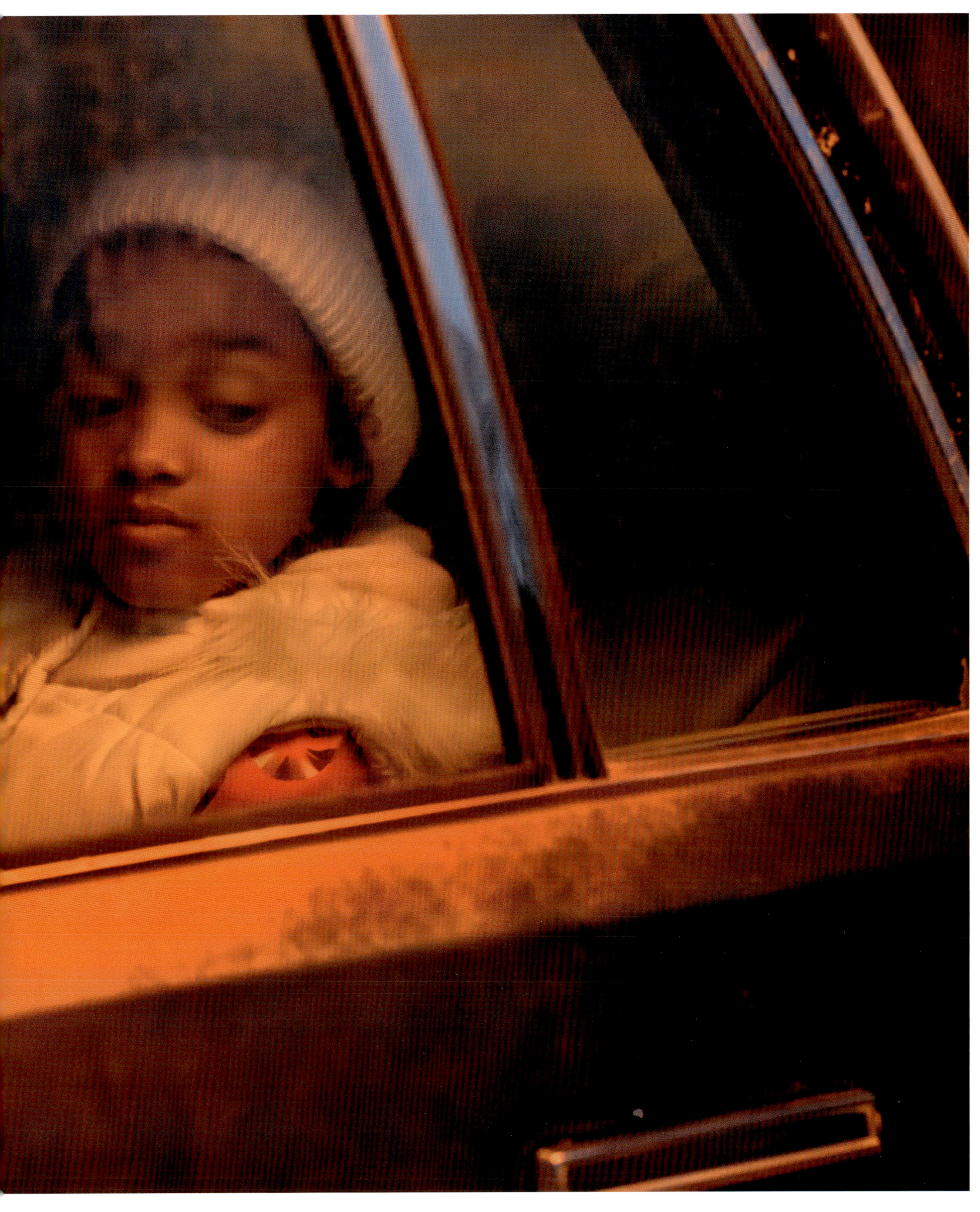

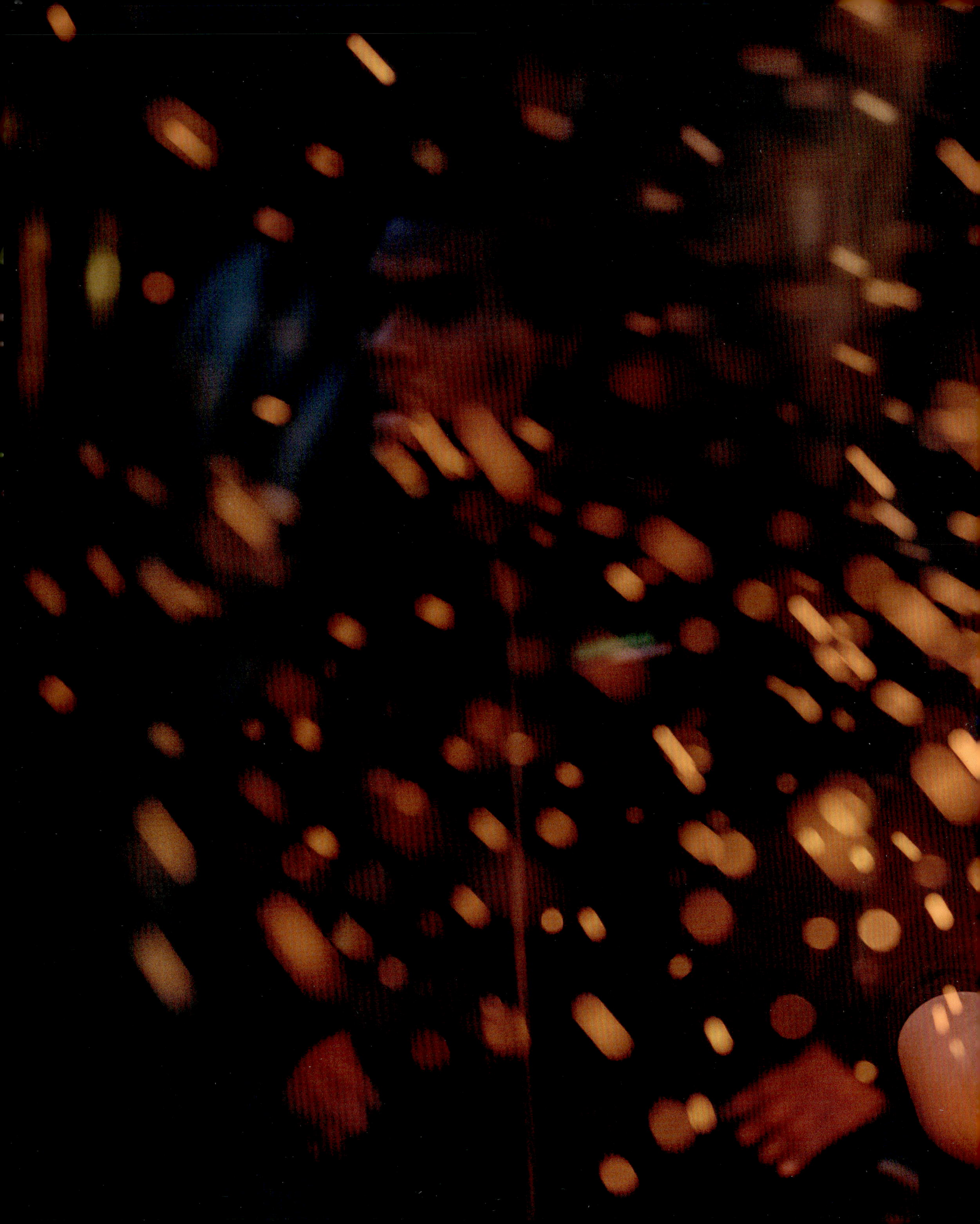

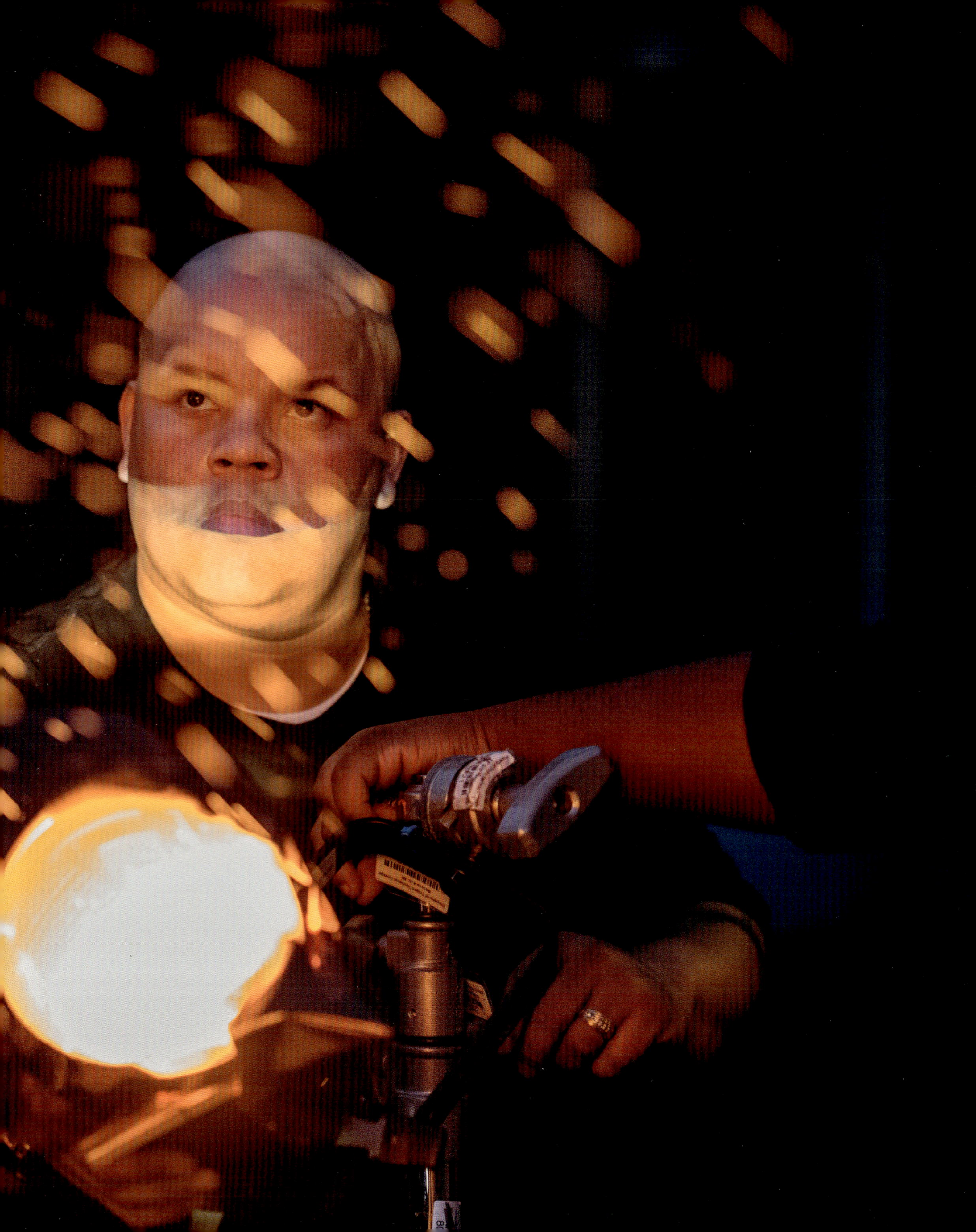

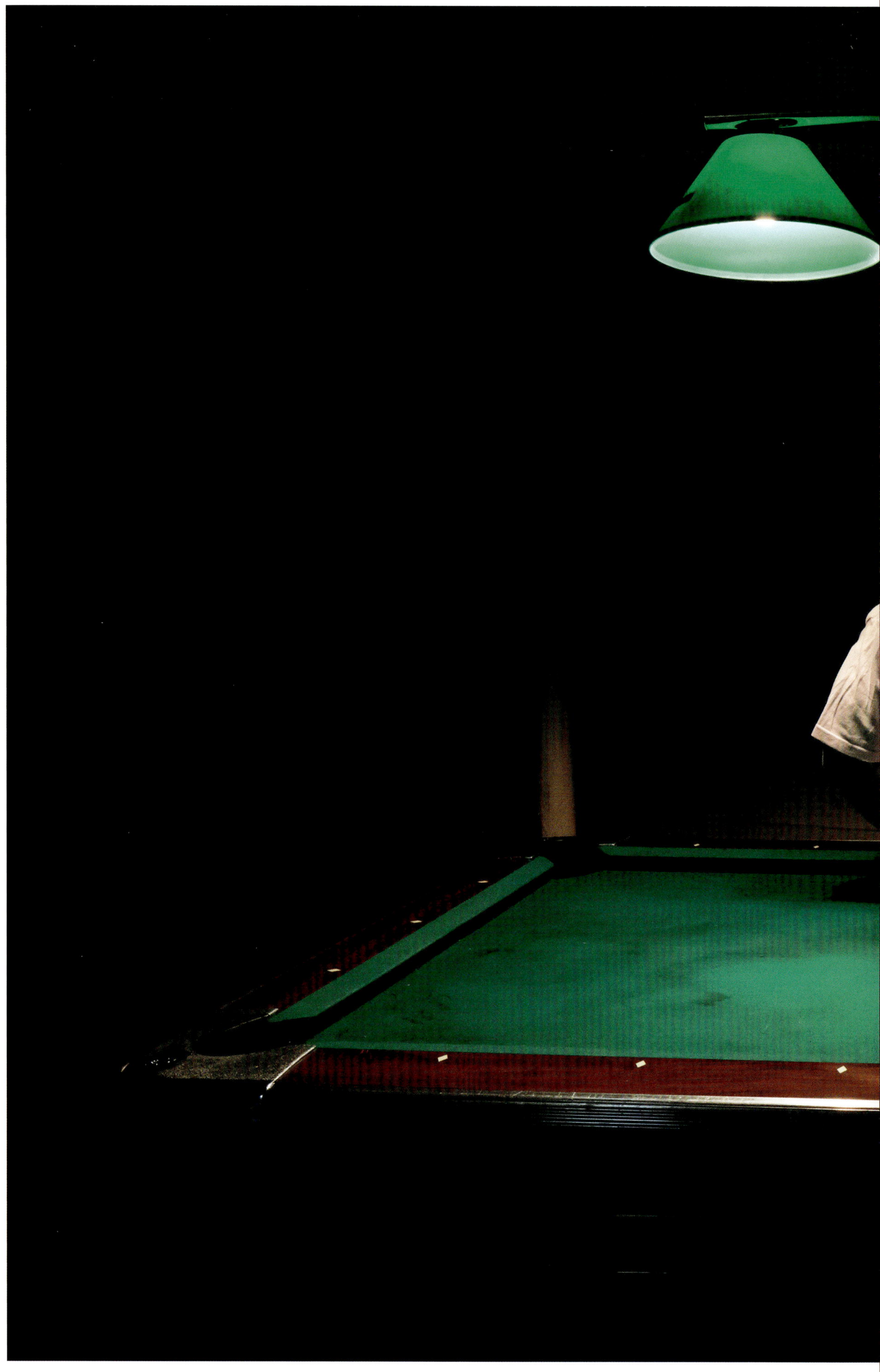

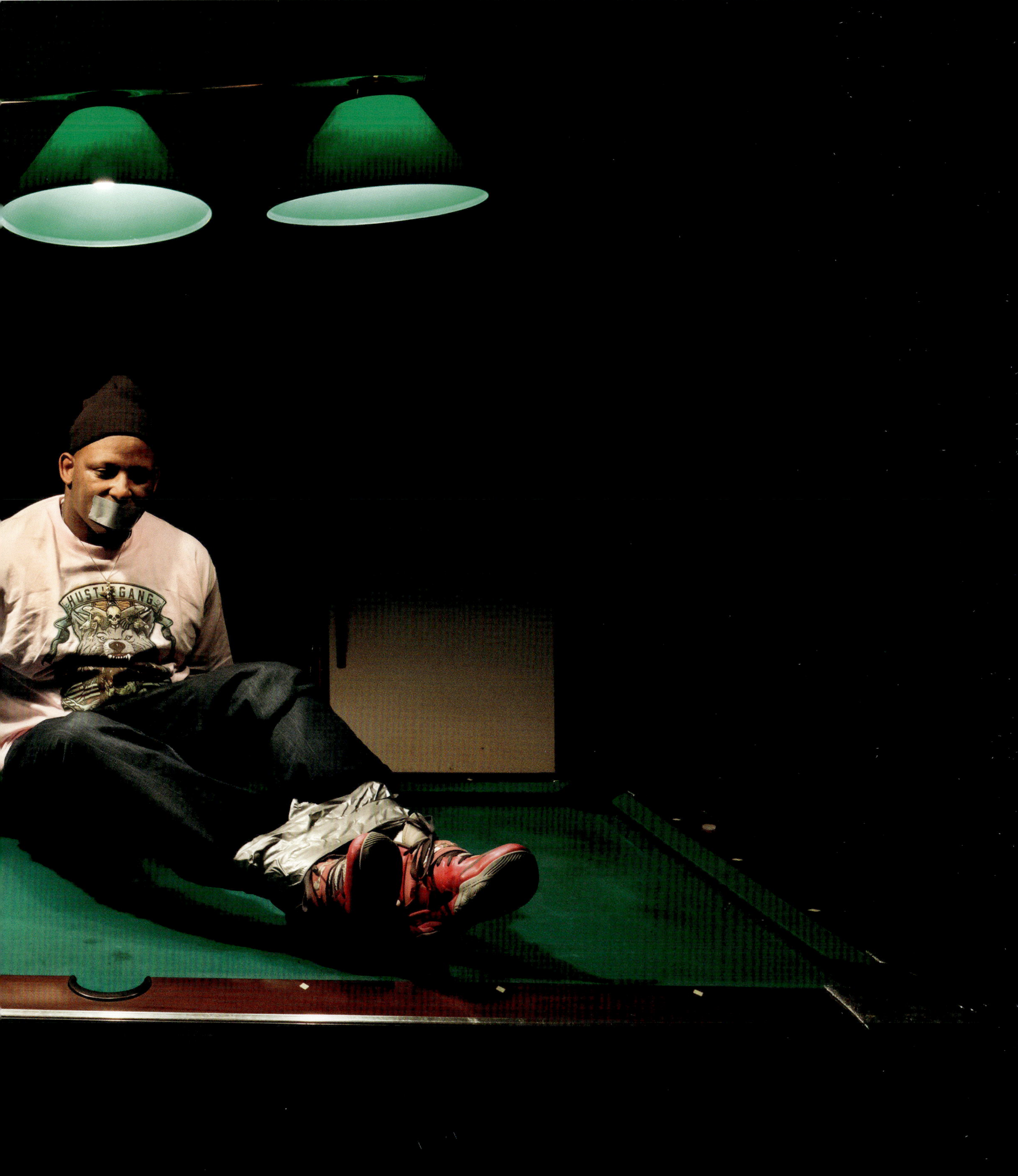

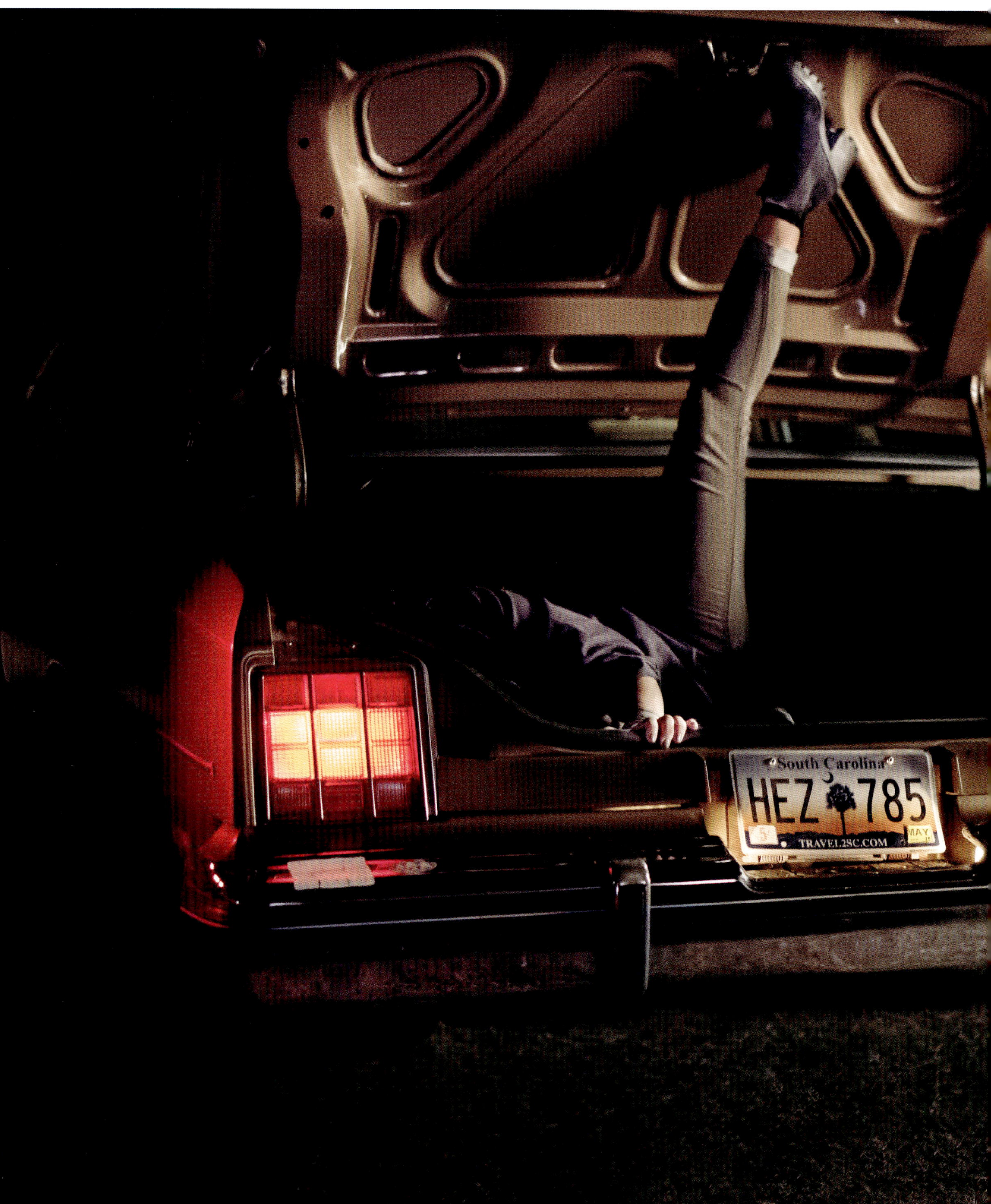

South Carolina
HEZ 785
TRAVEL2SC.COM
MAY

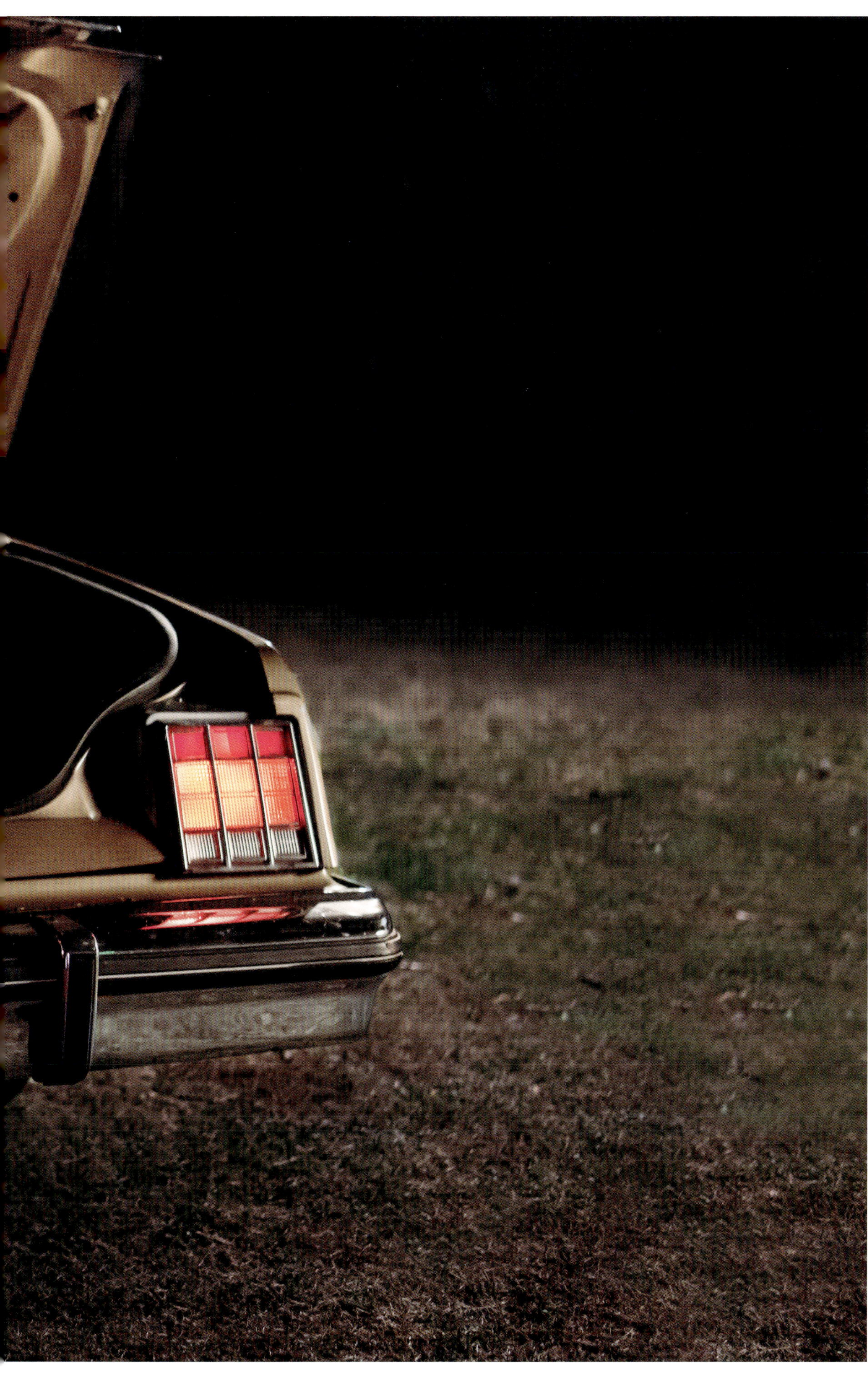

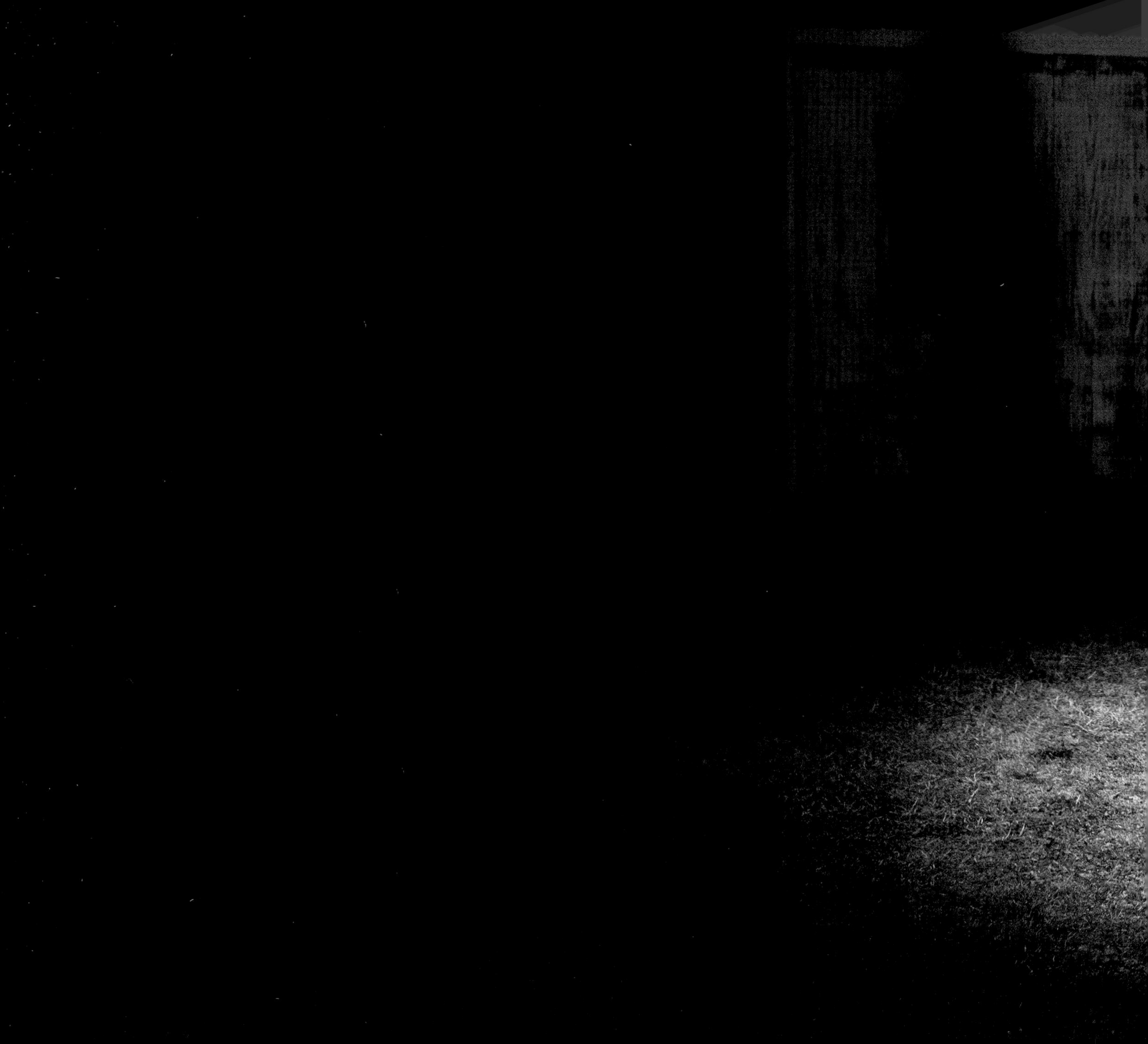

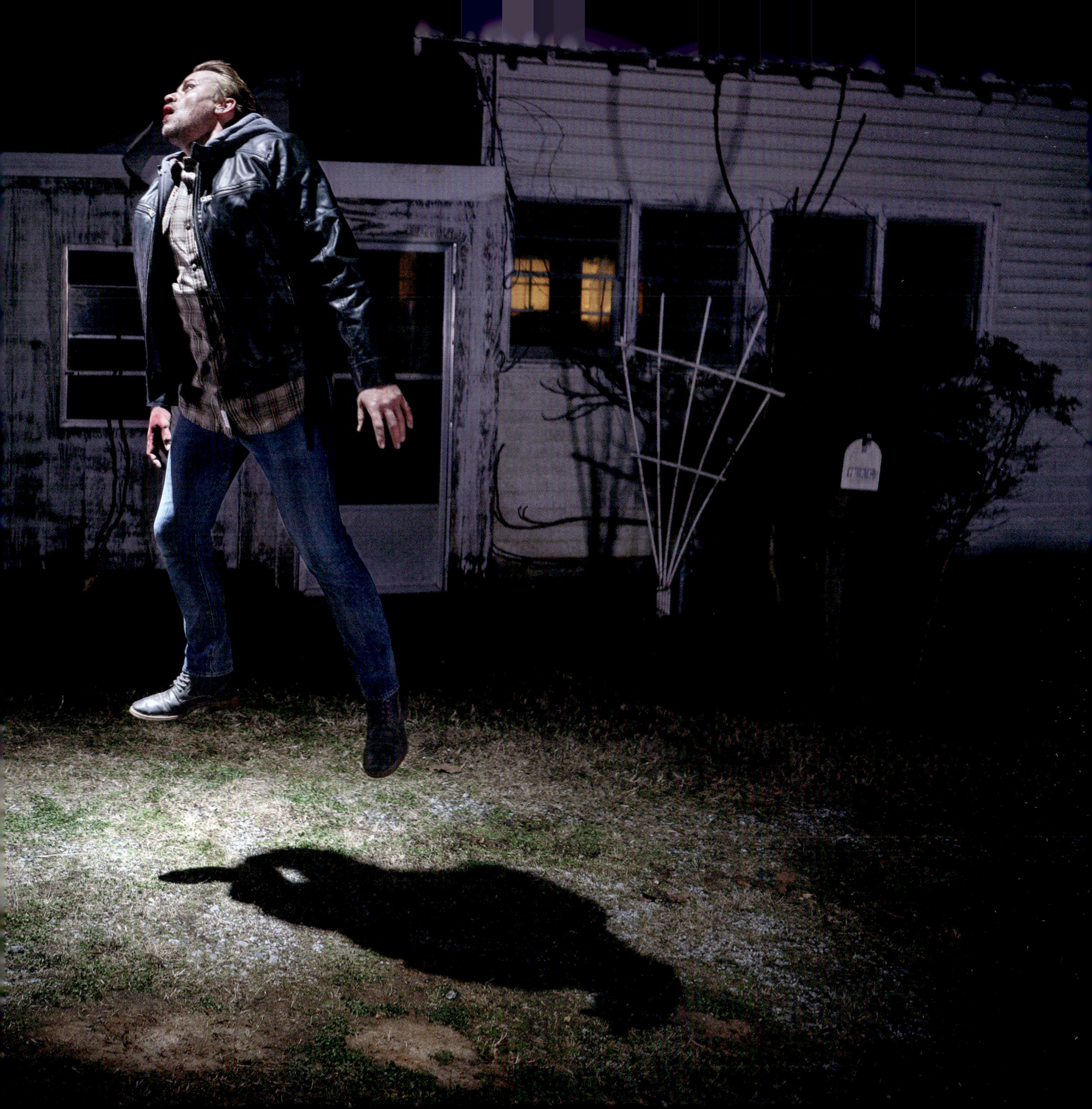

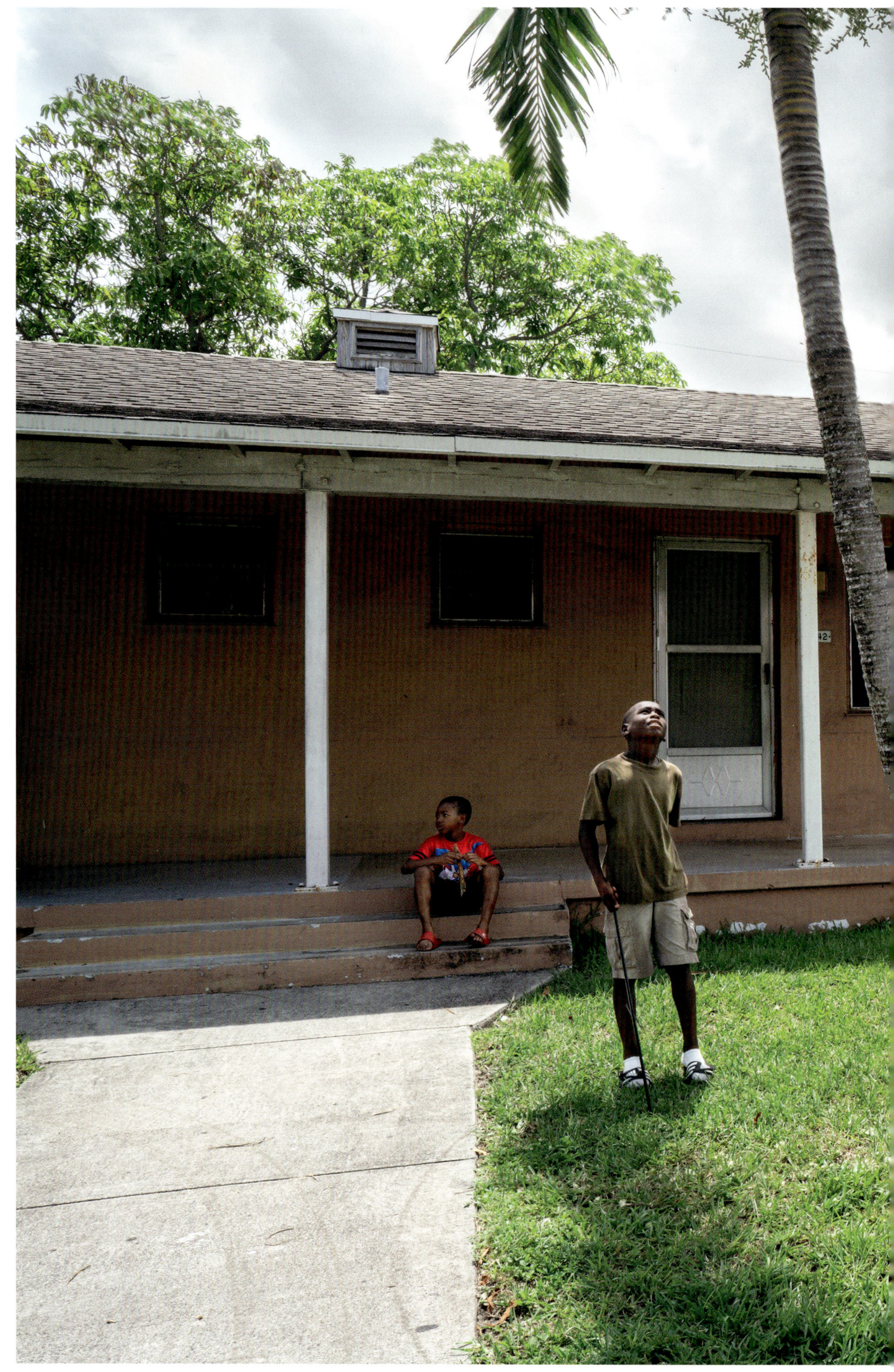

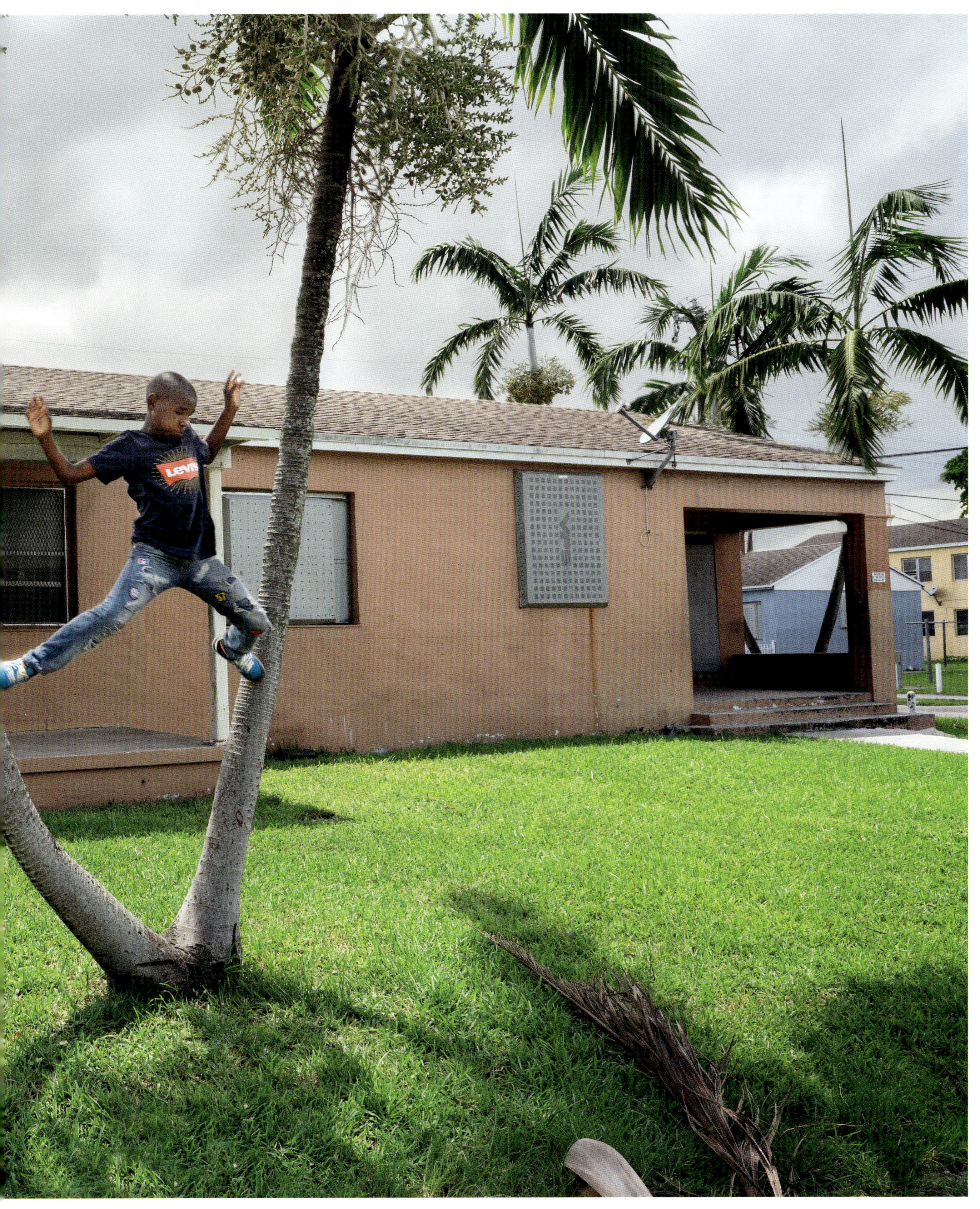

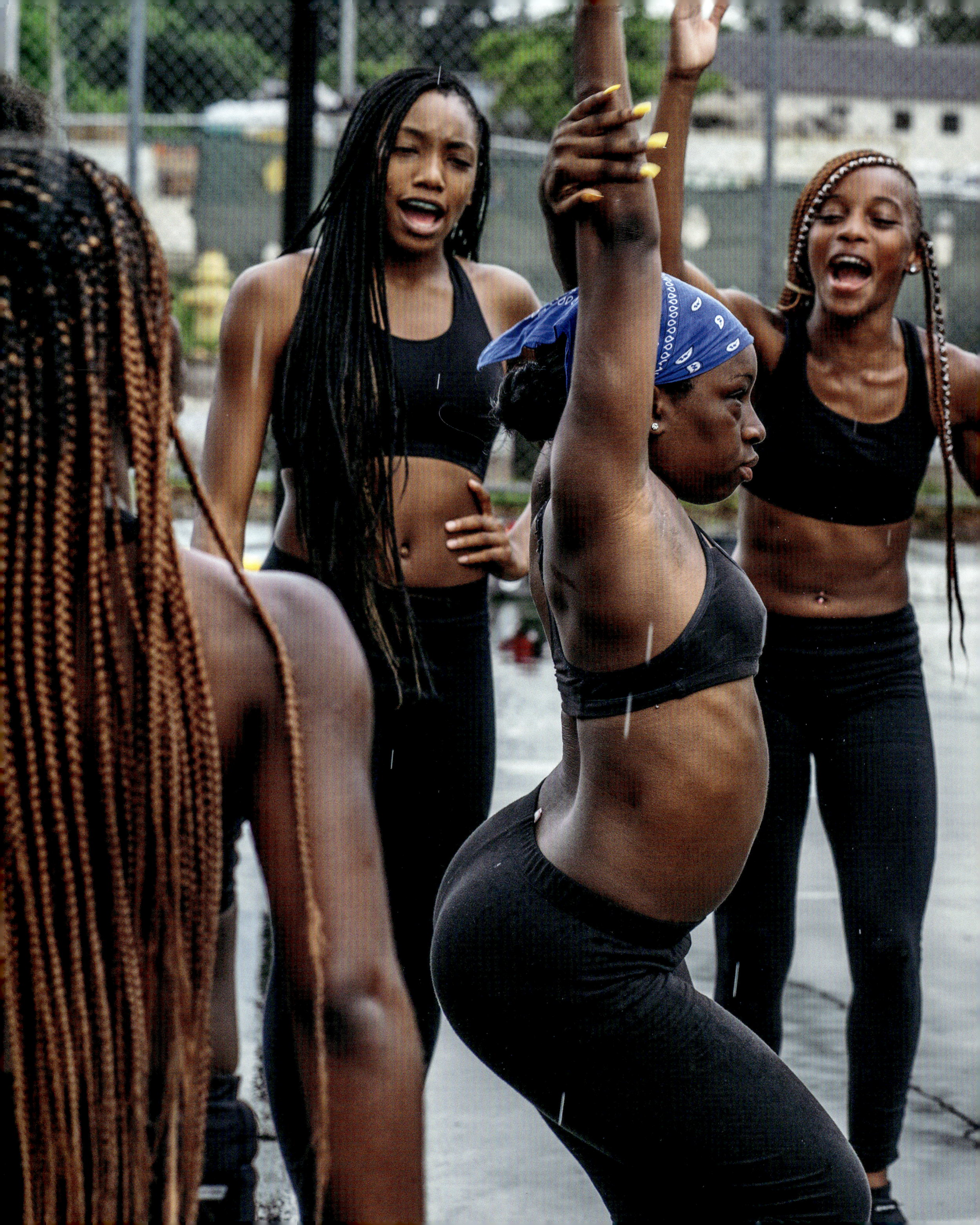

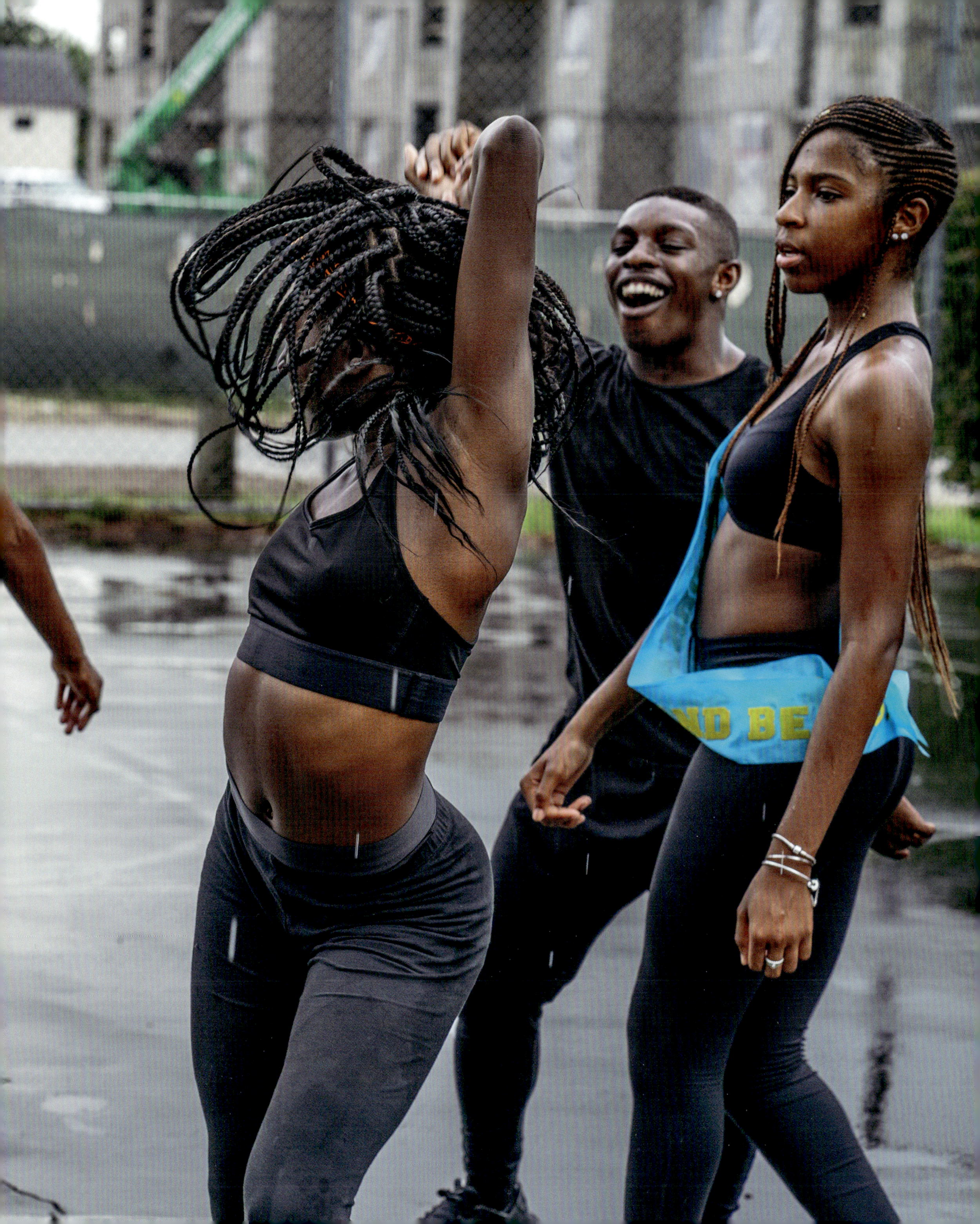

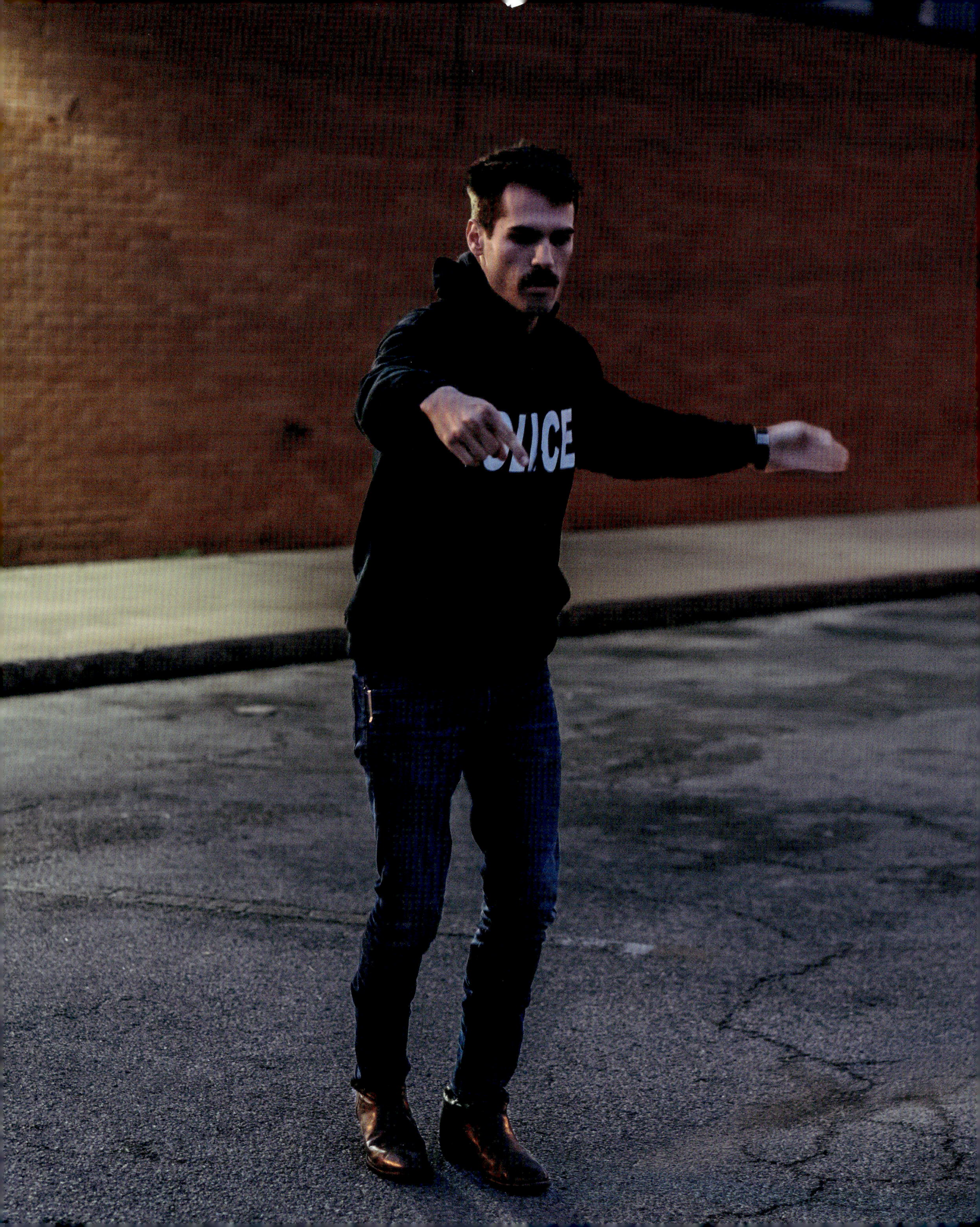

OLICE

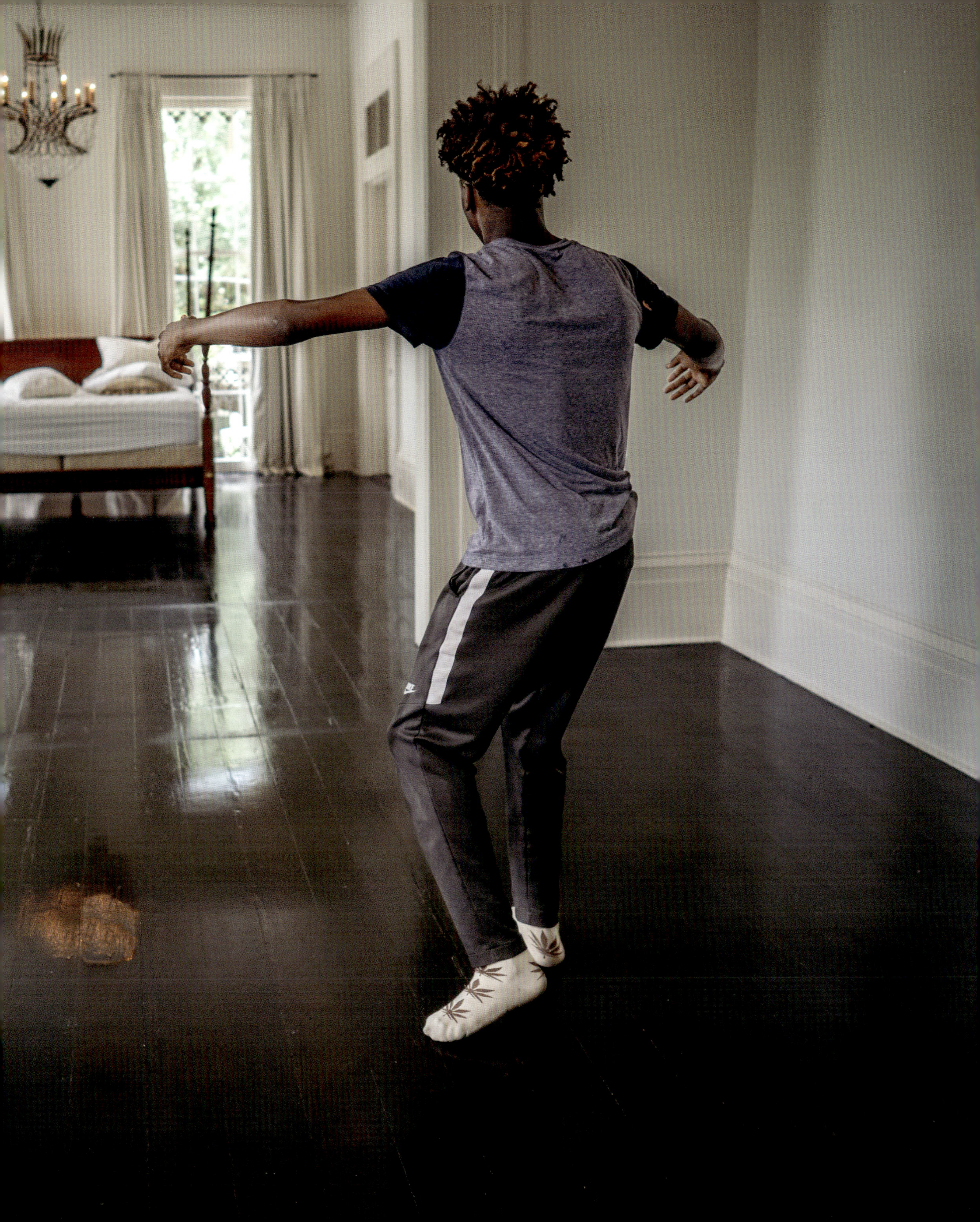

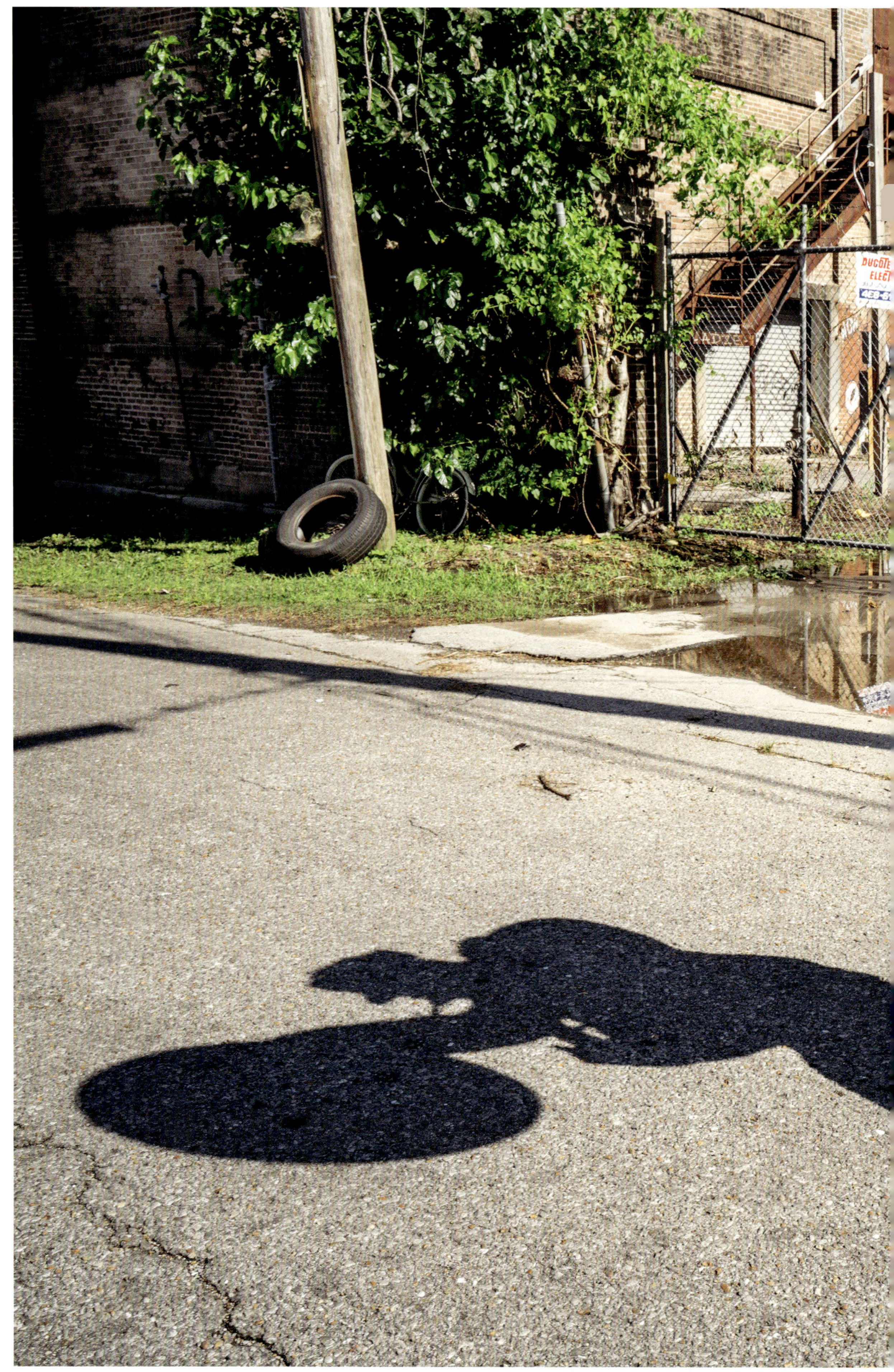

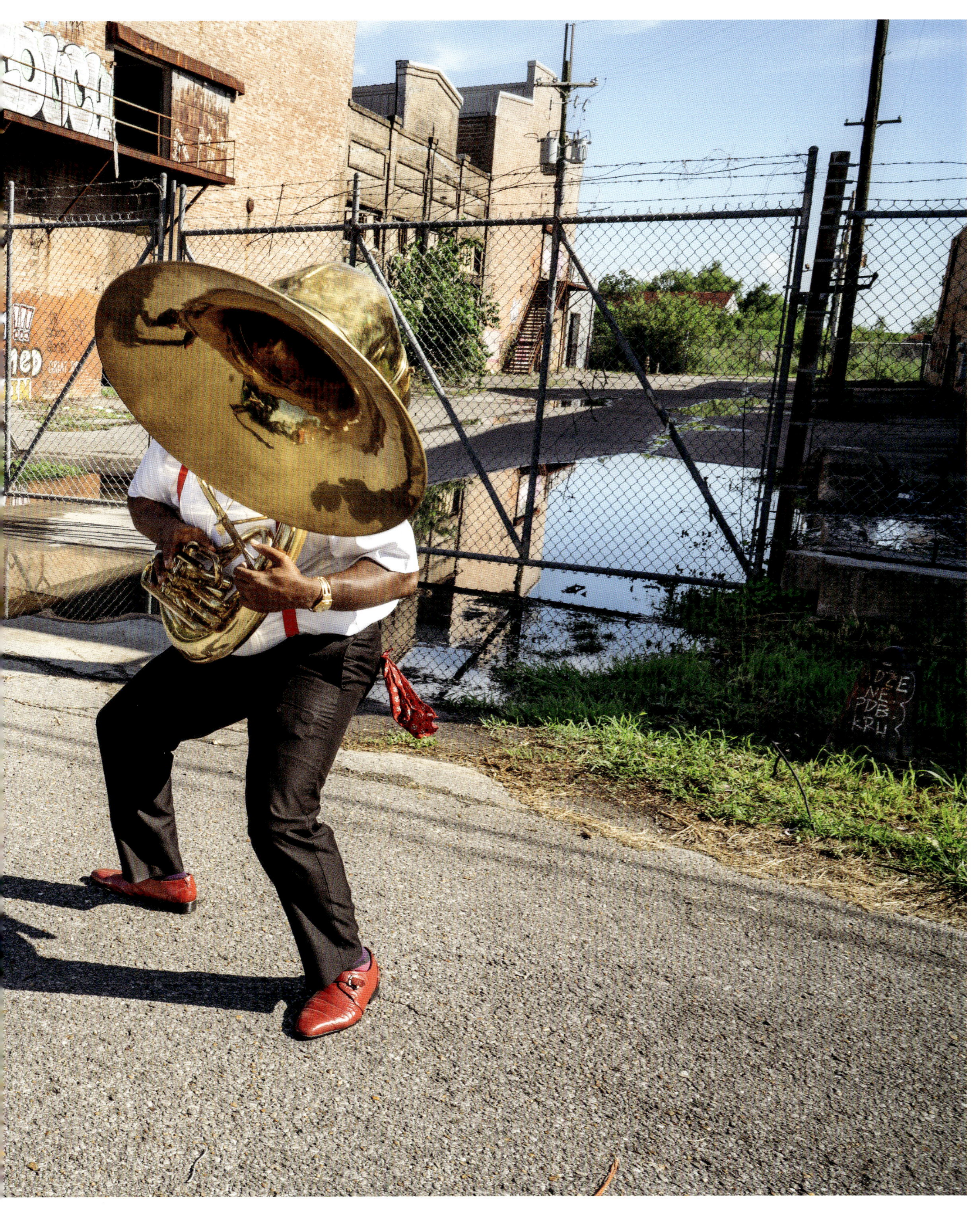

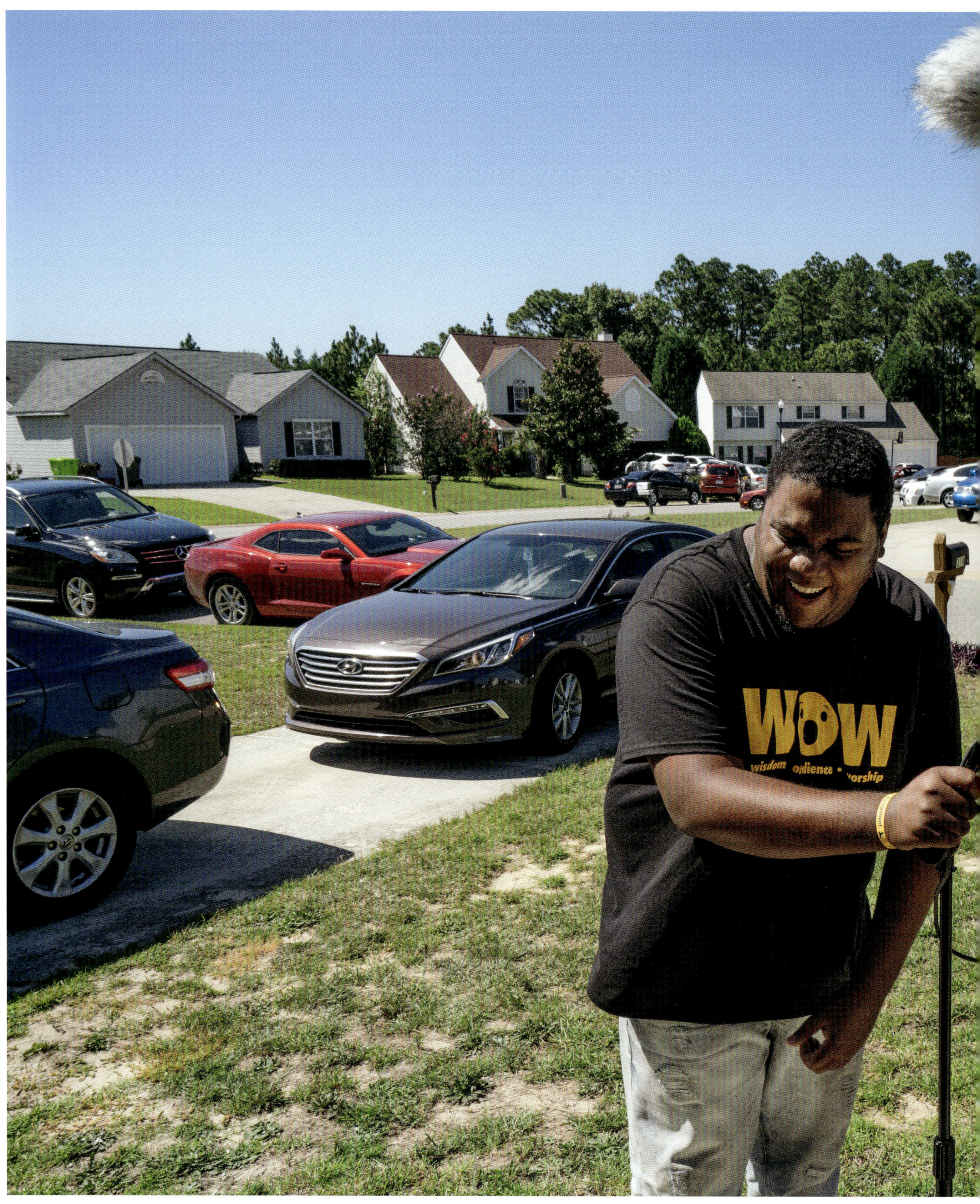

WOW
wisdom • obedience • worship

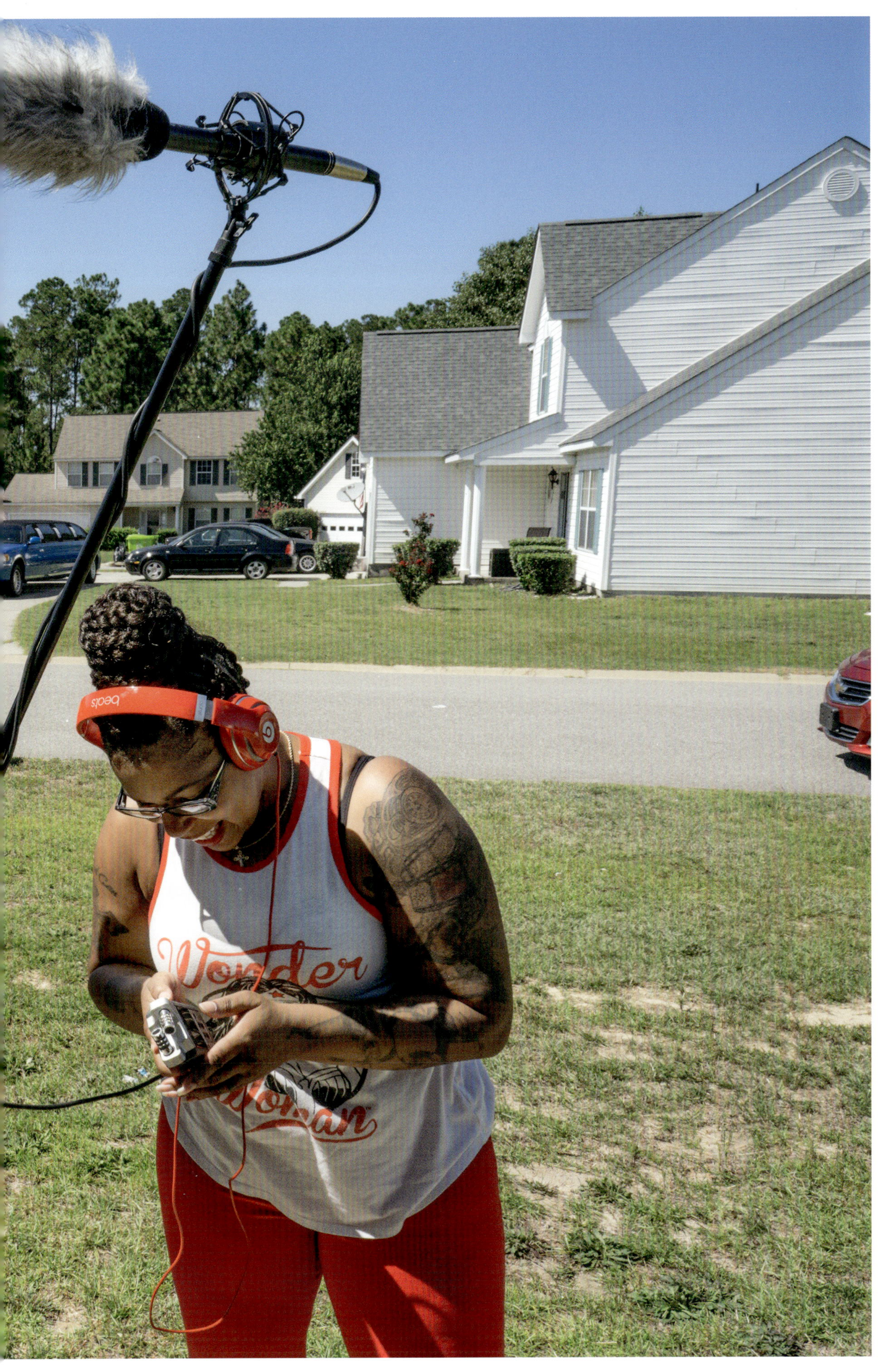

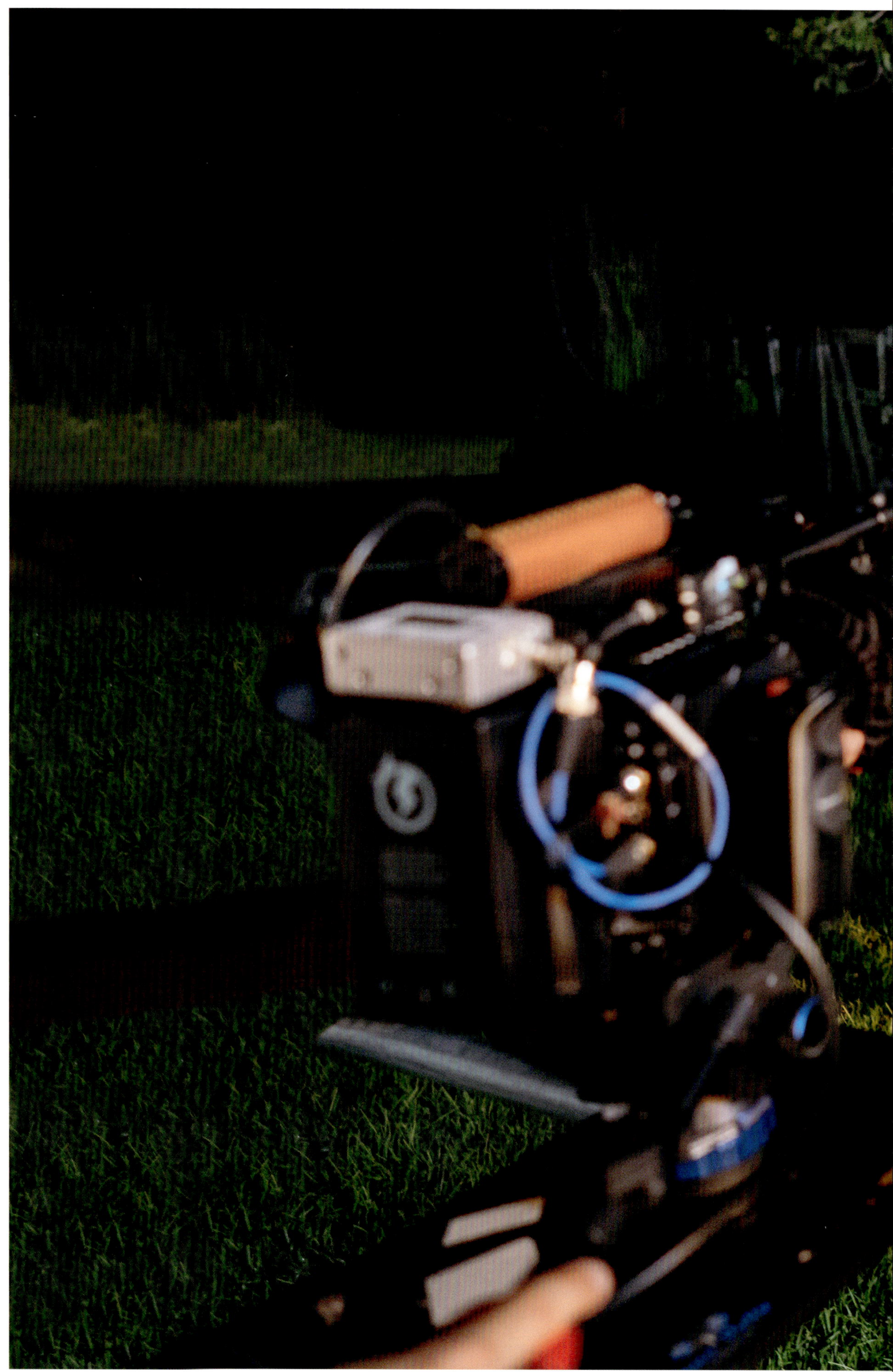

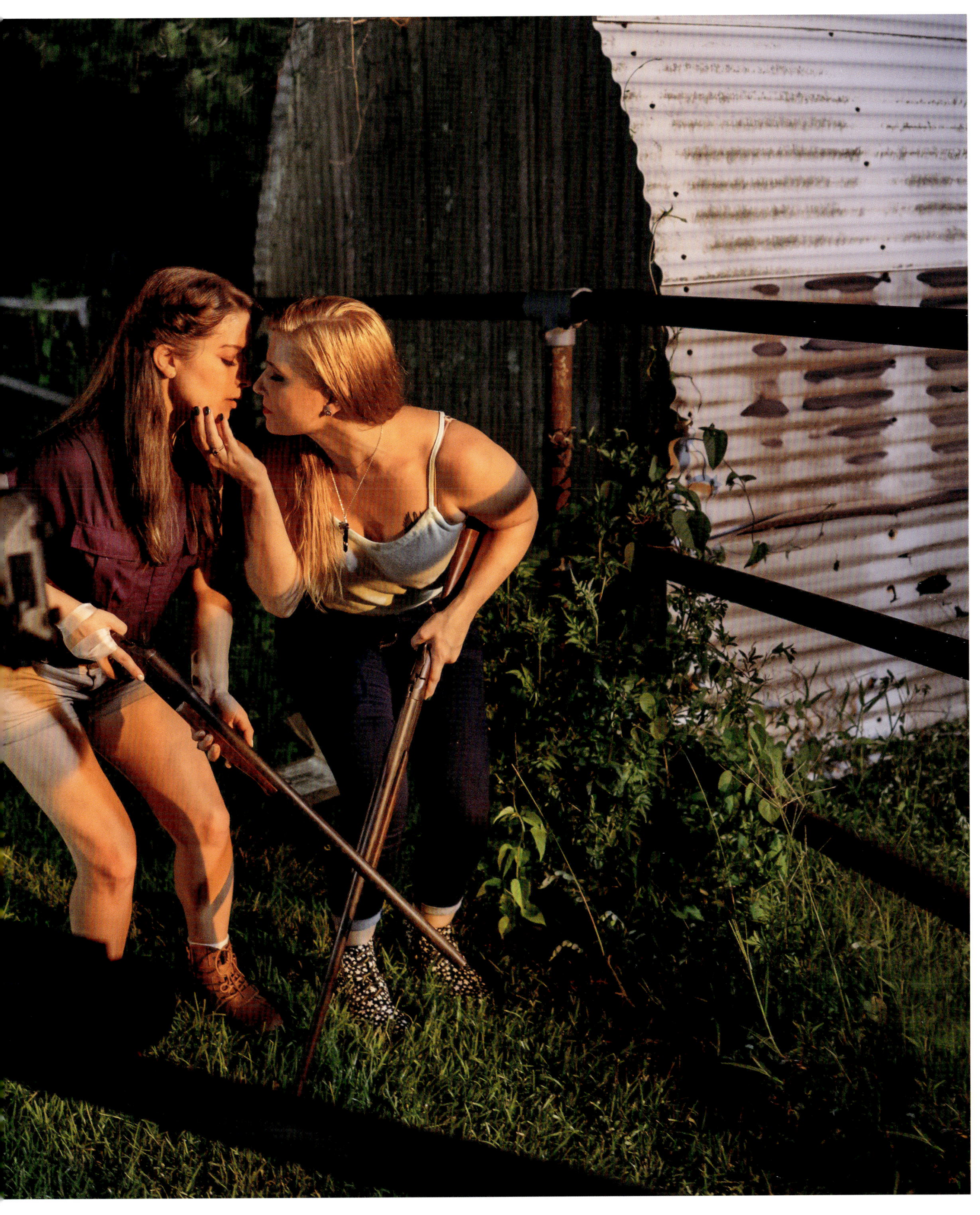

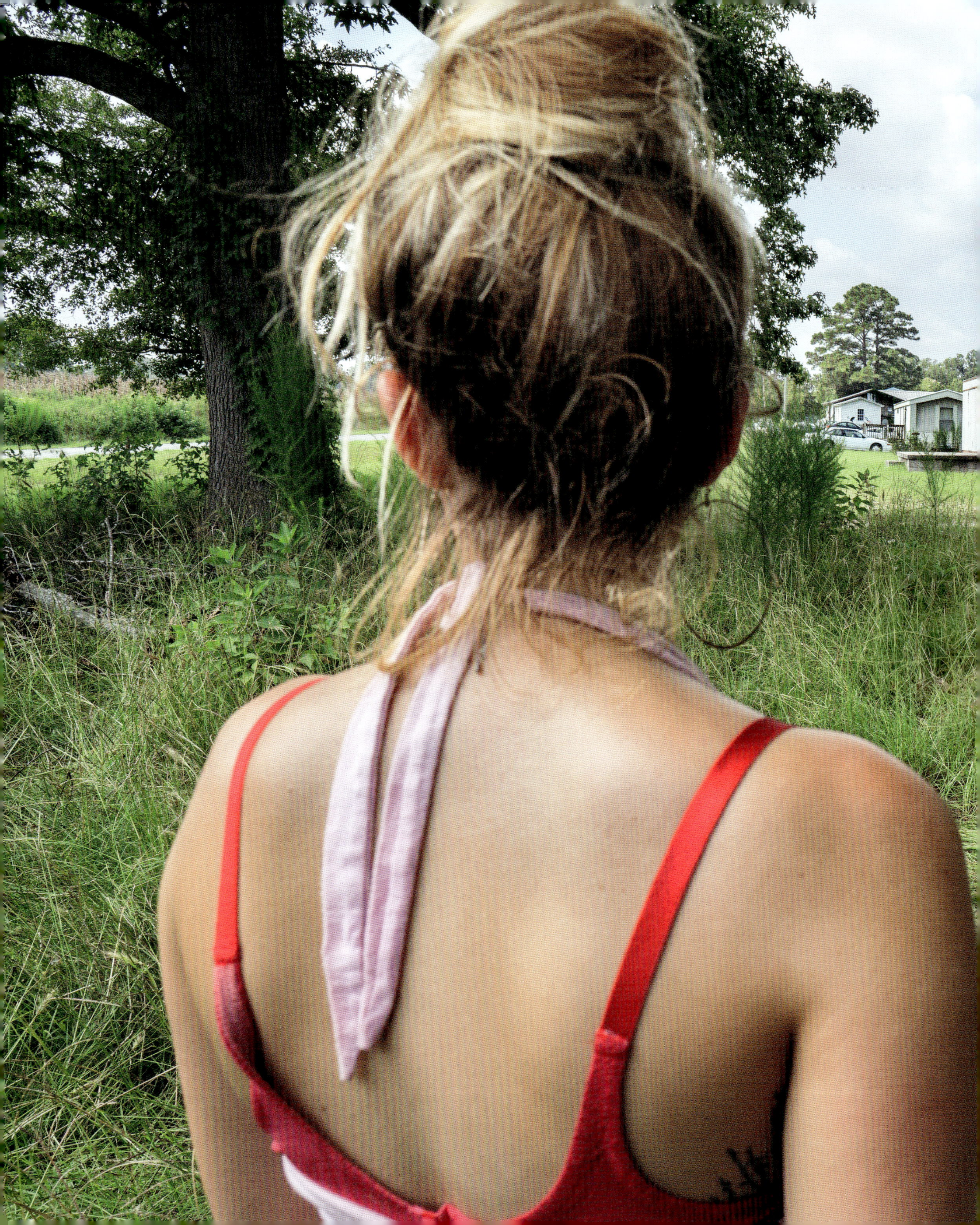

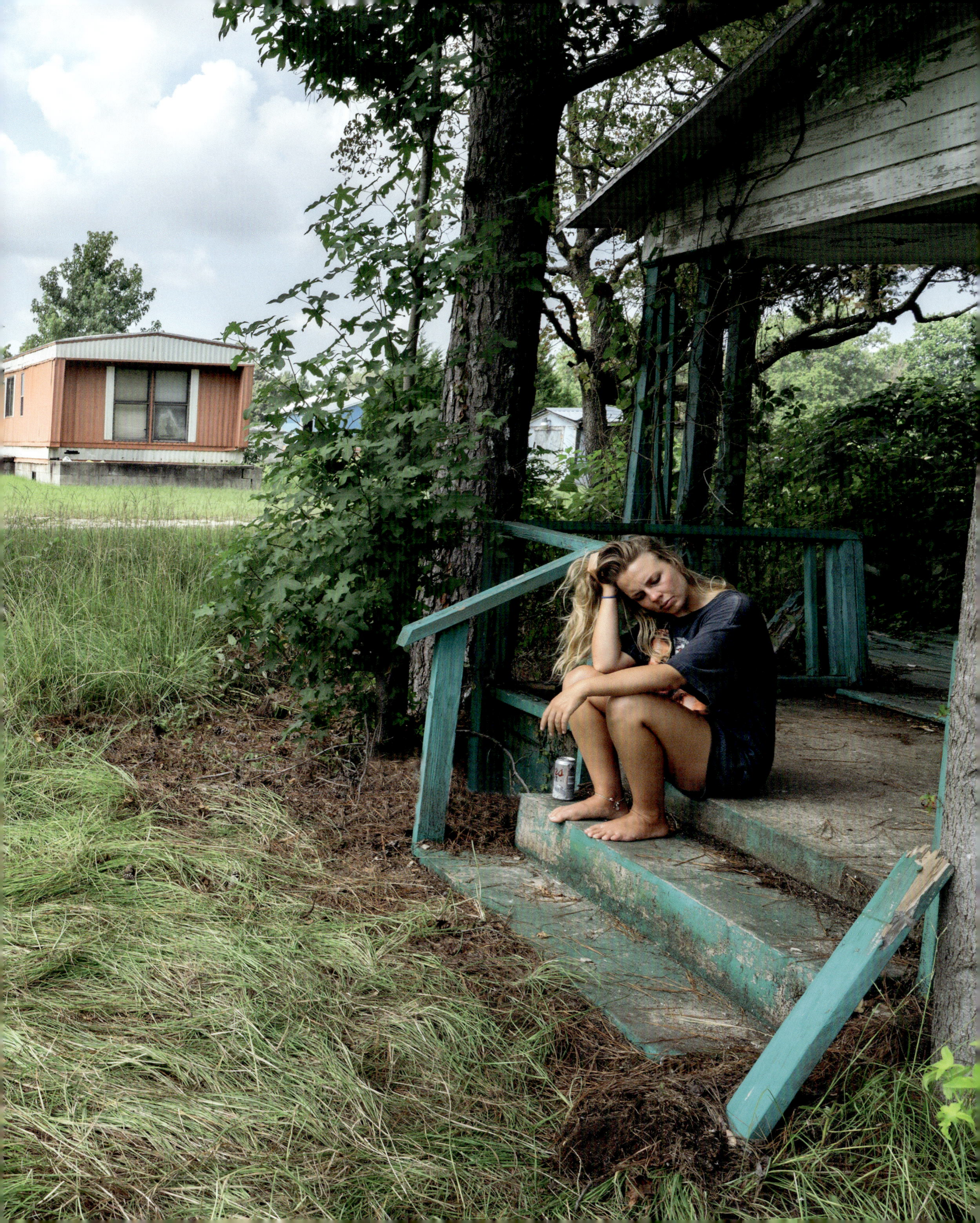

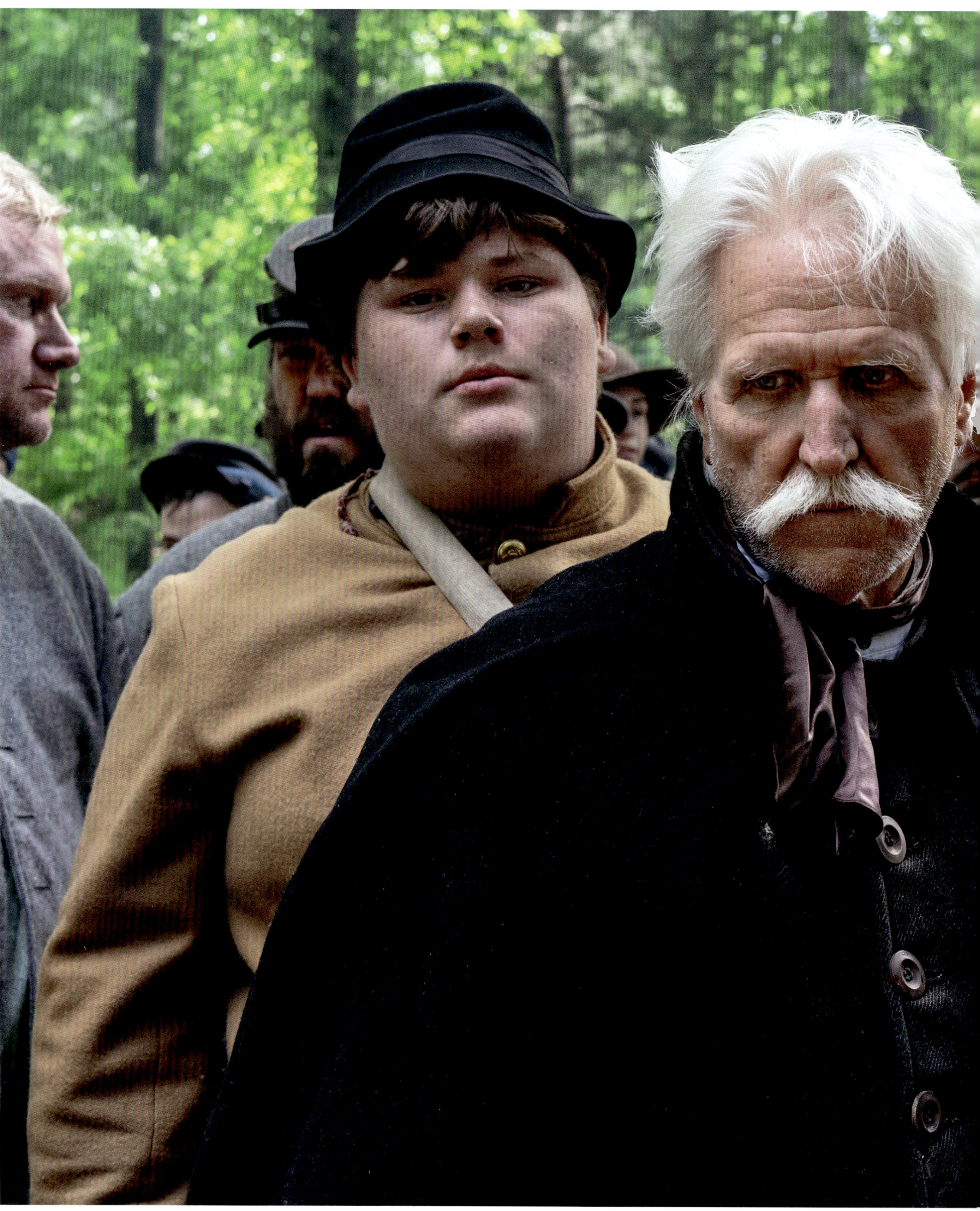

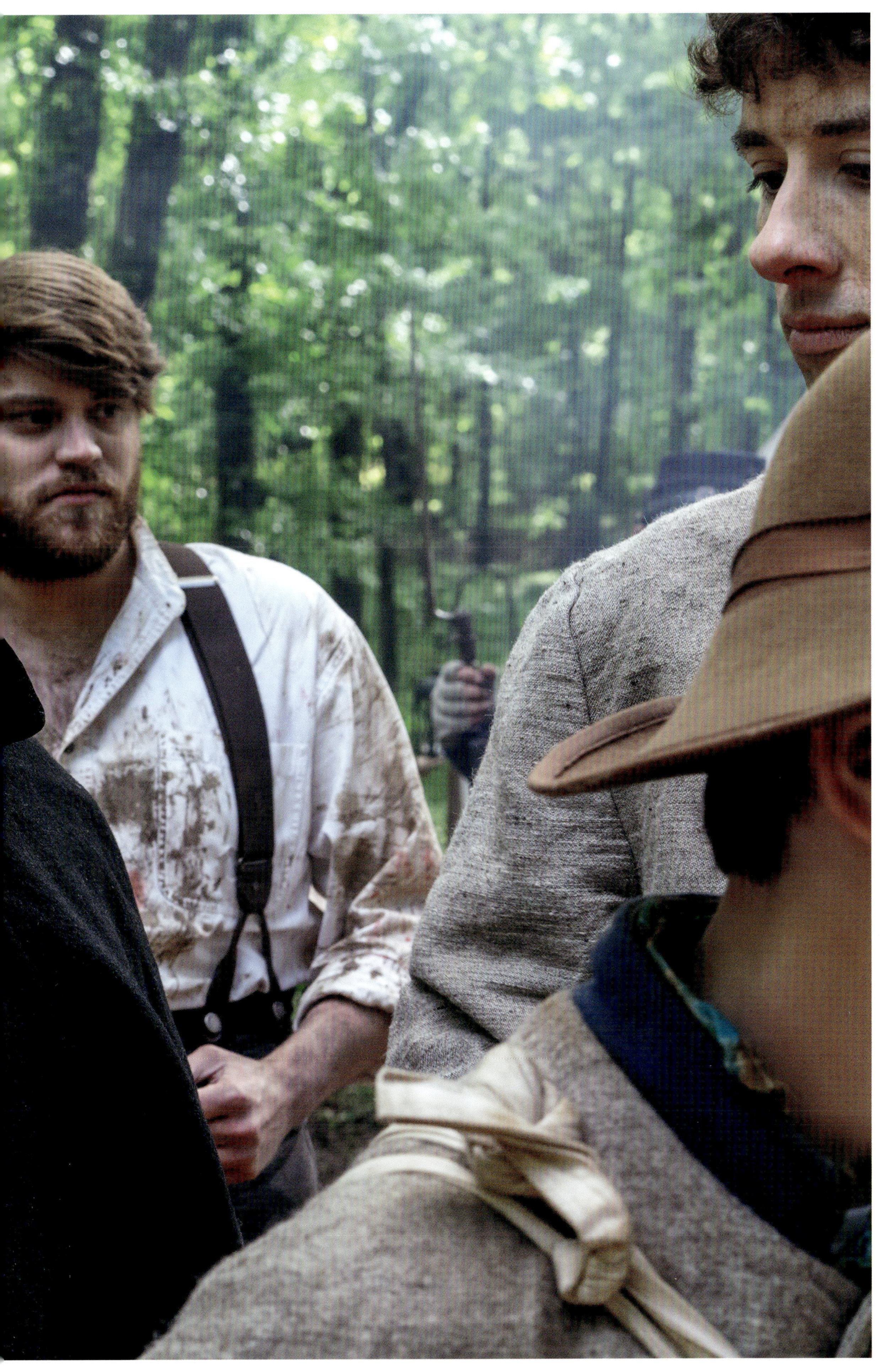

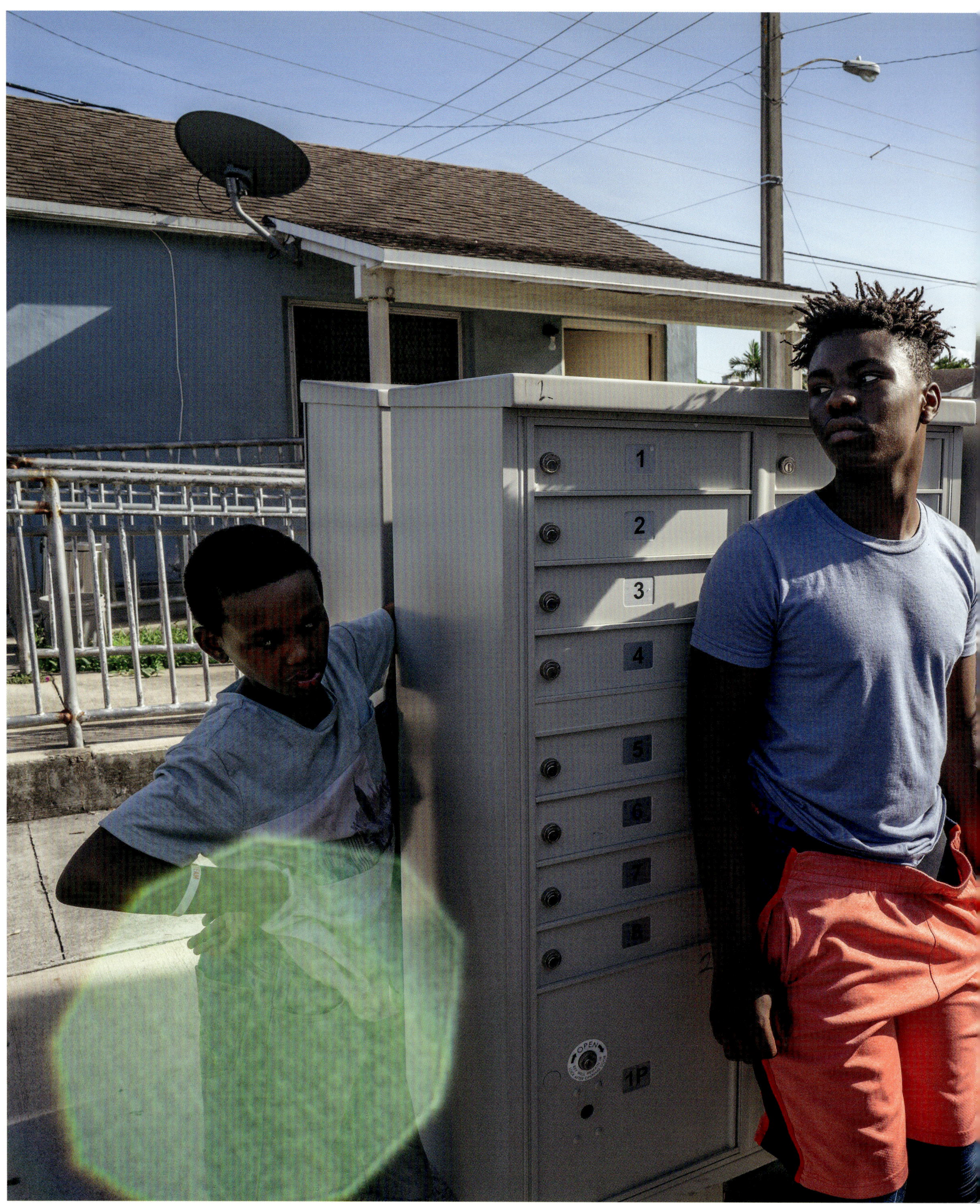

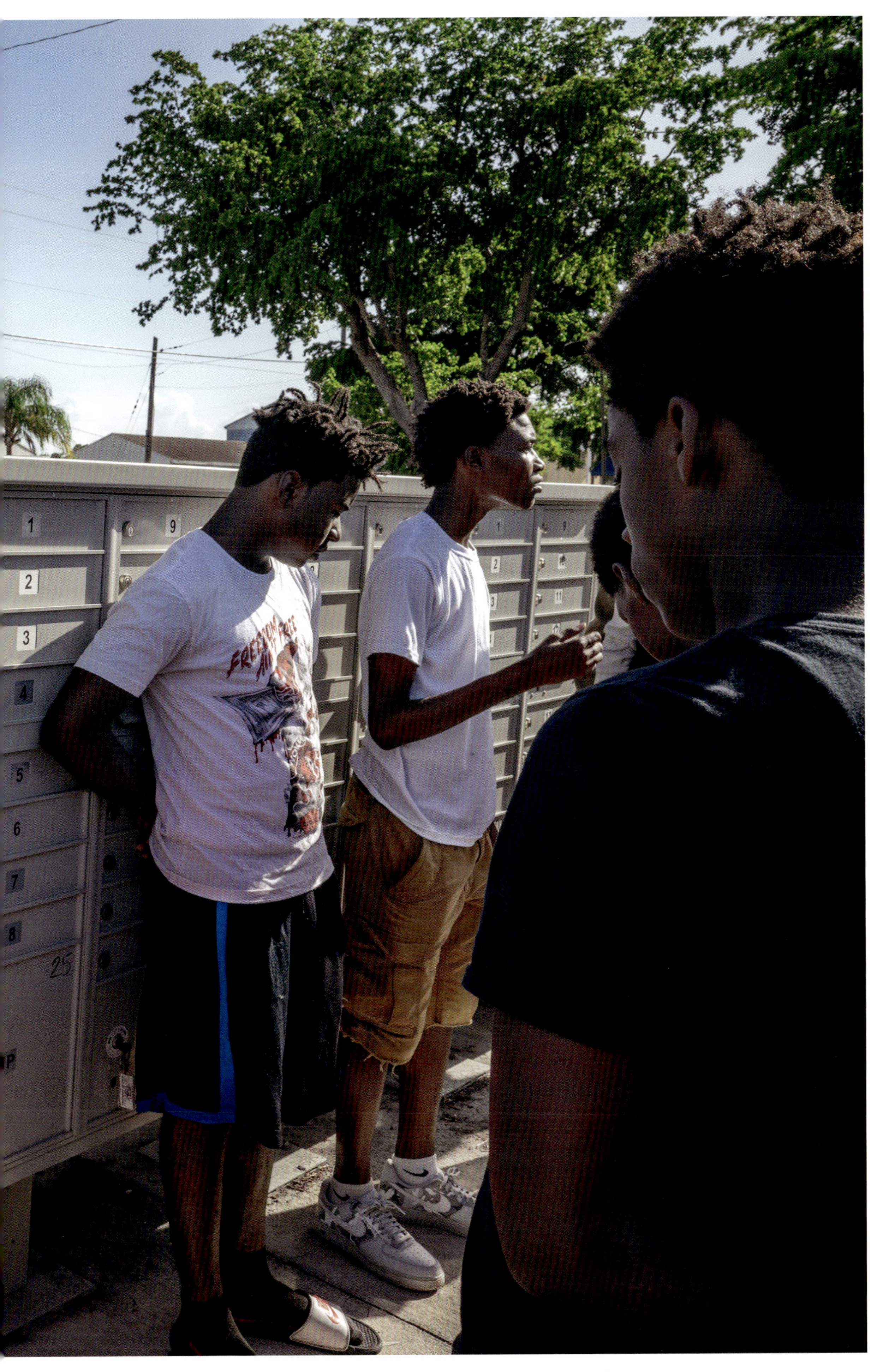

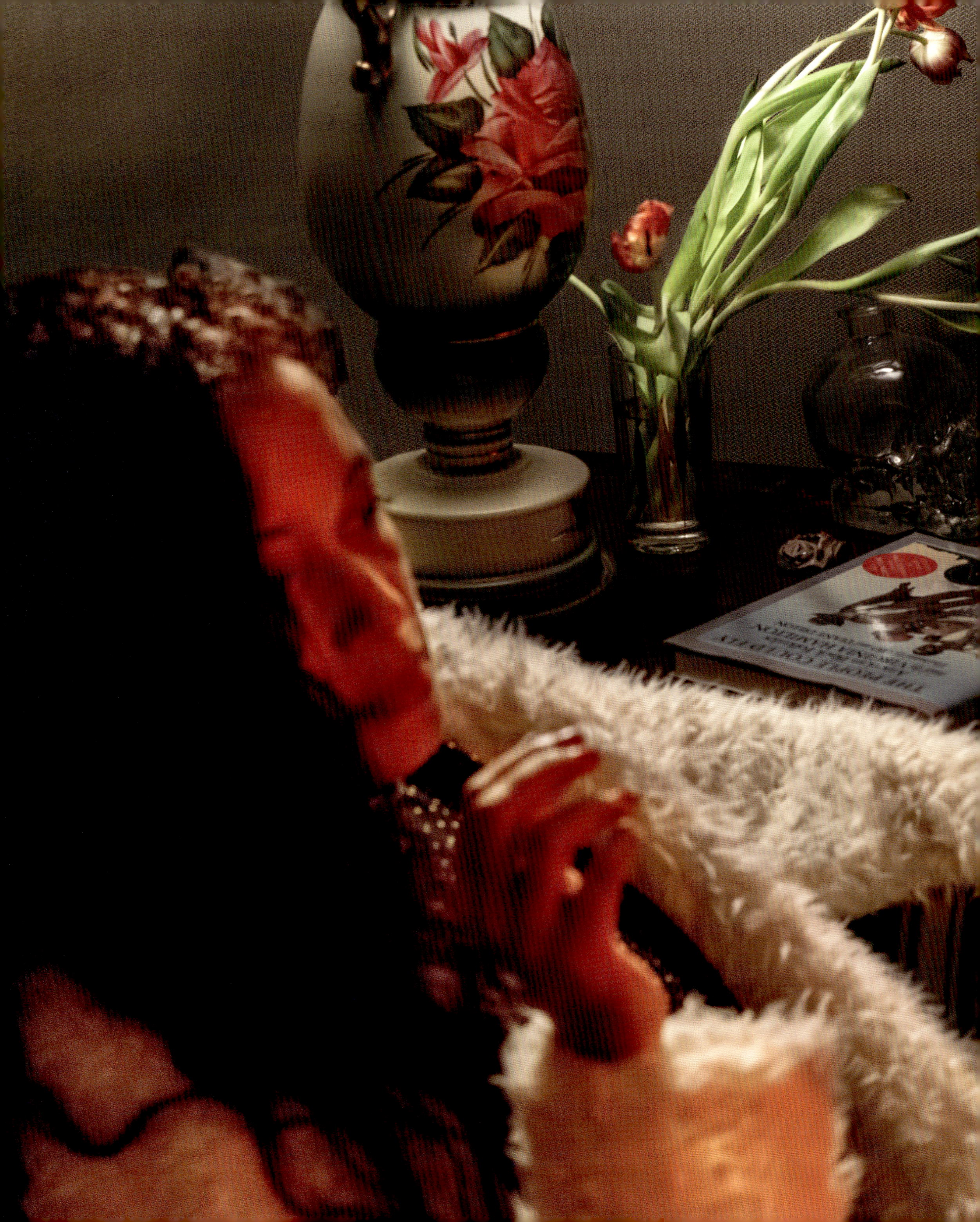

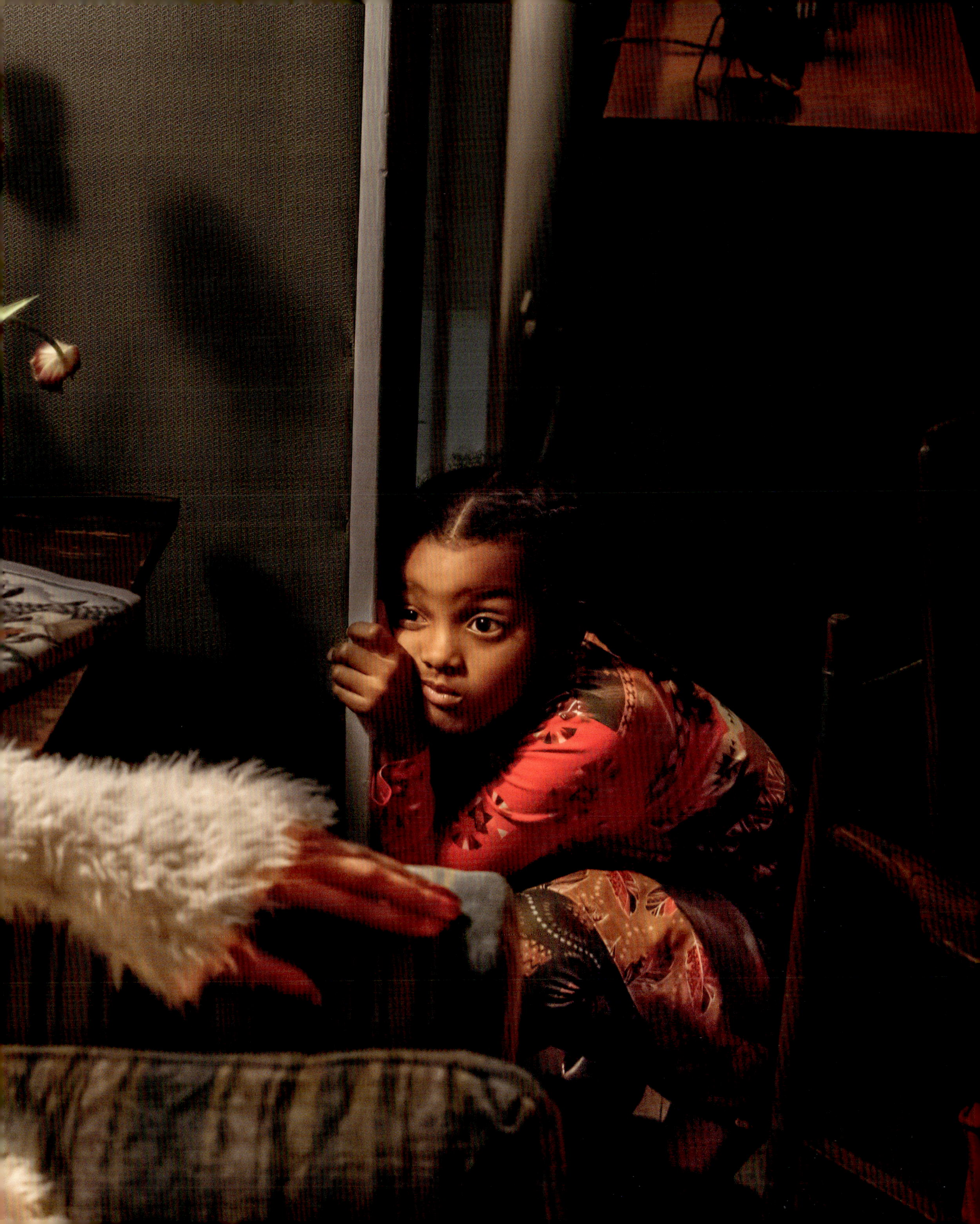

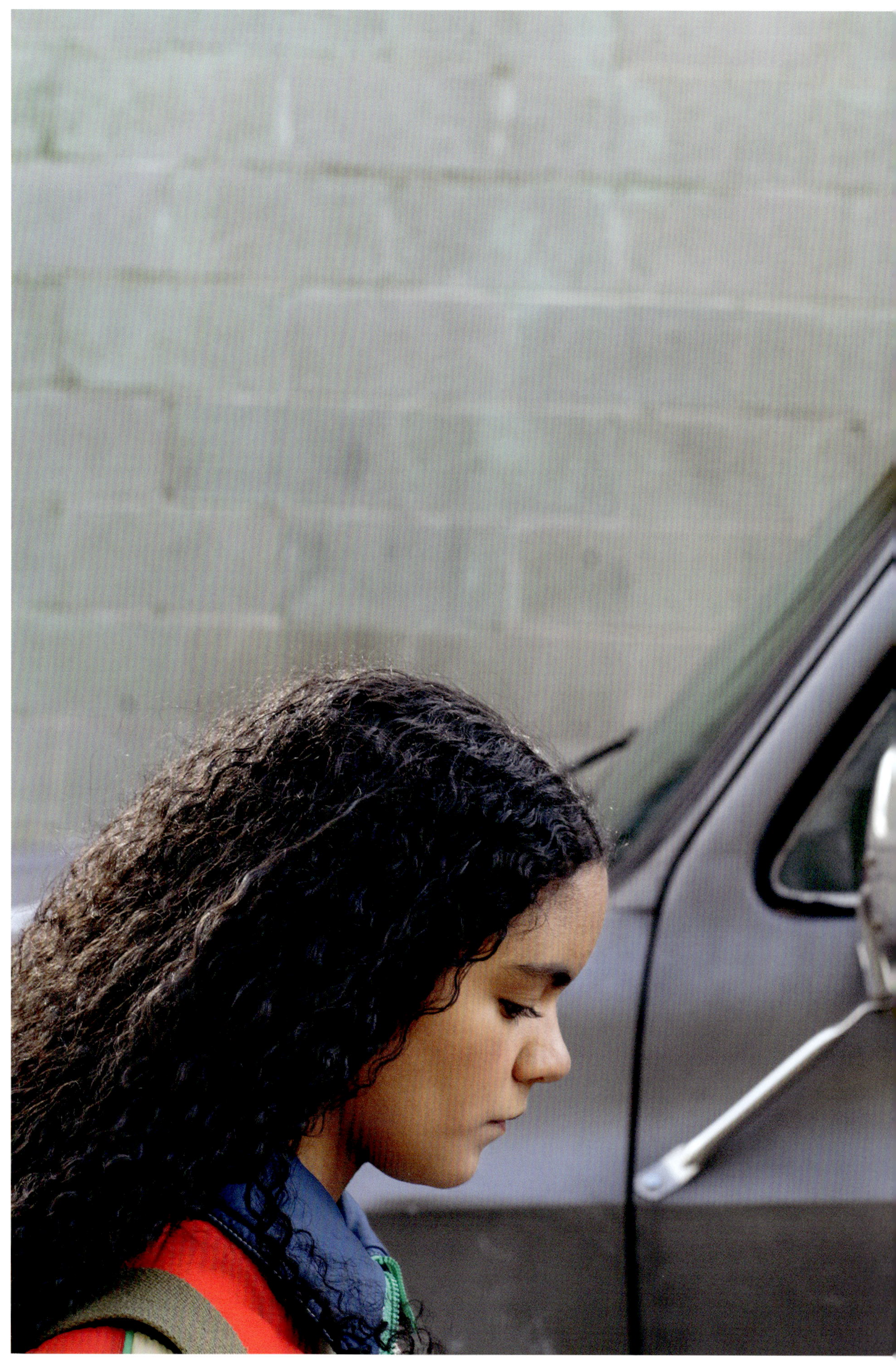

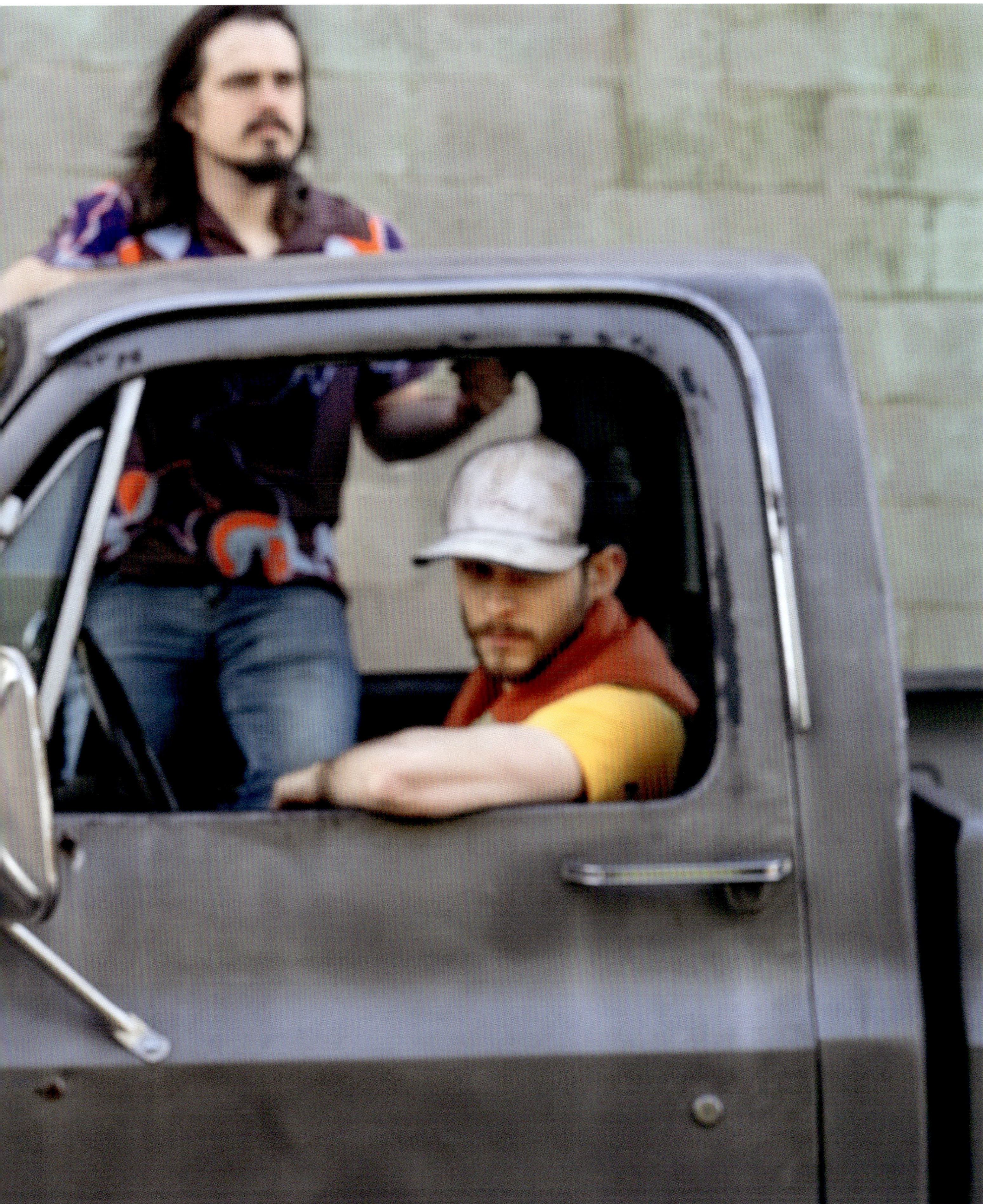

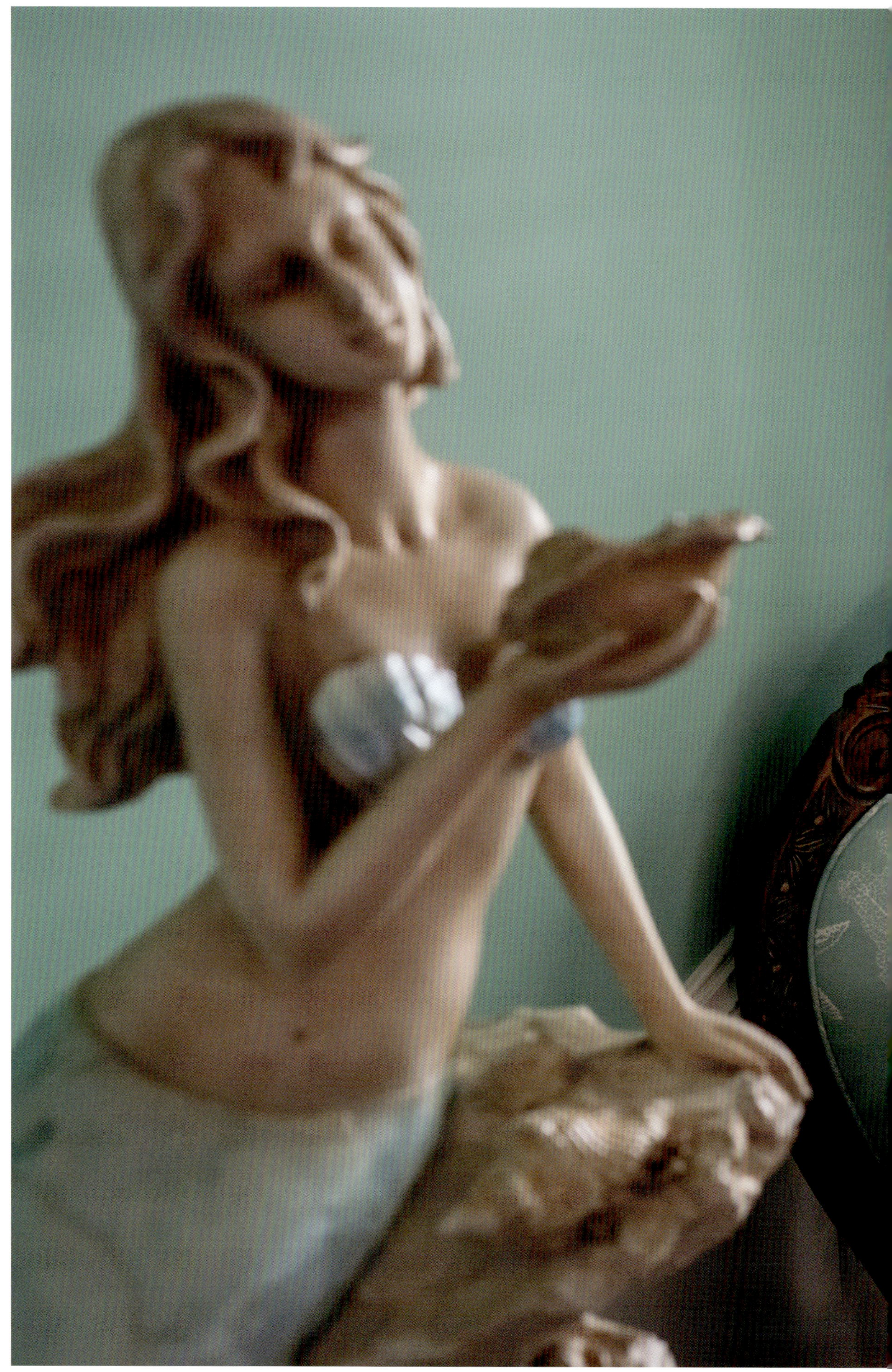

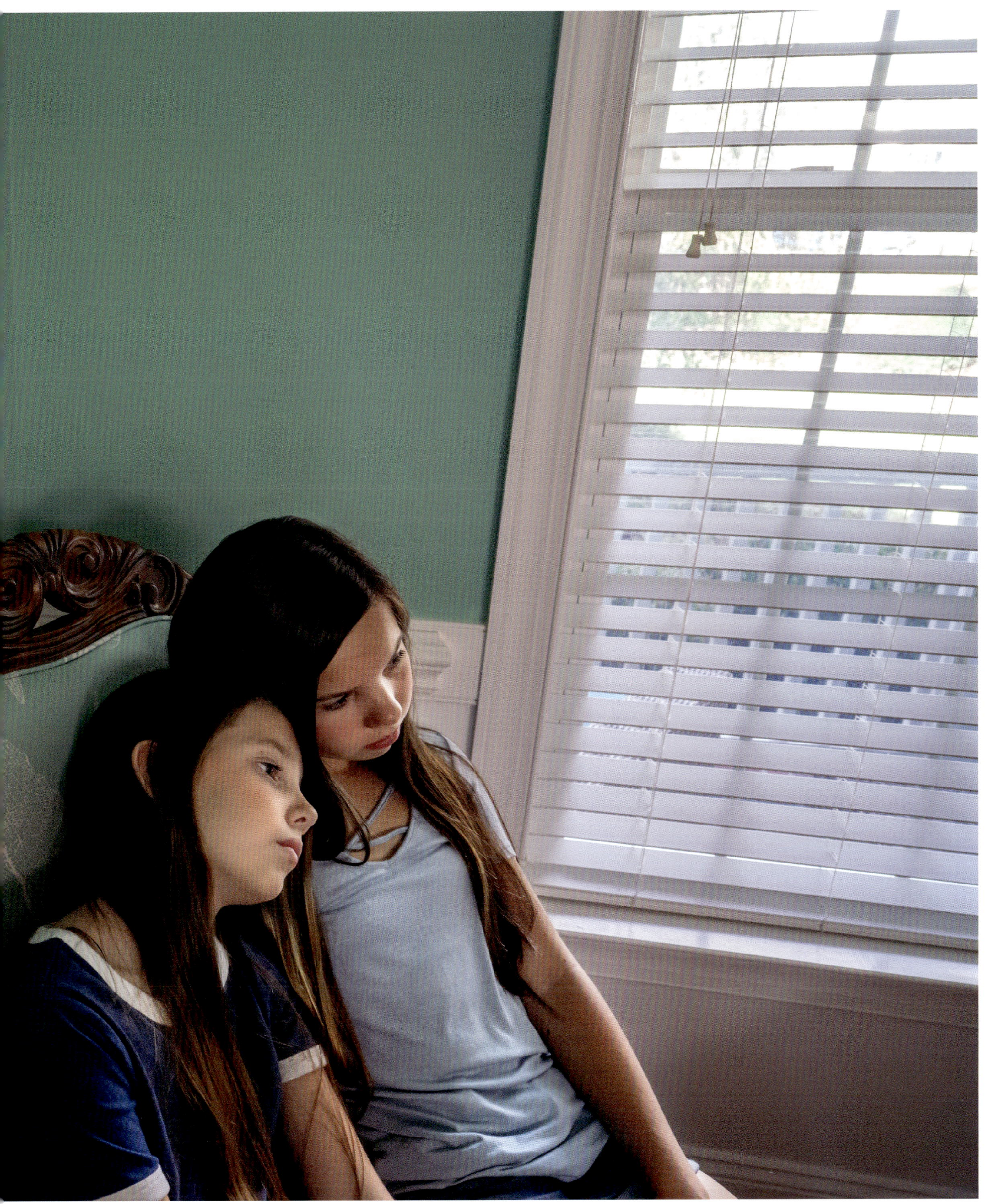

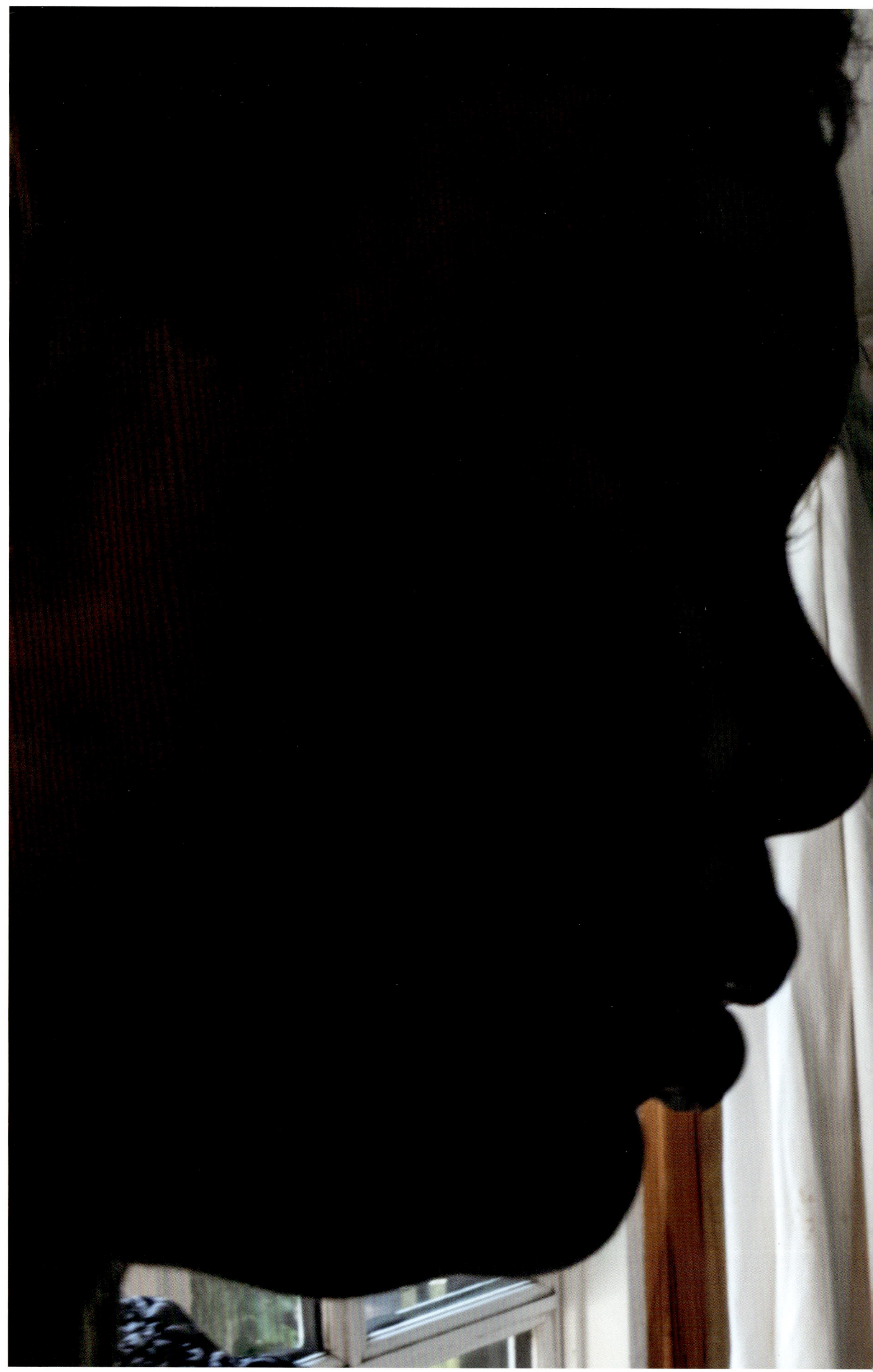

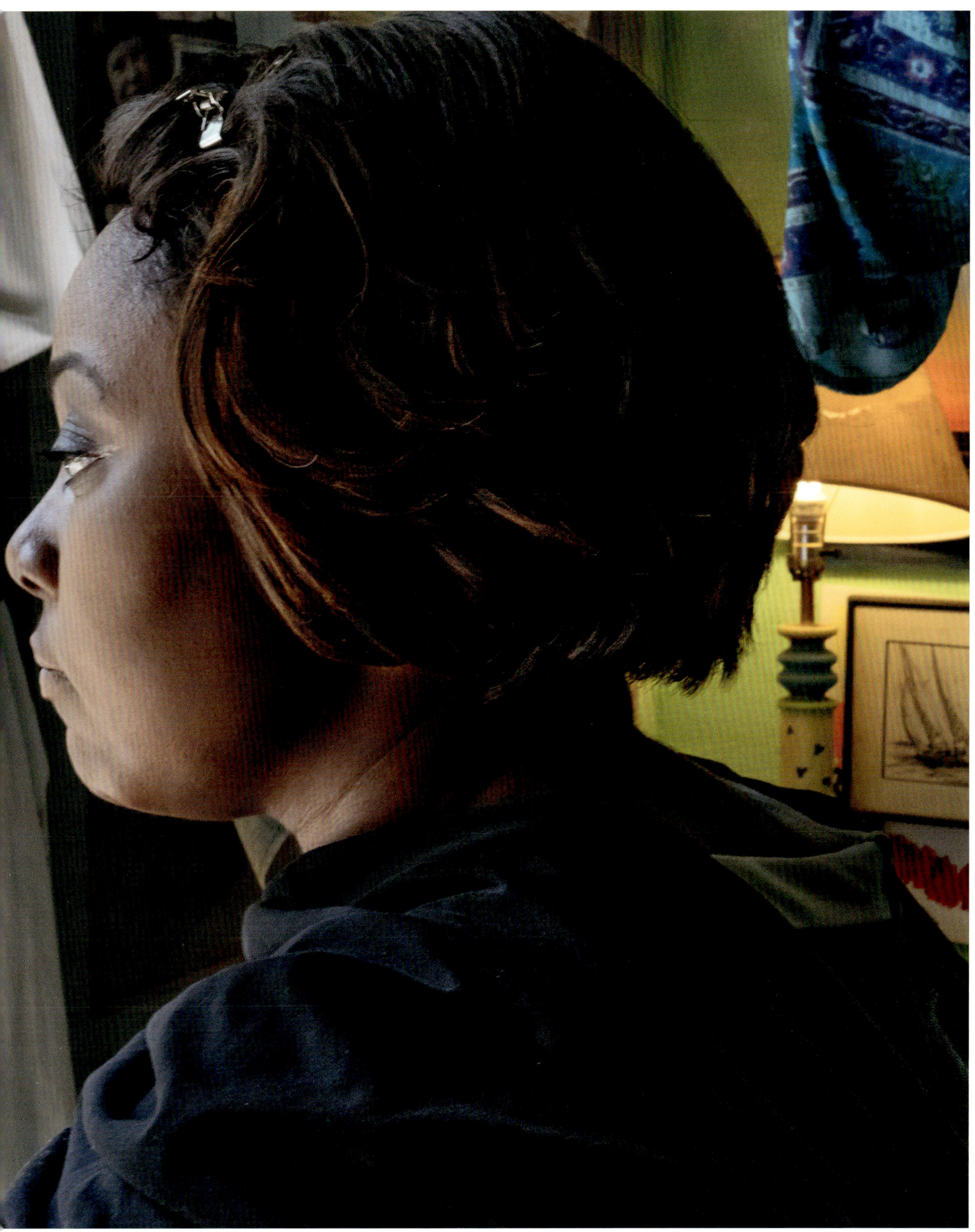

2012
u don't Stay Here
t Go No Further Than
Hallway
Darkroom
Outside - Thats were u Stay
Liven Room
eam don't cum down my
way to No One room
ss
ya'll Ask
u Dont Like
GOO!

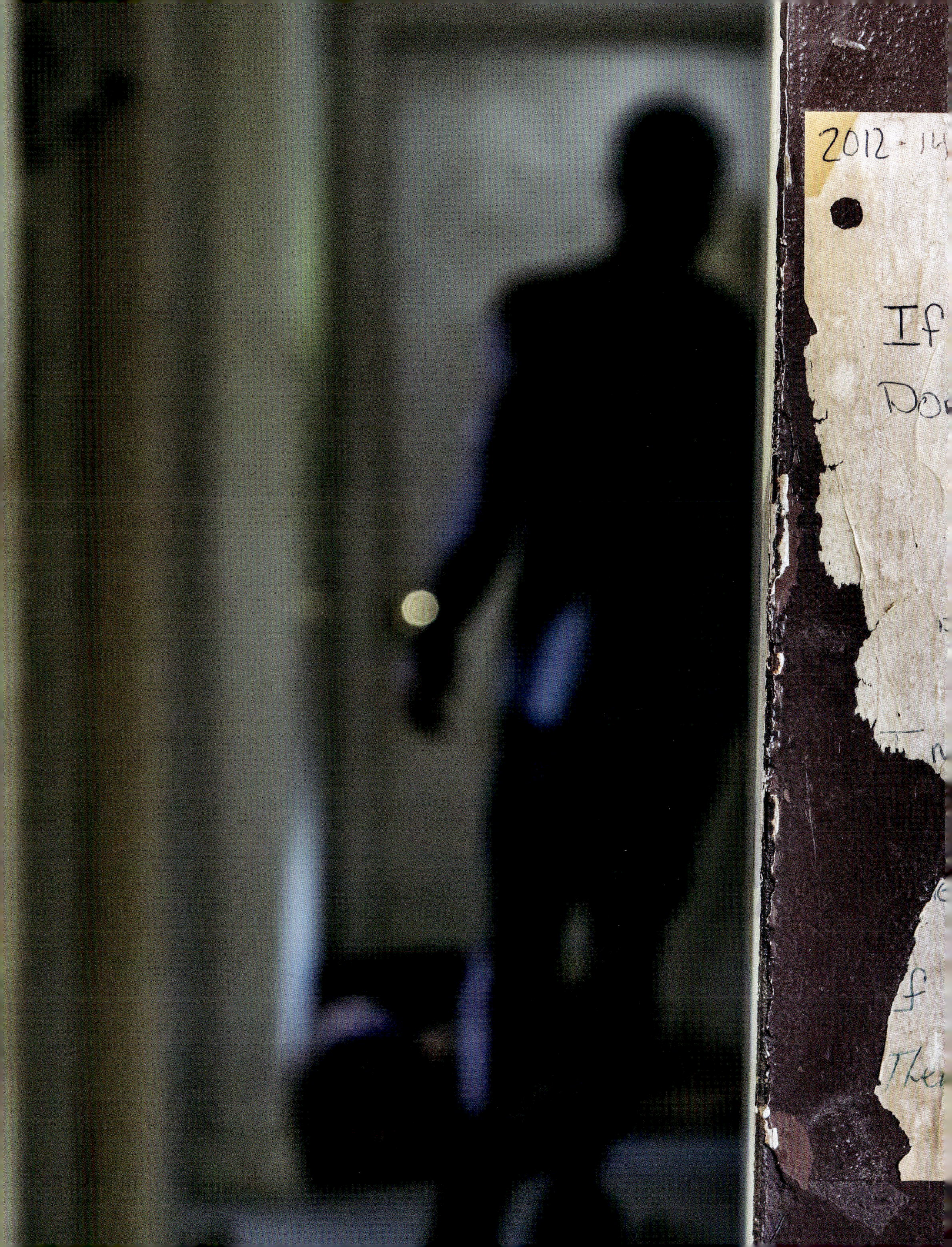

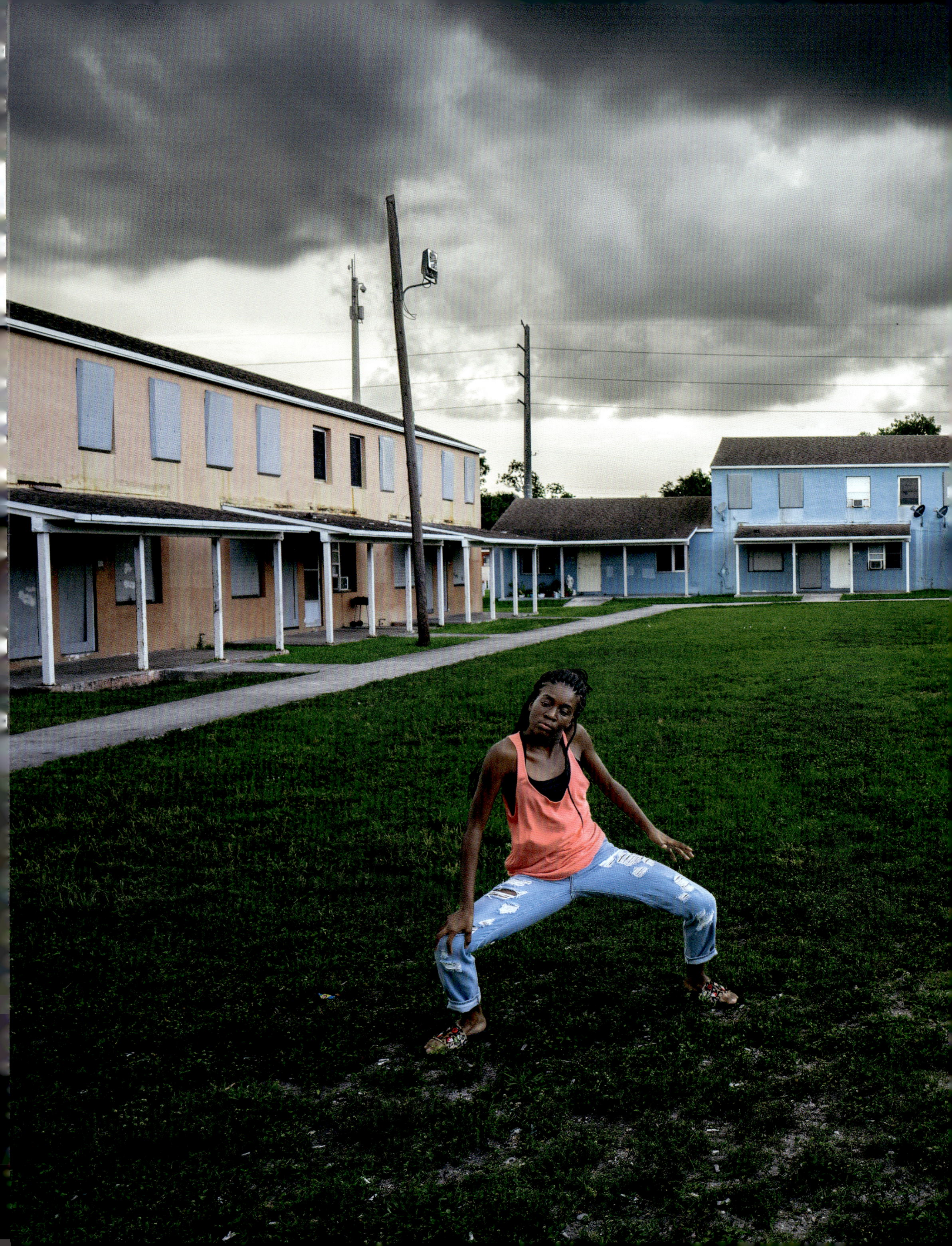

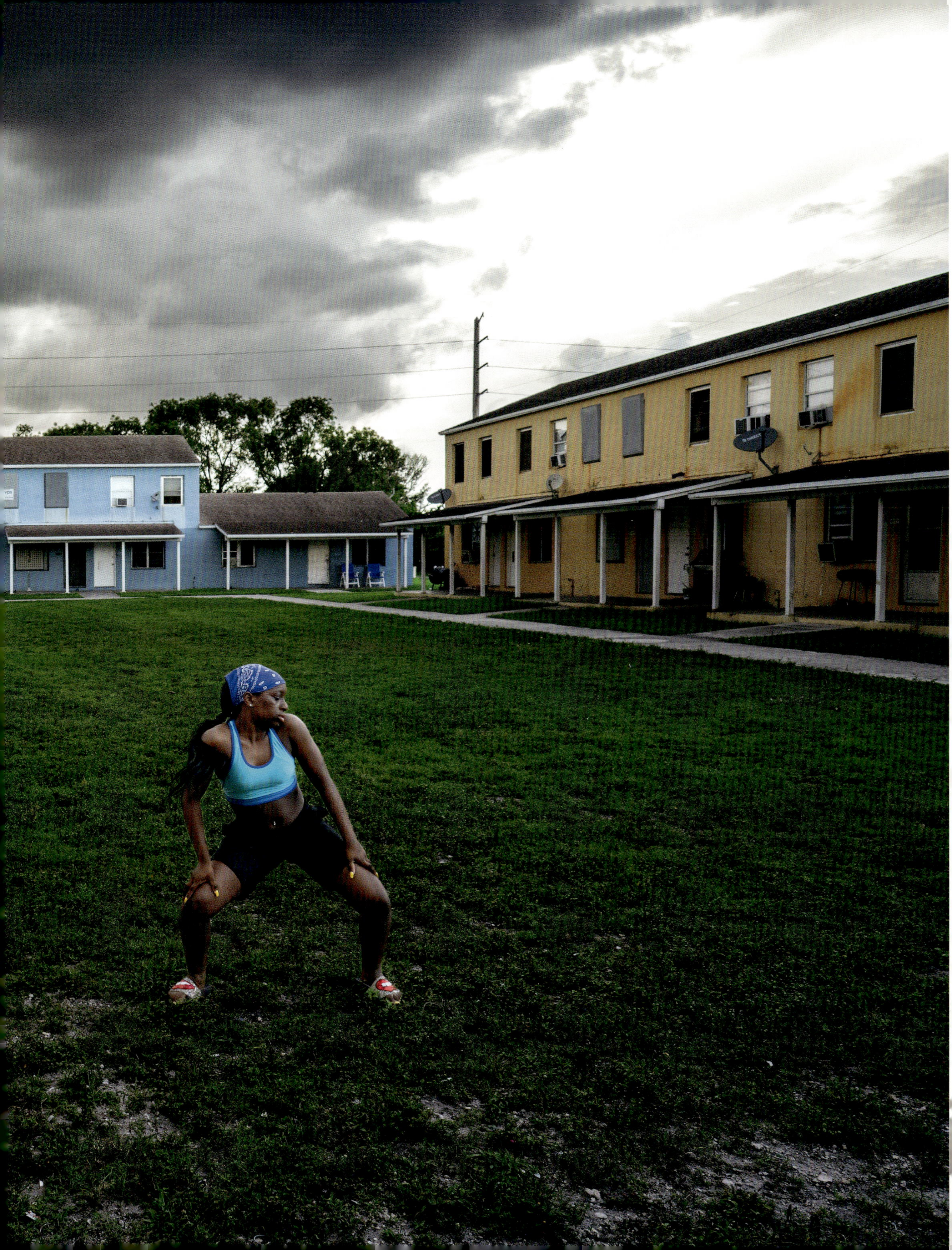

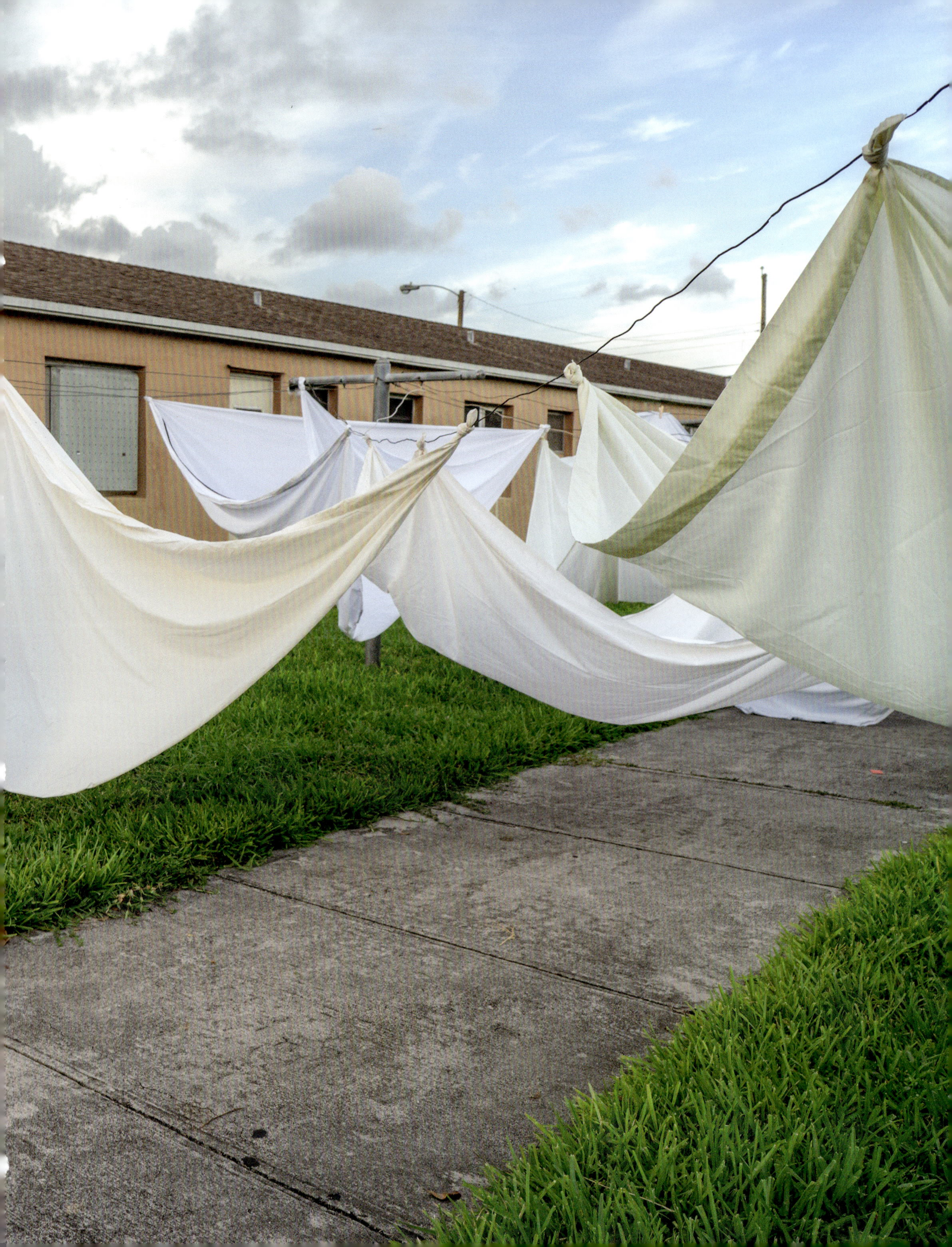

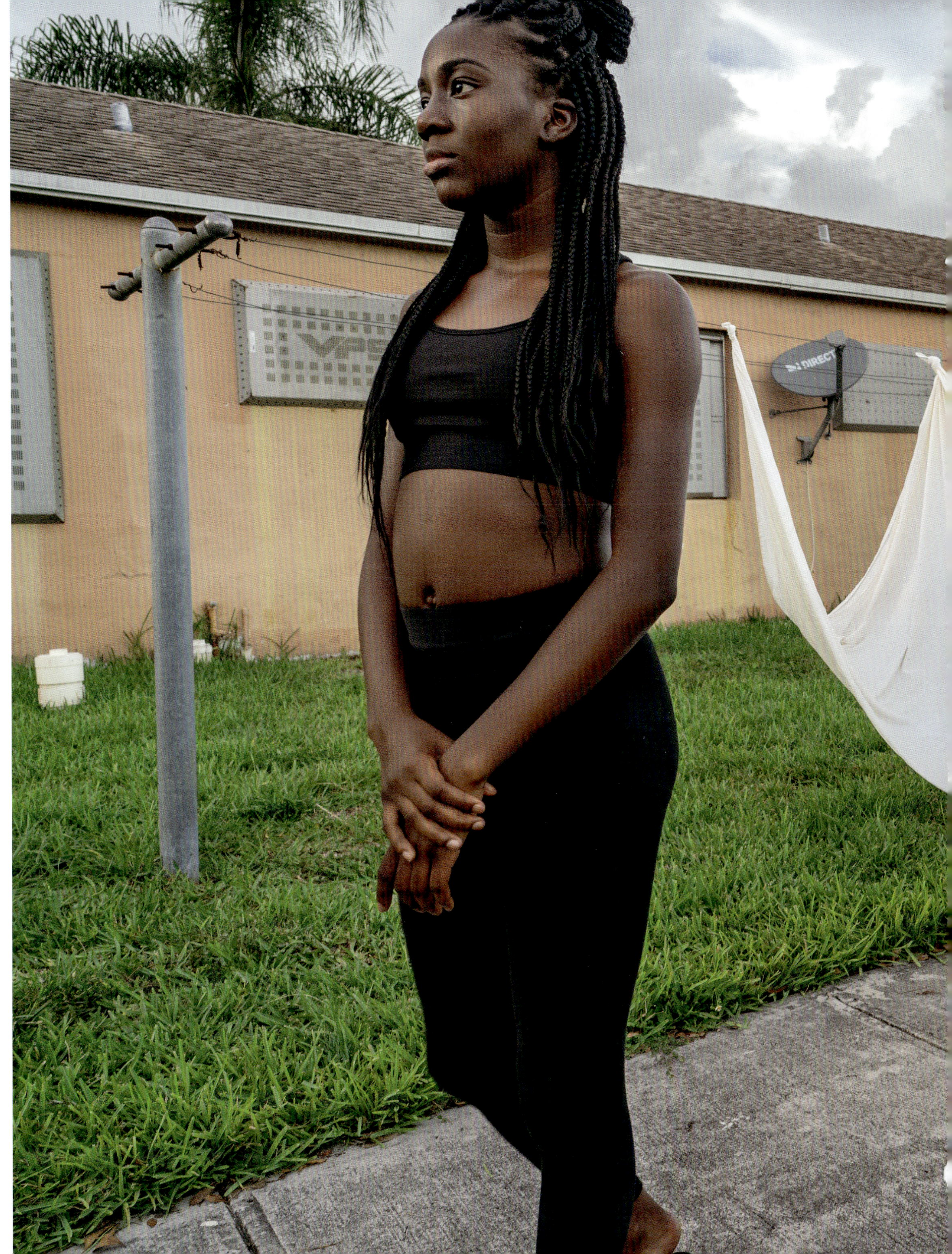

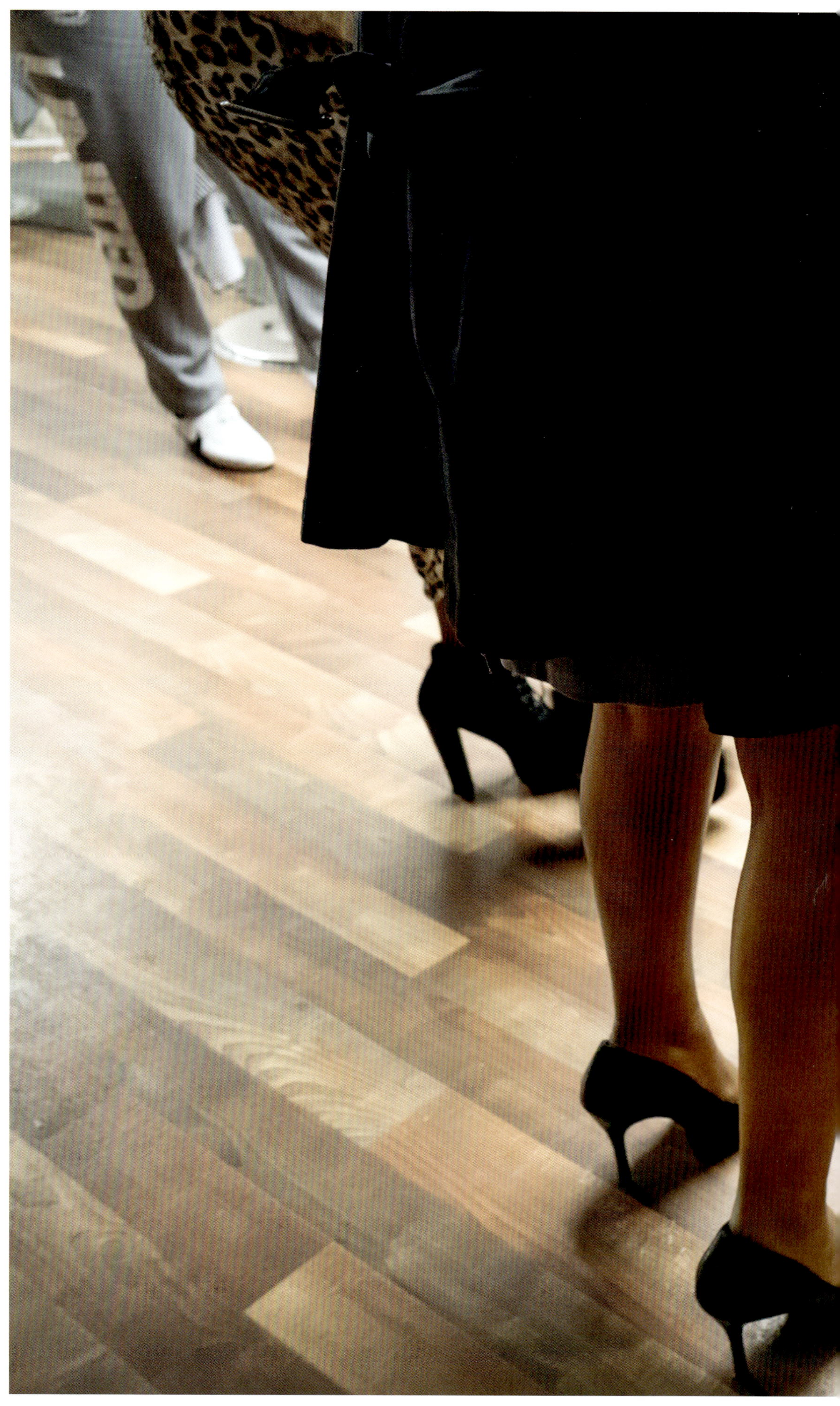

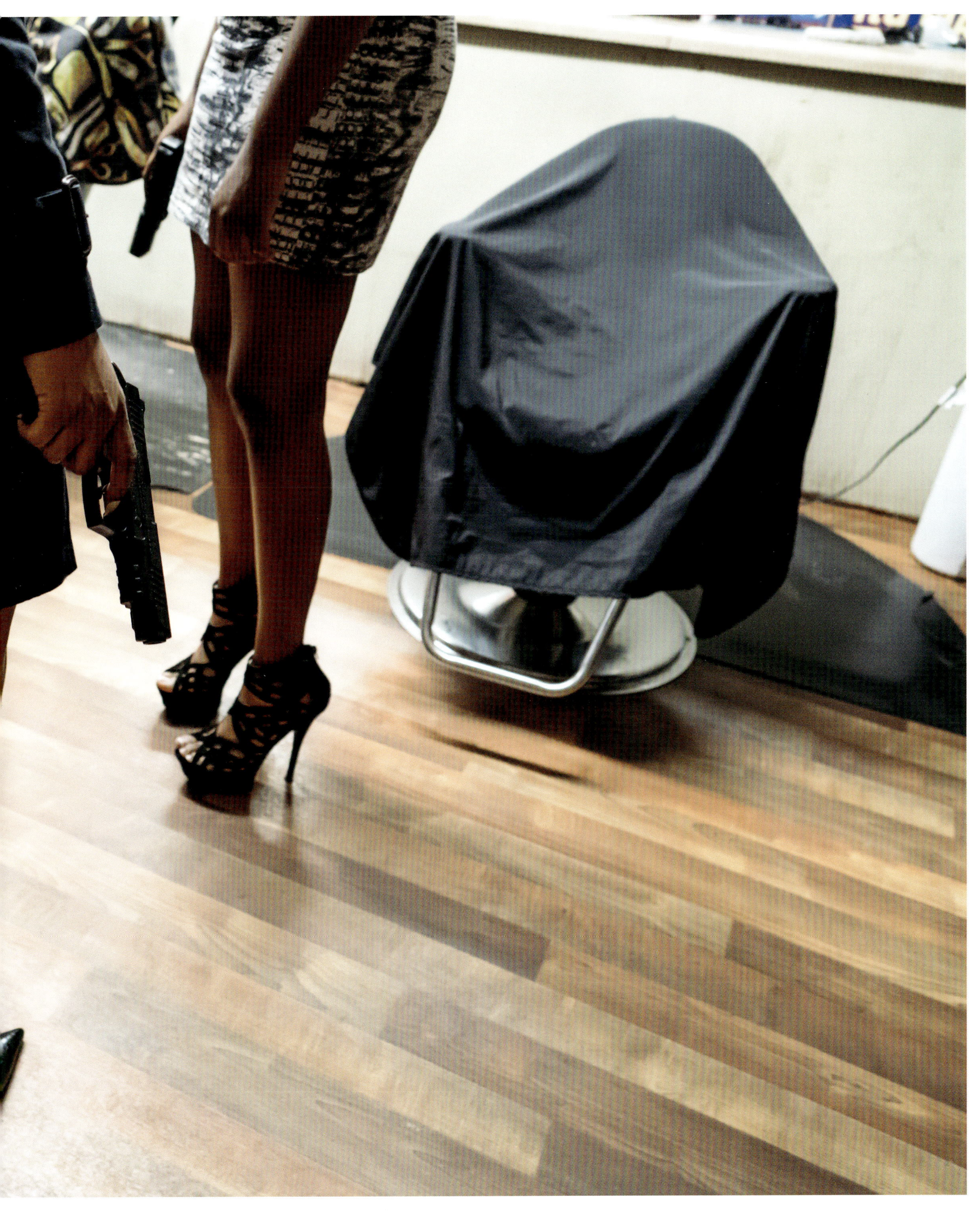

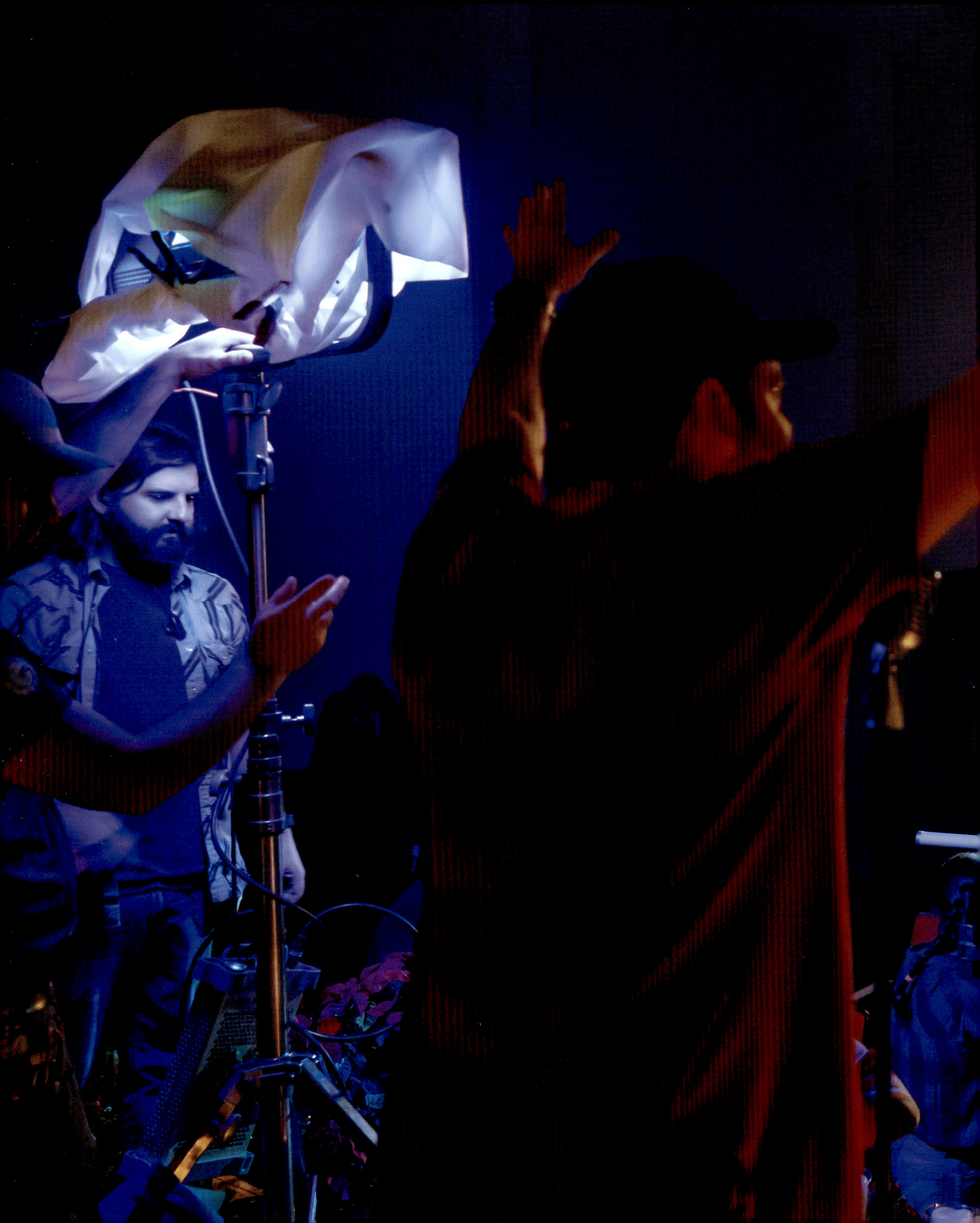

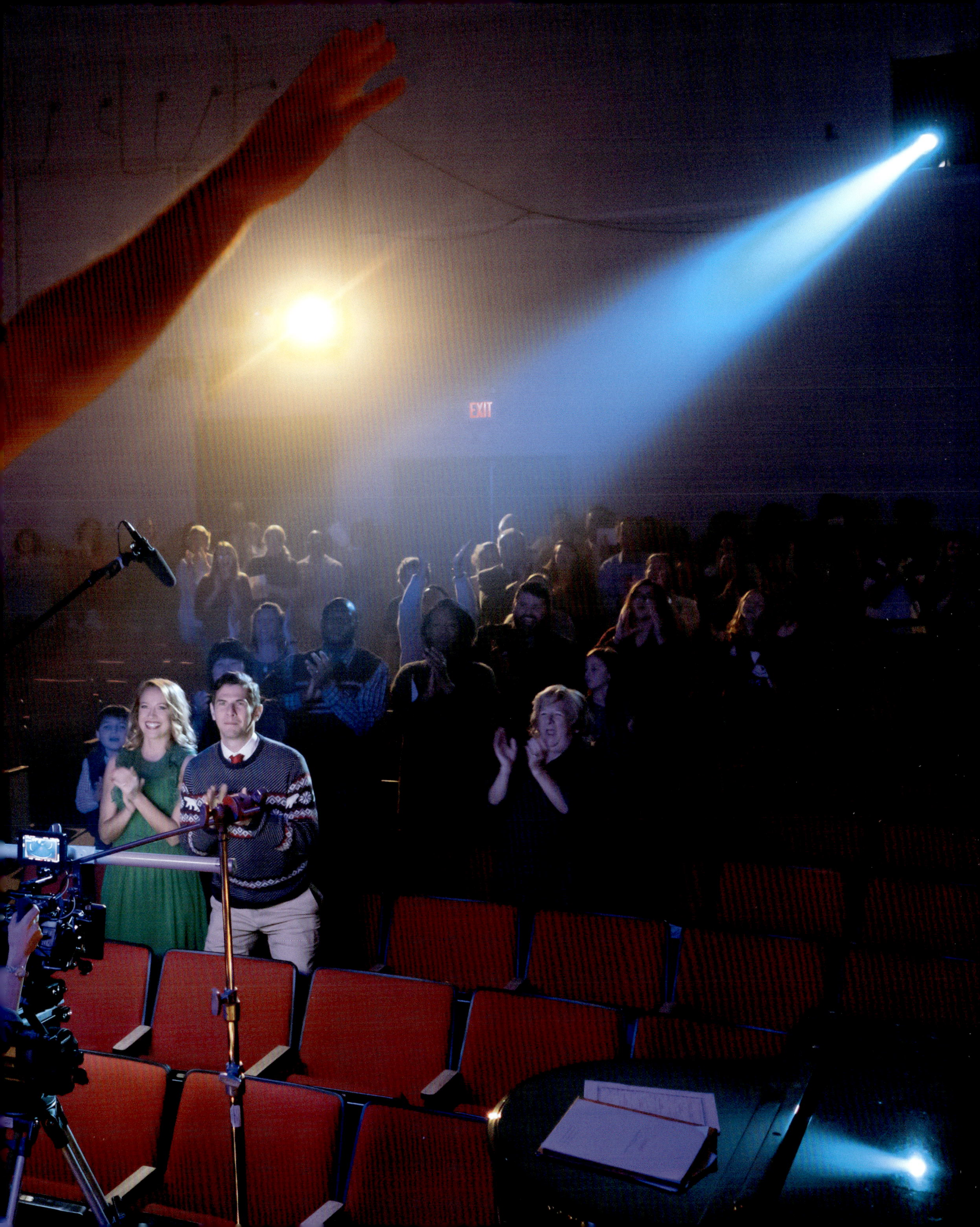
EXIT

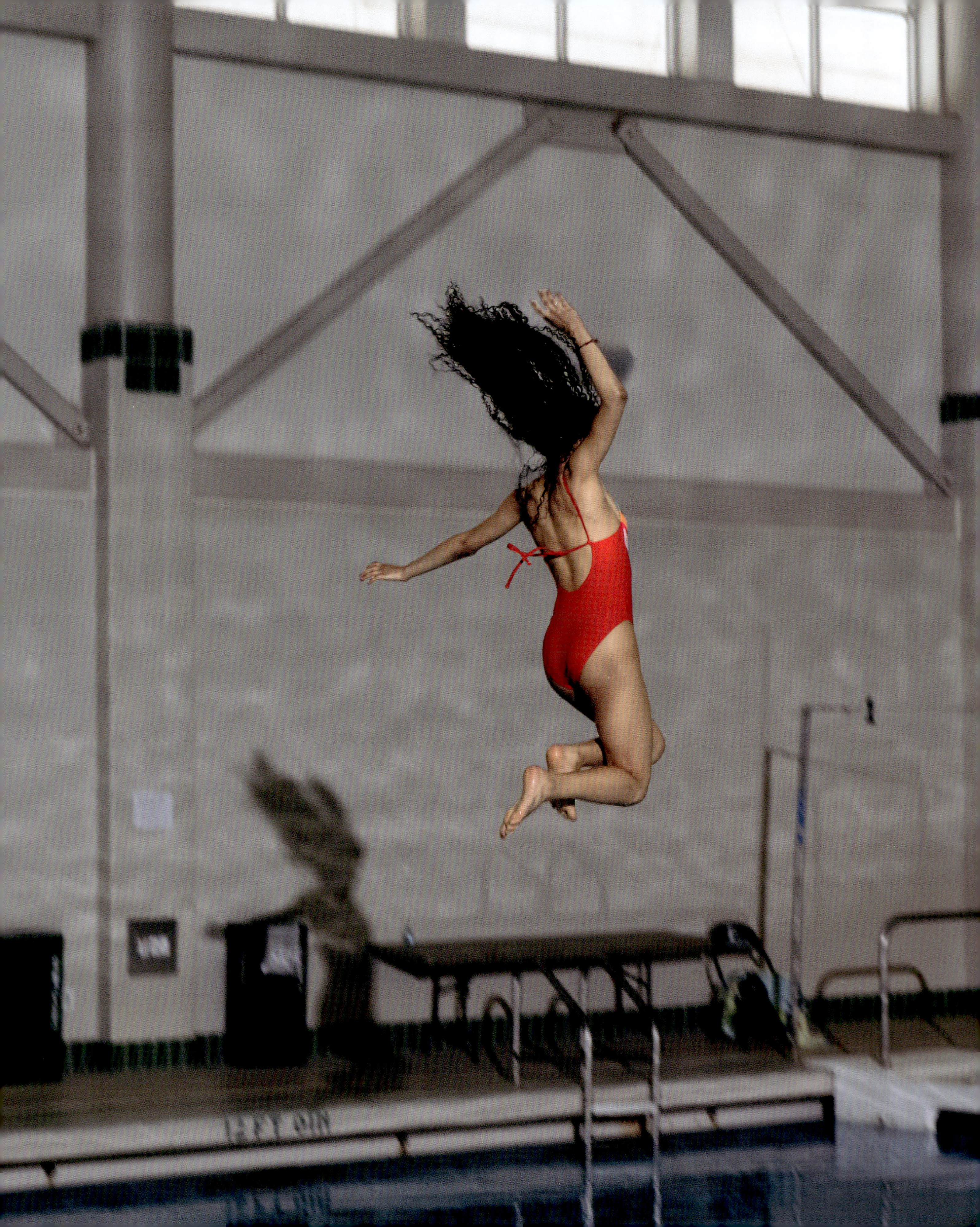

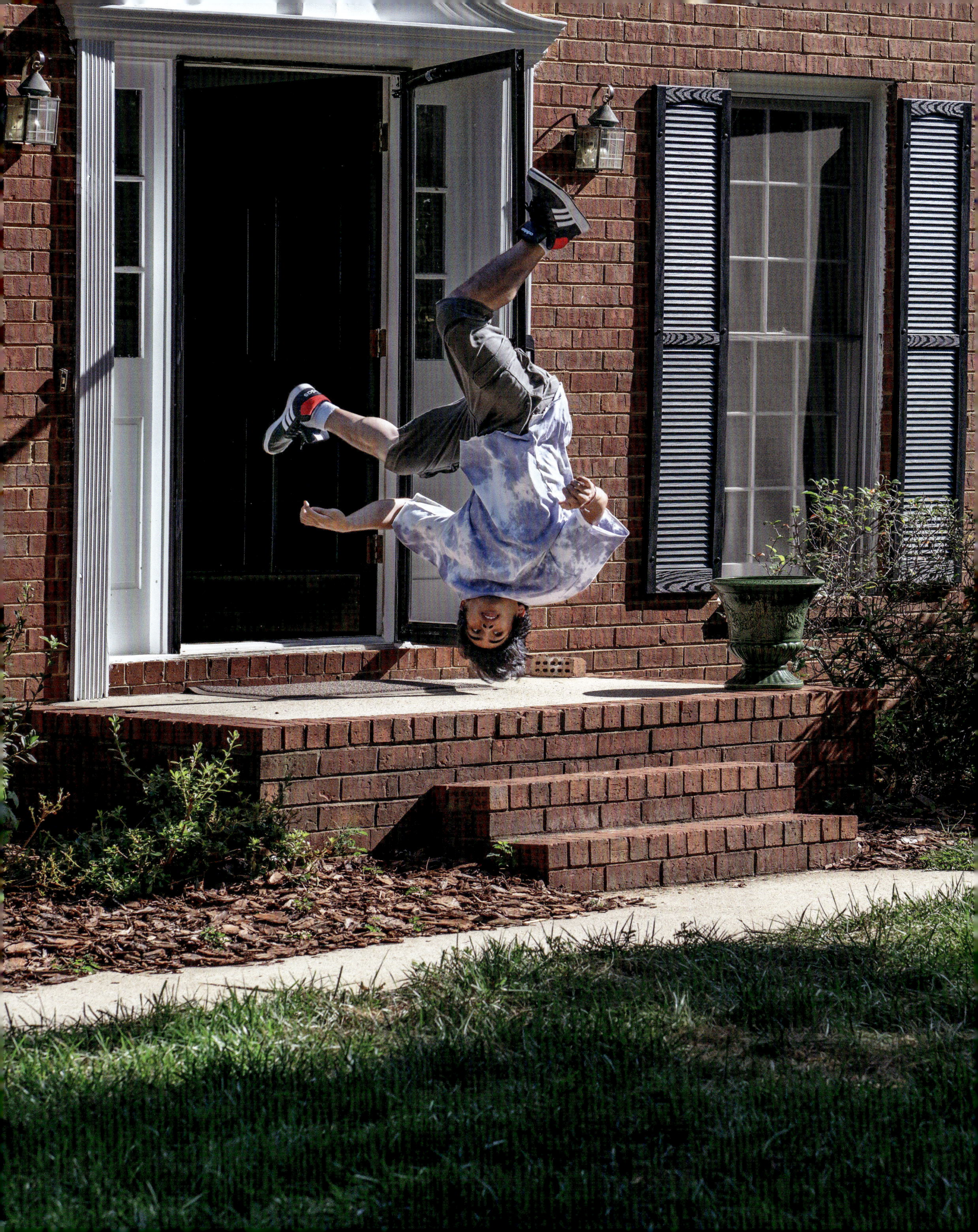

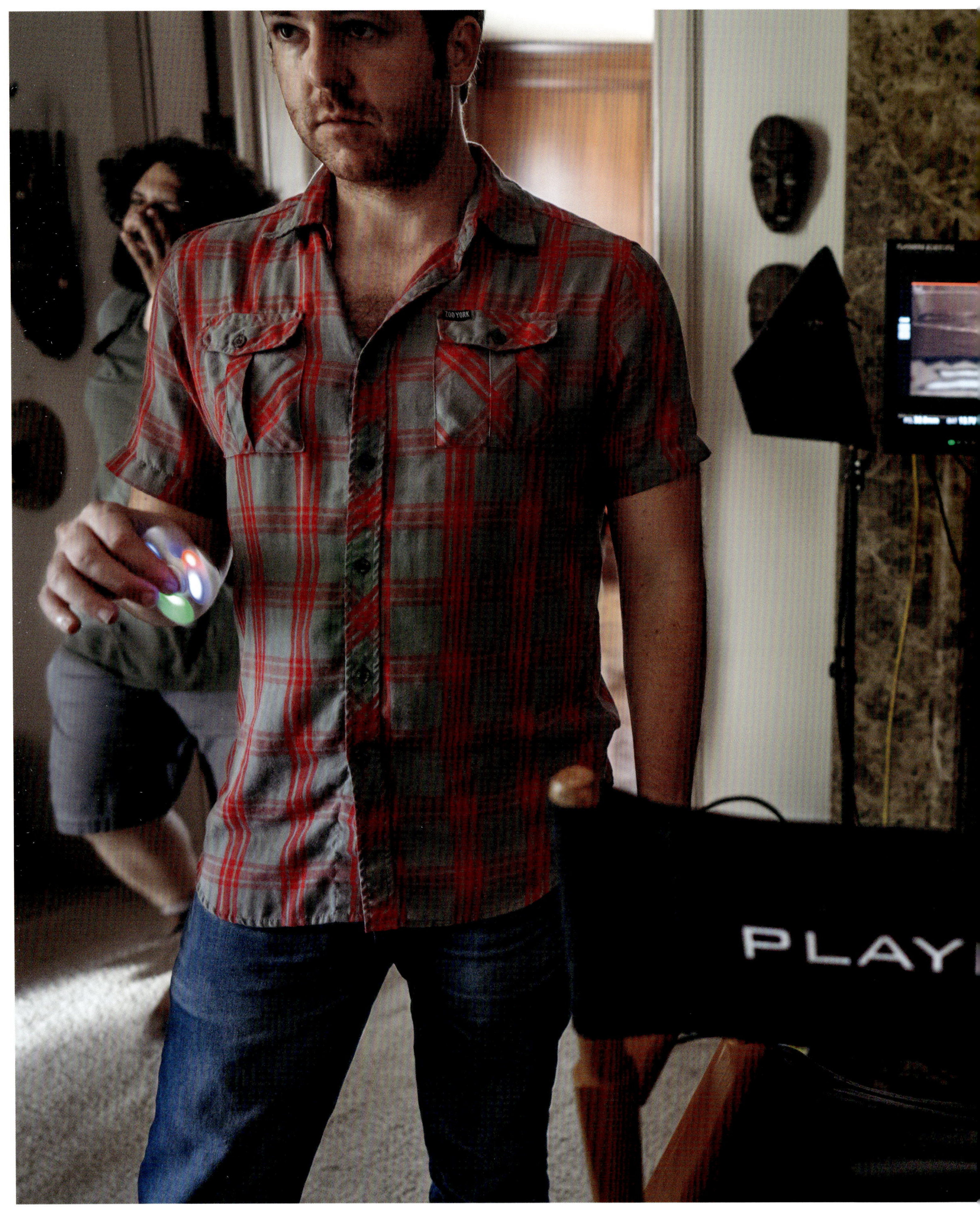

ZOO YORK
PLAY

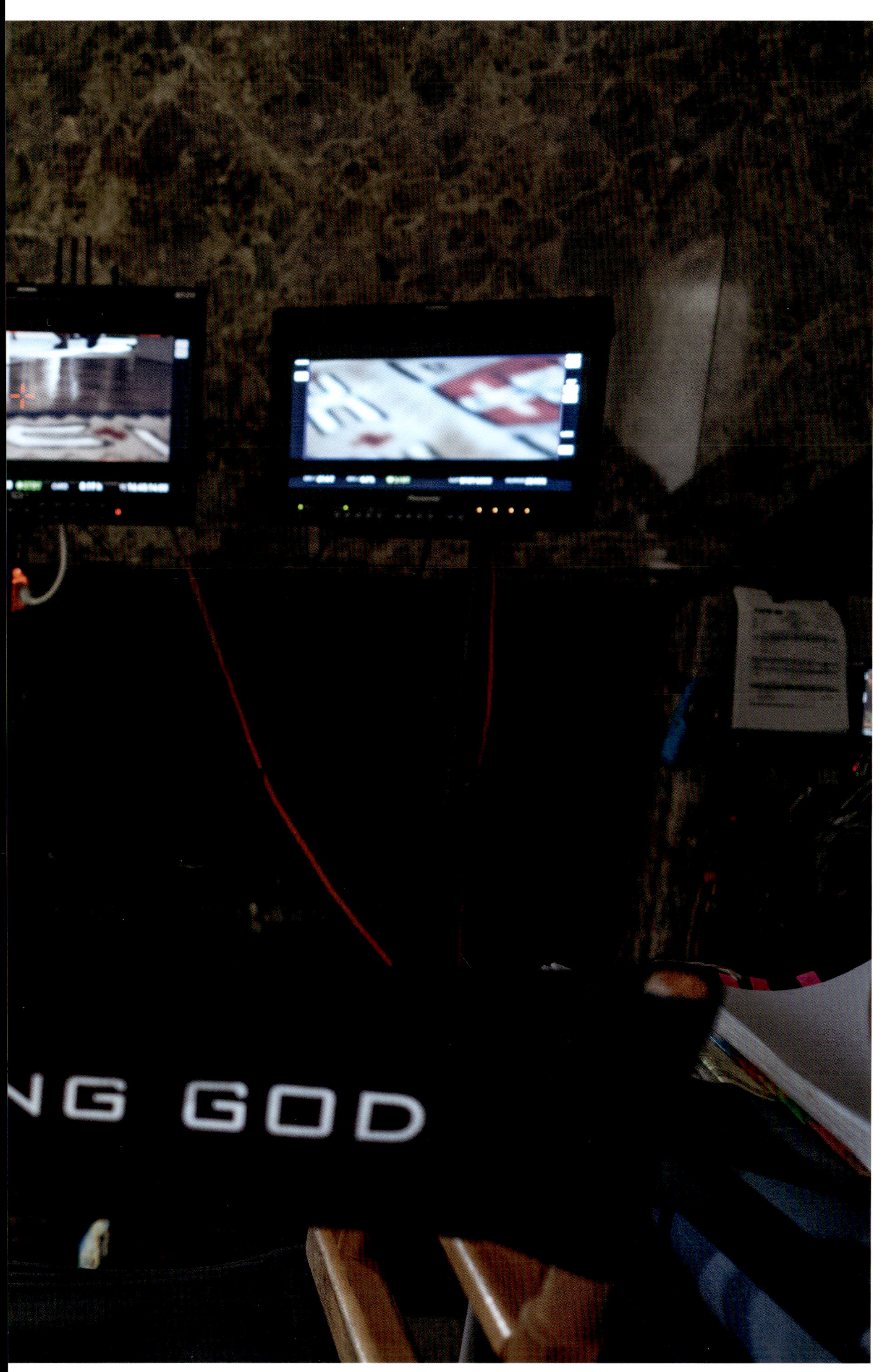
NG GOD

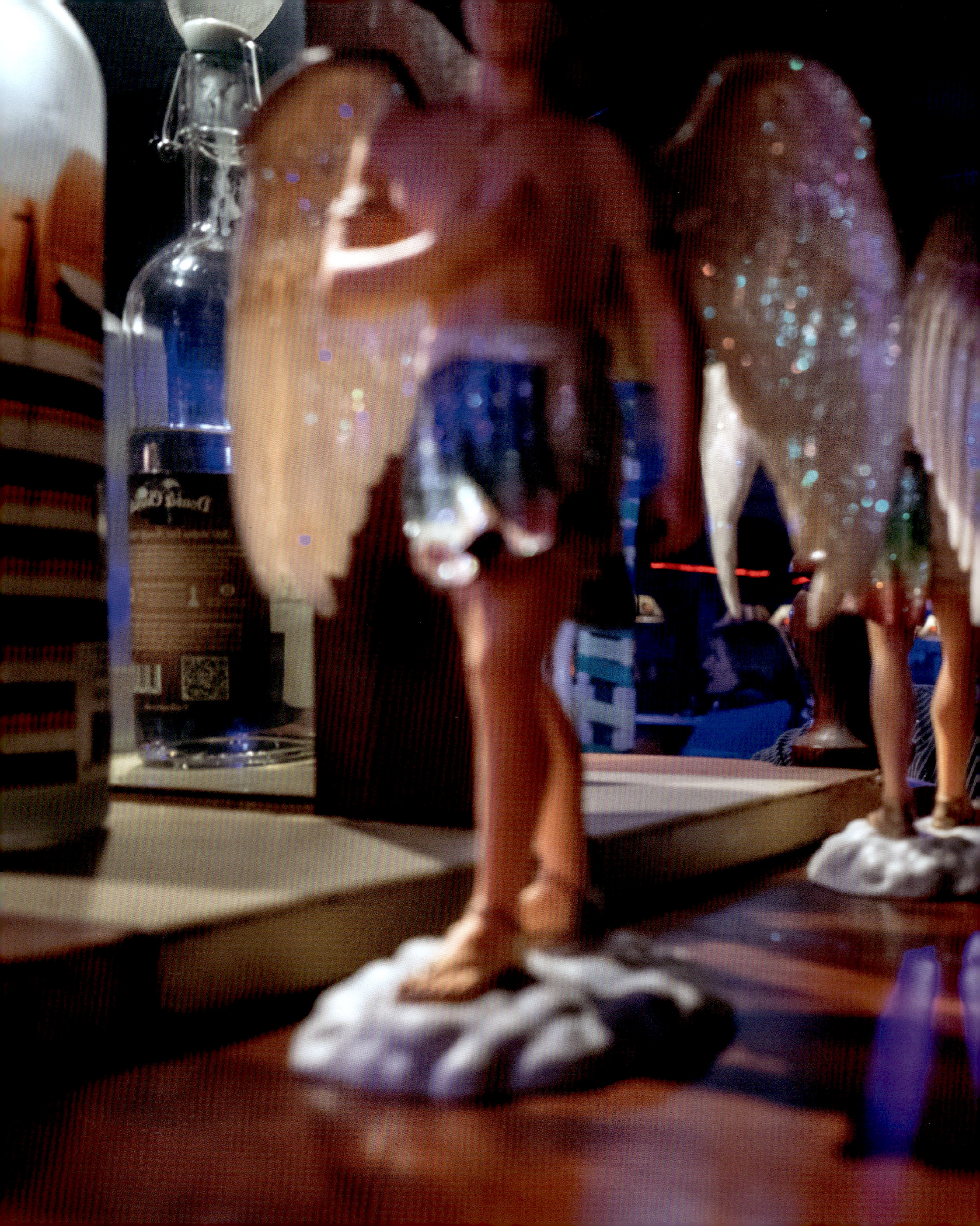

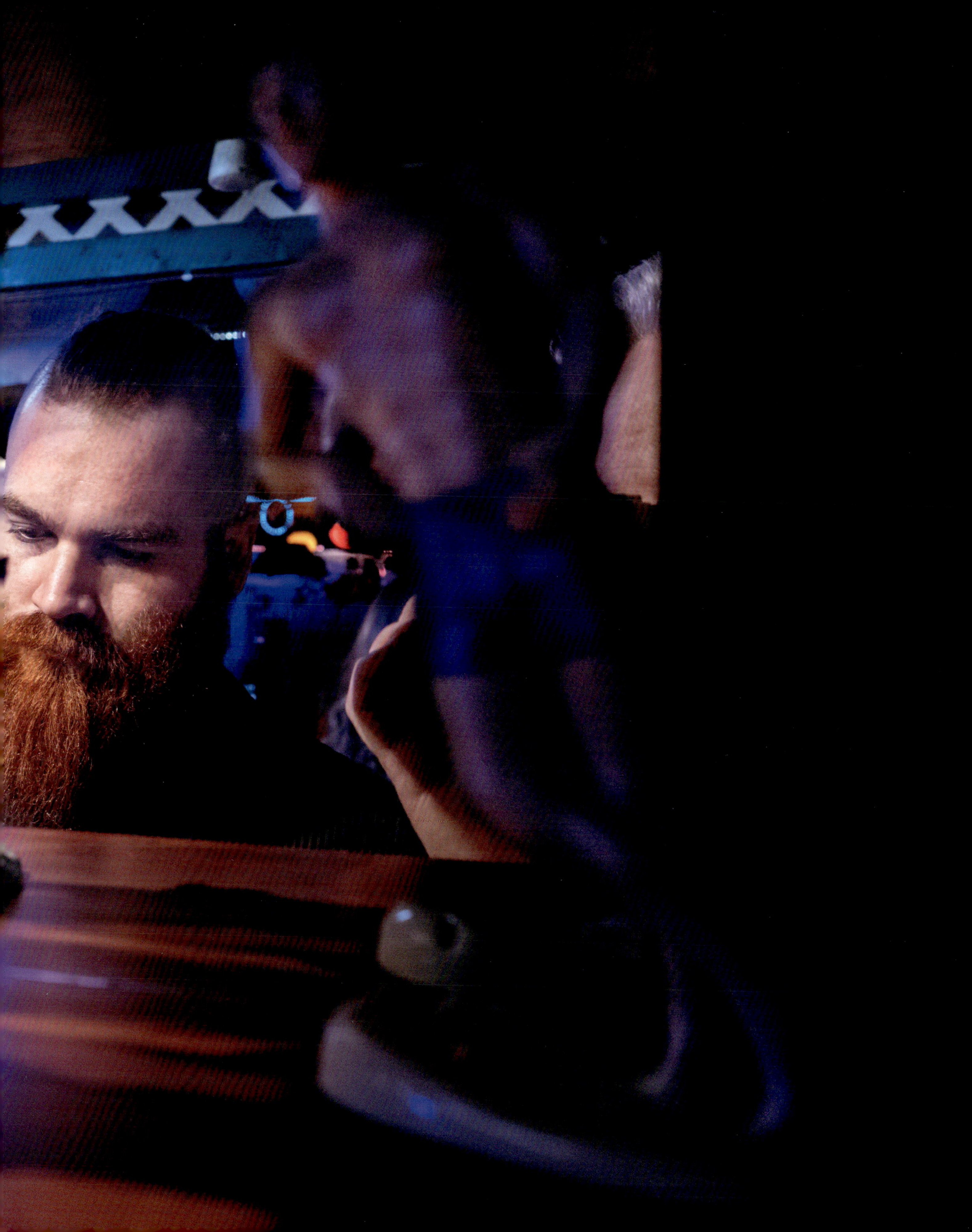

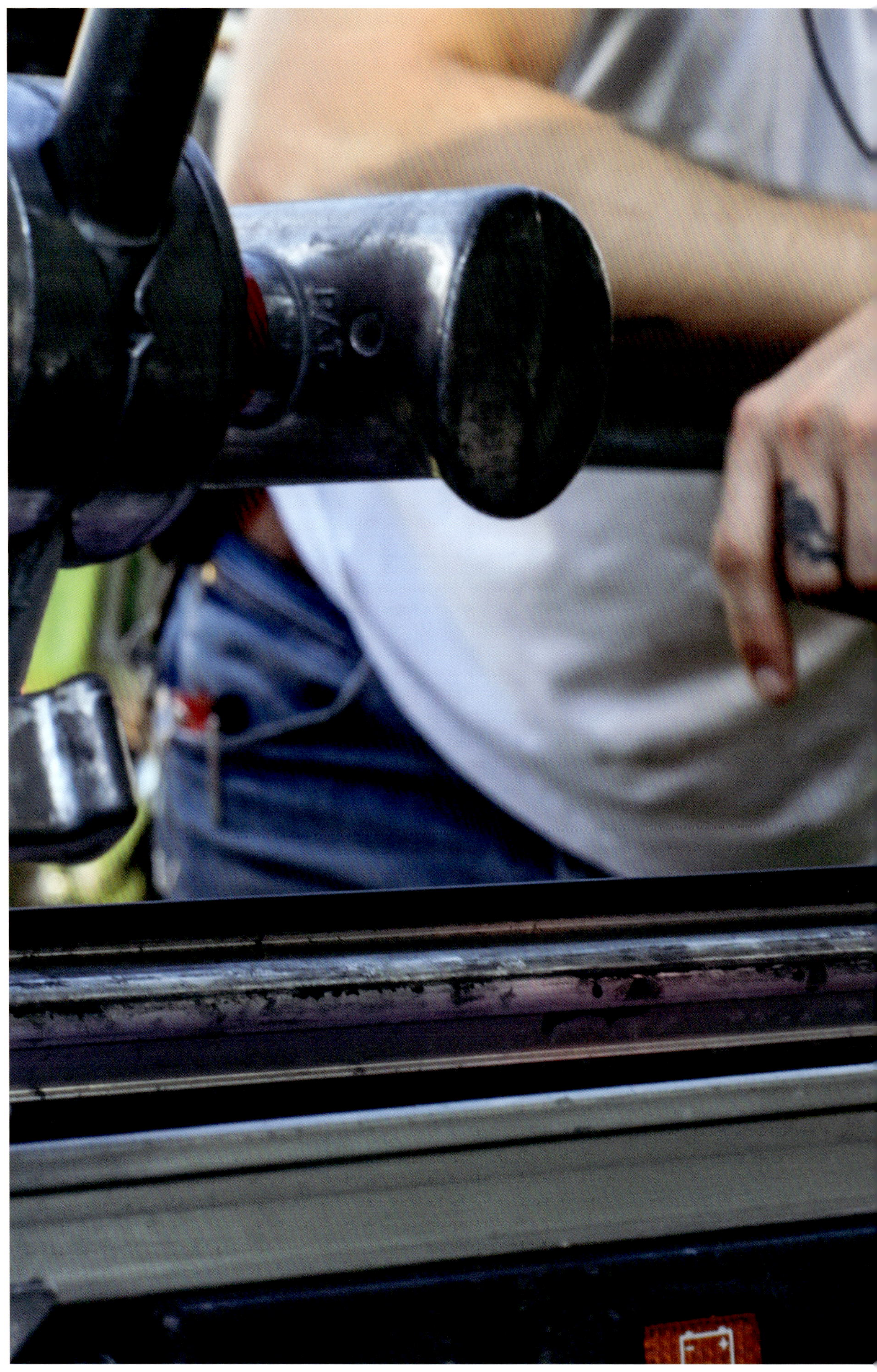

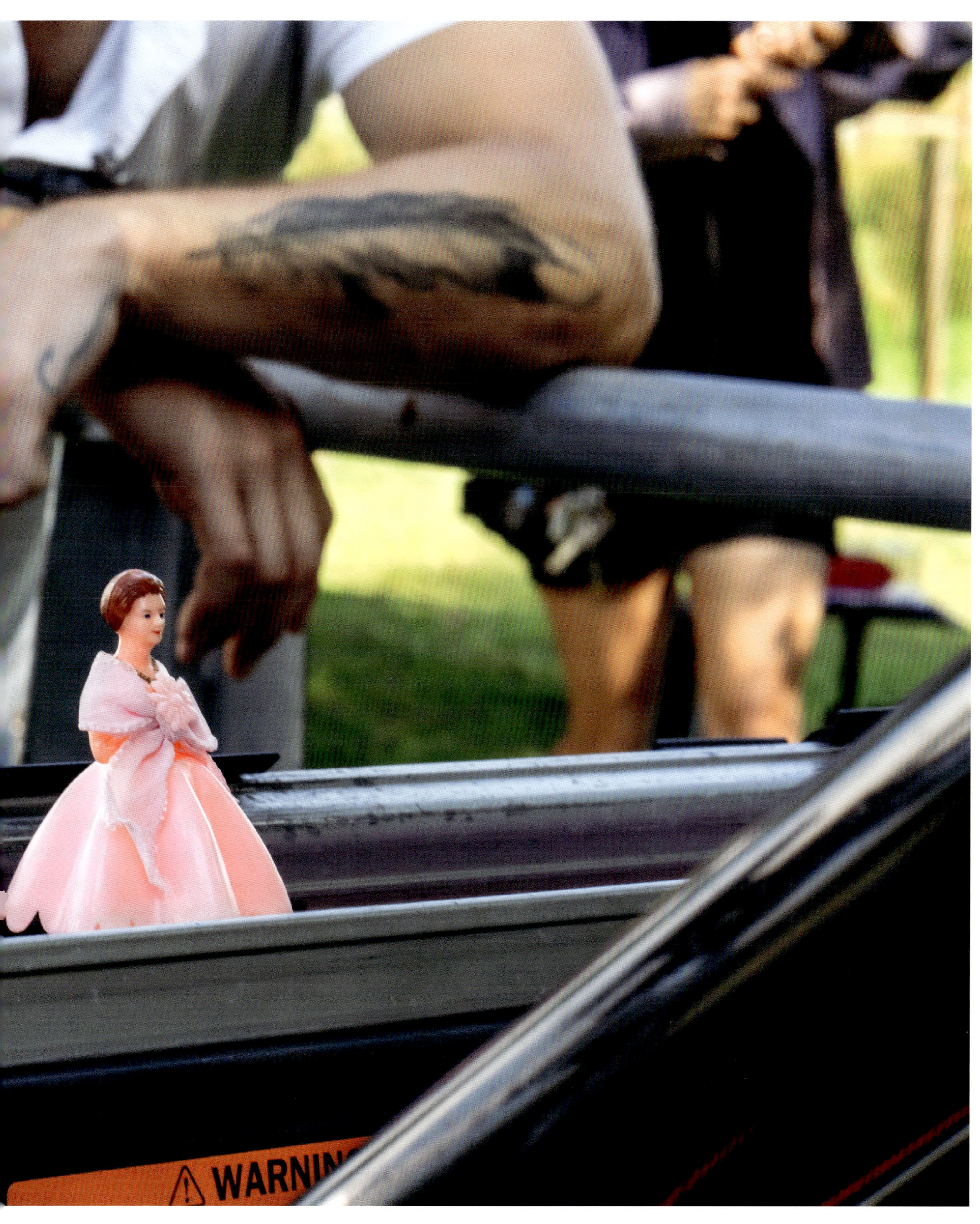

⚠ WARNING

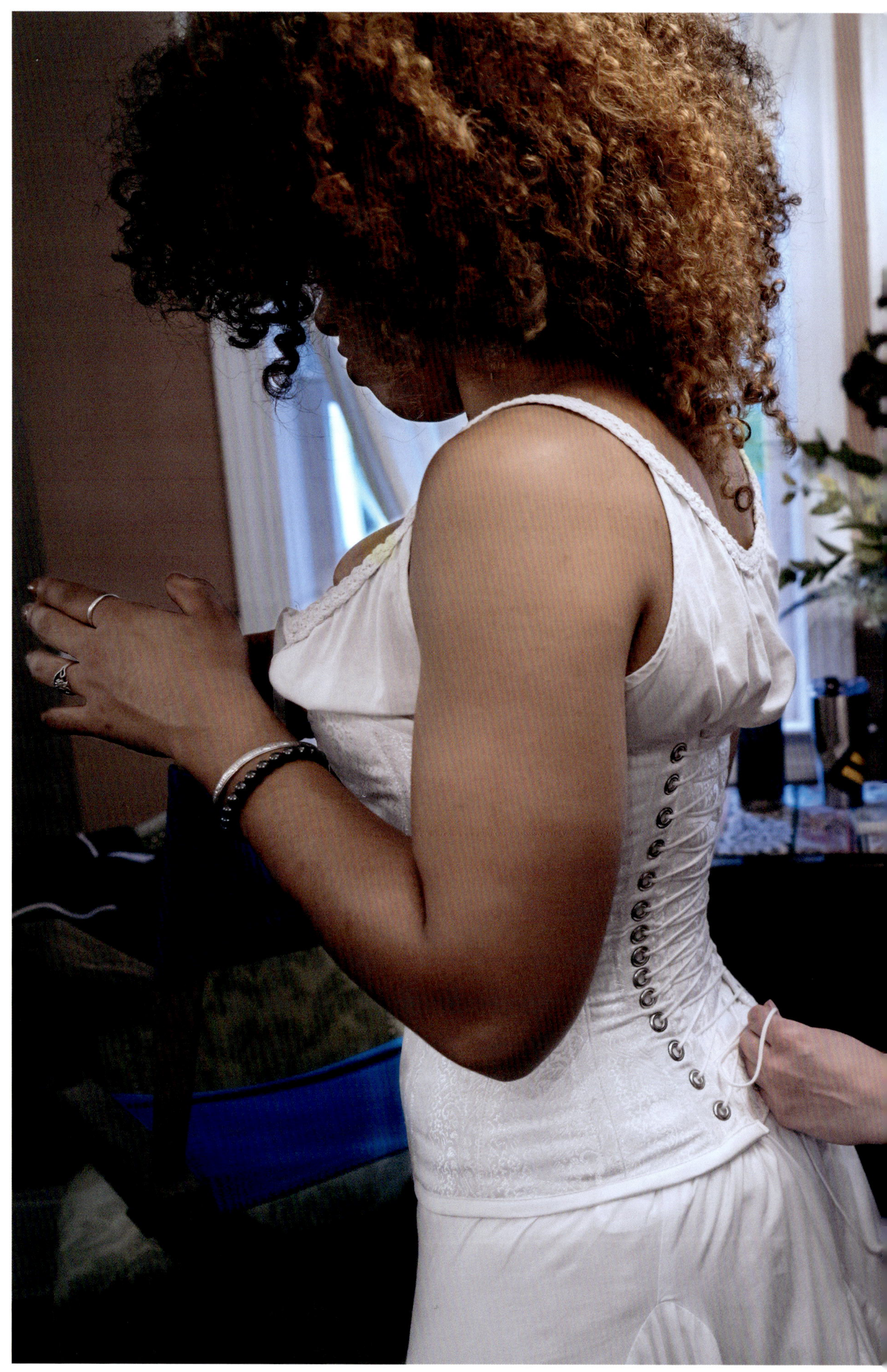

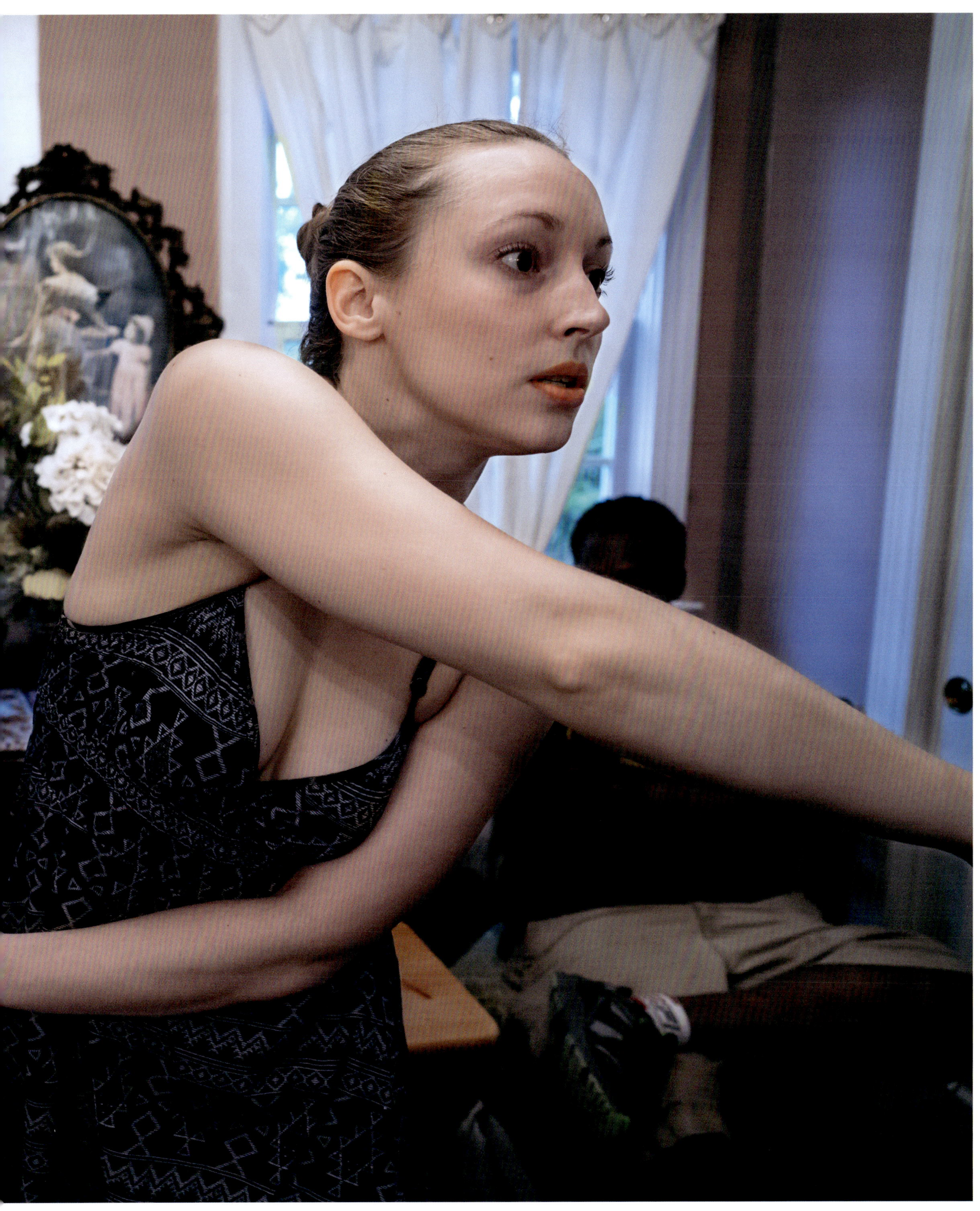

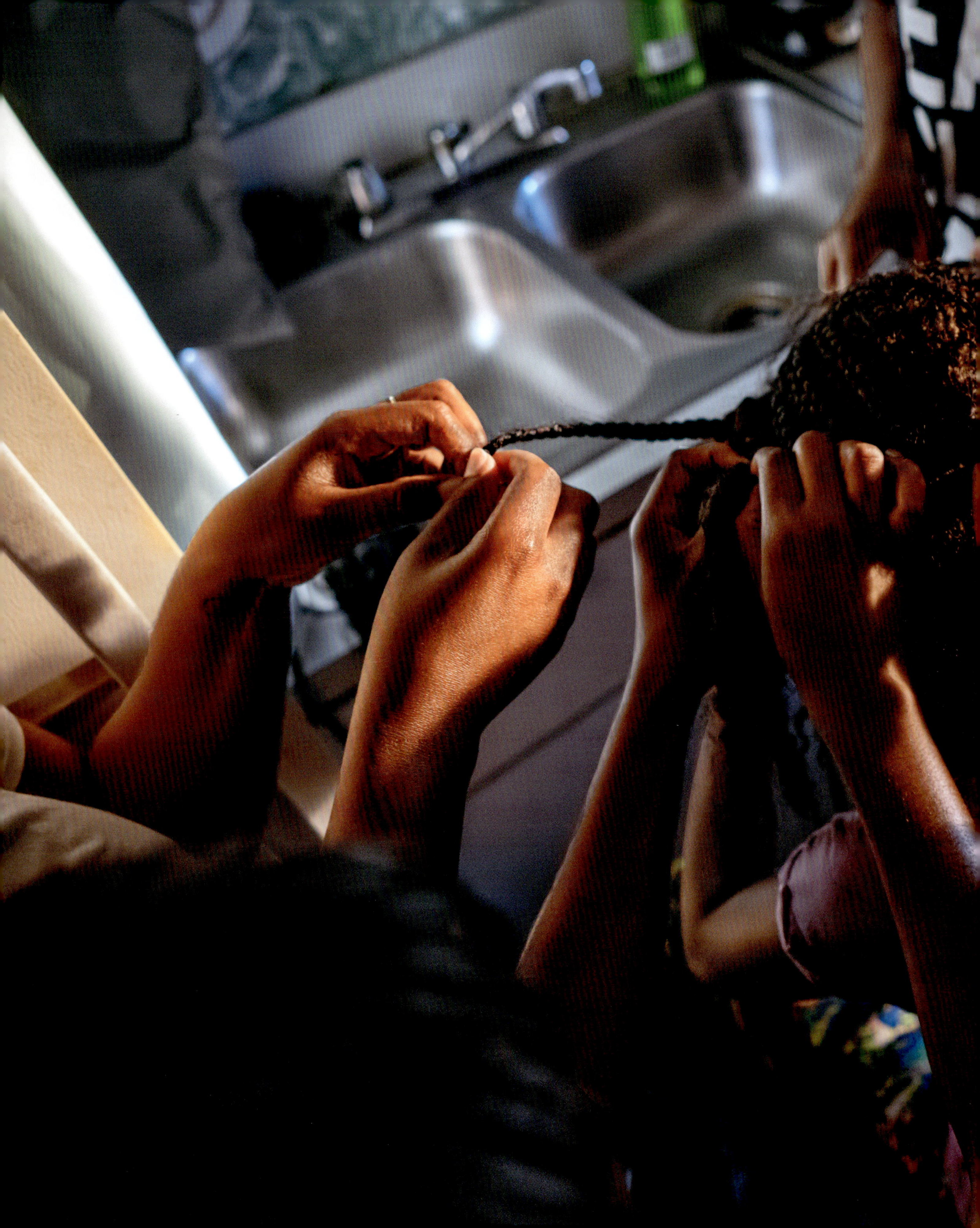

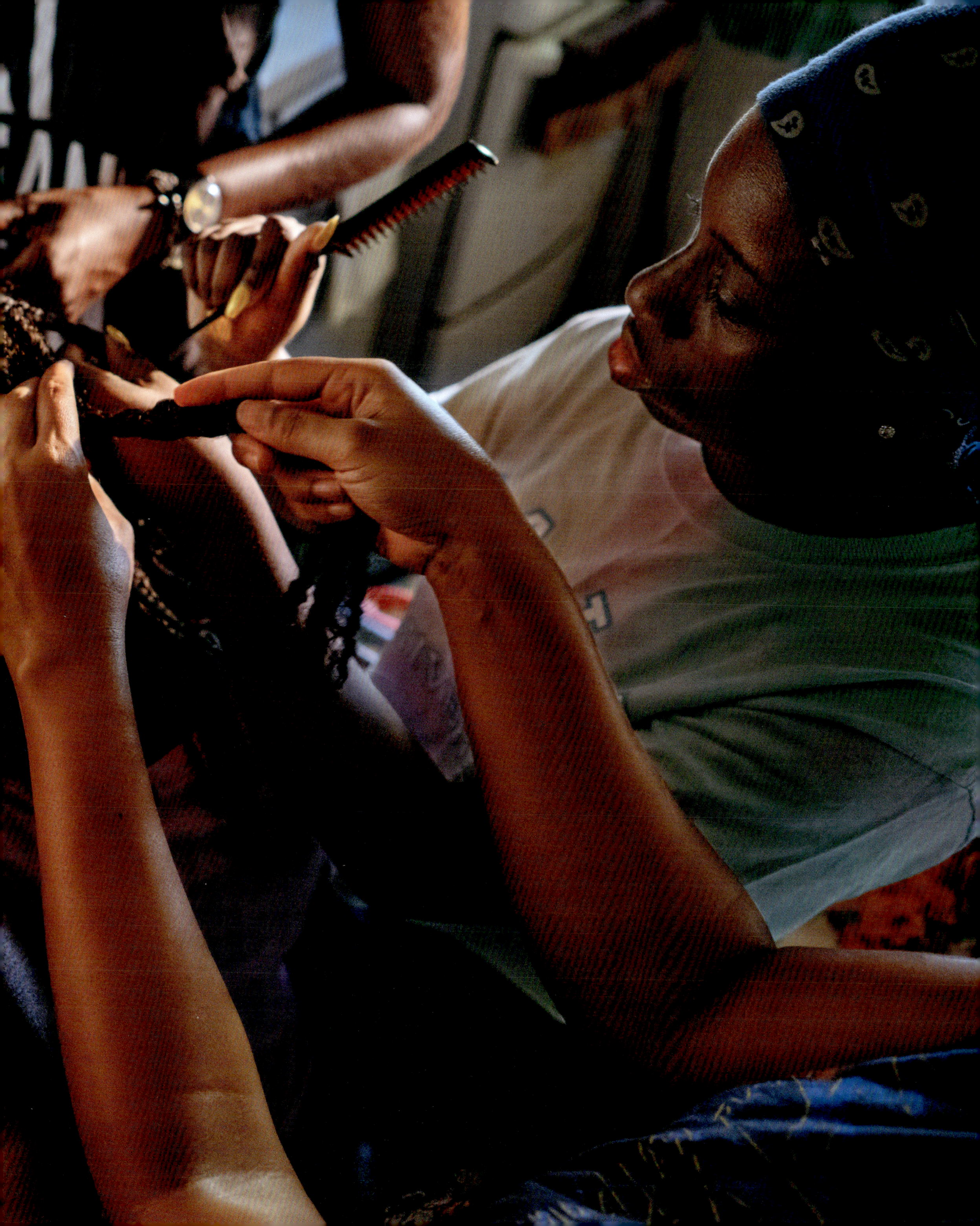

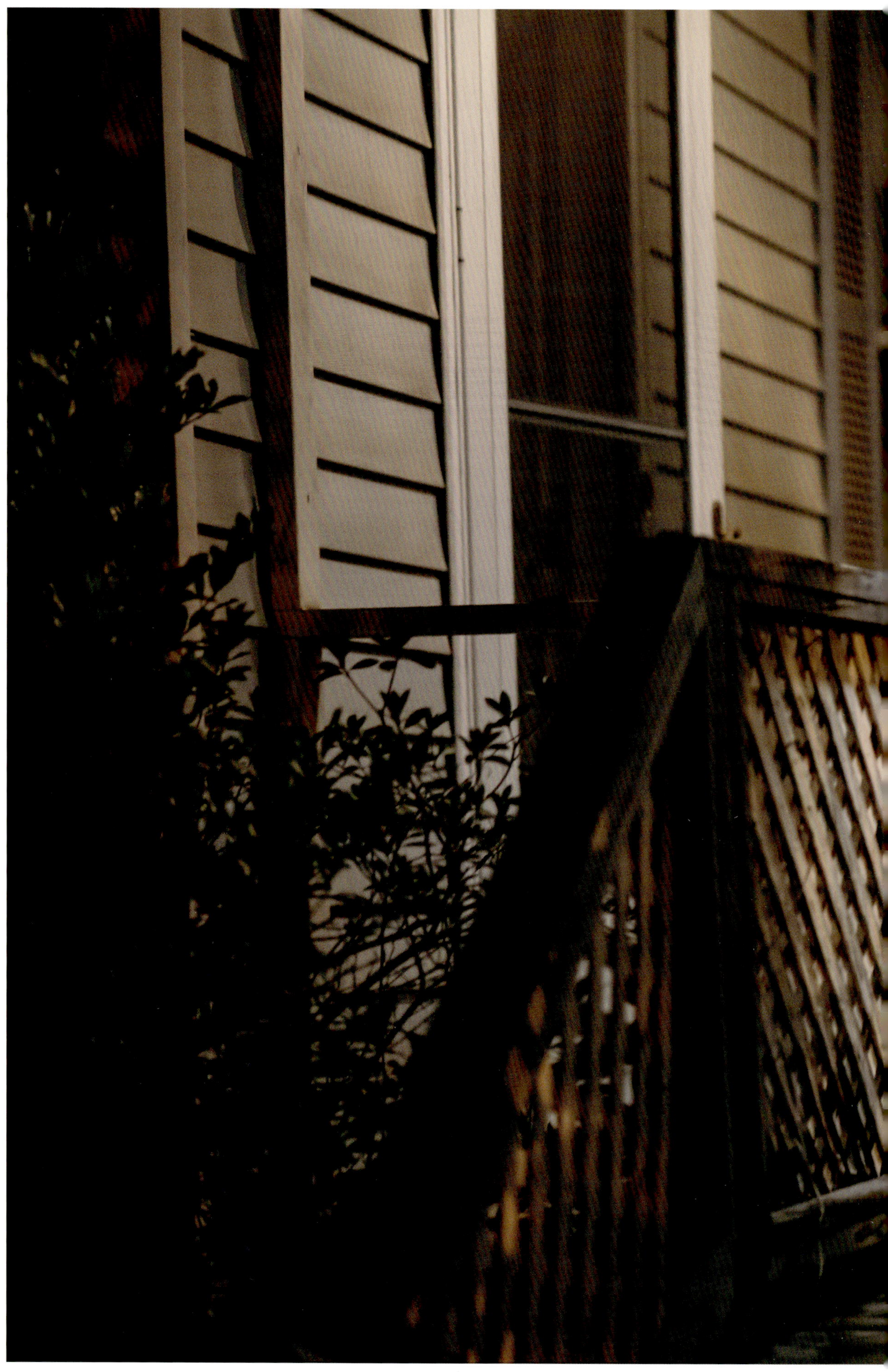

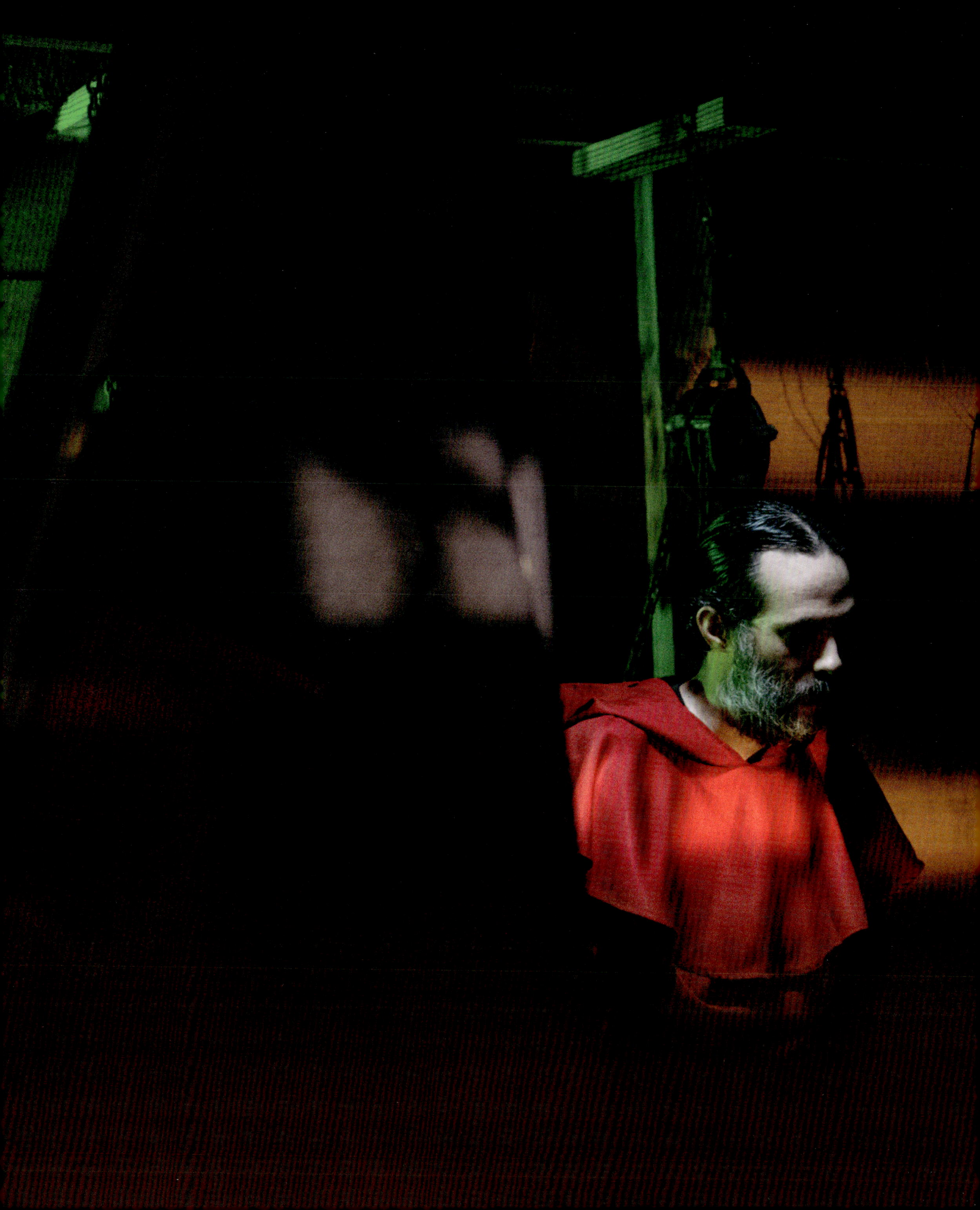

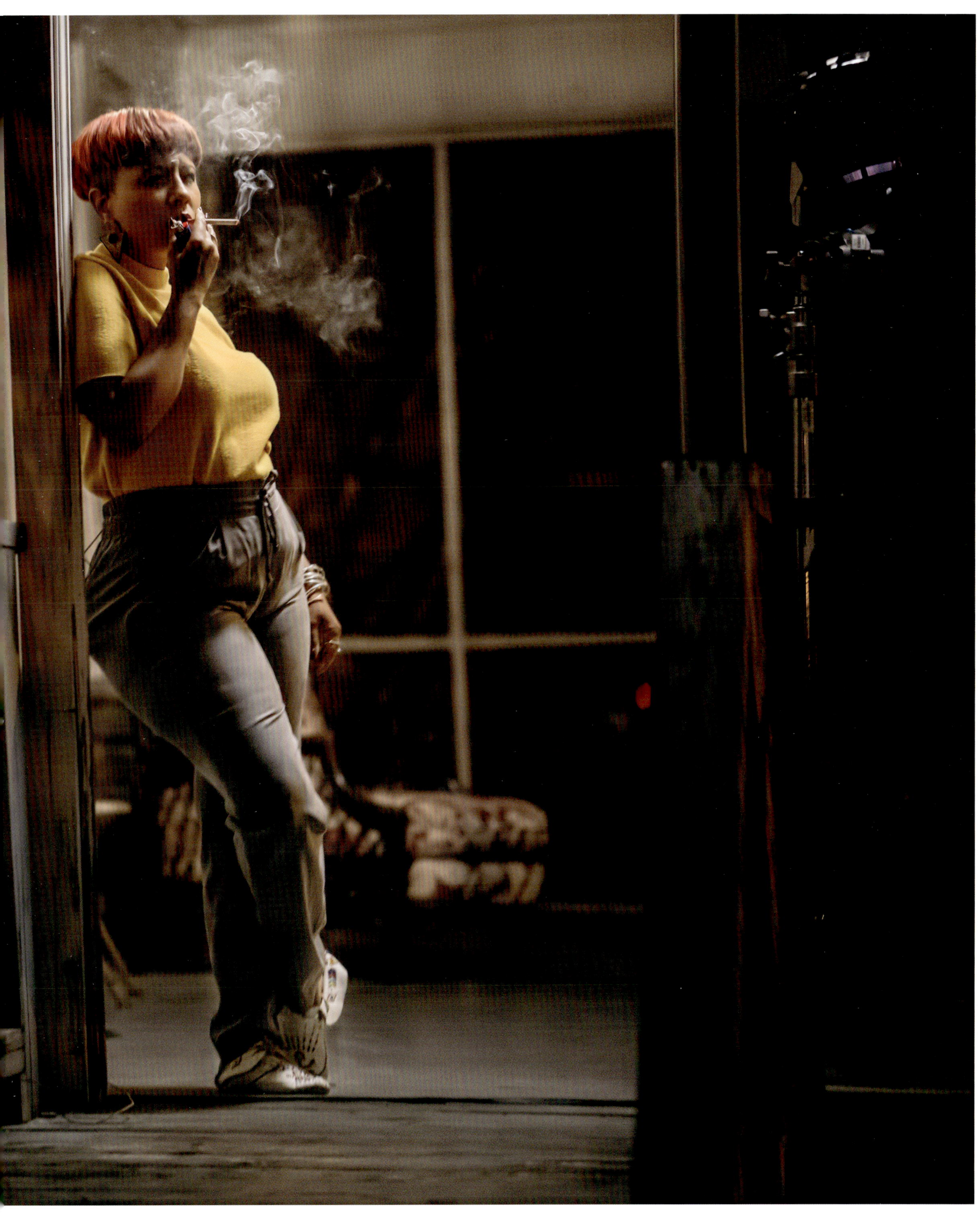

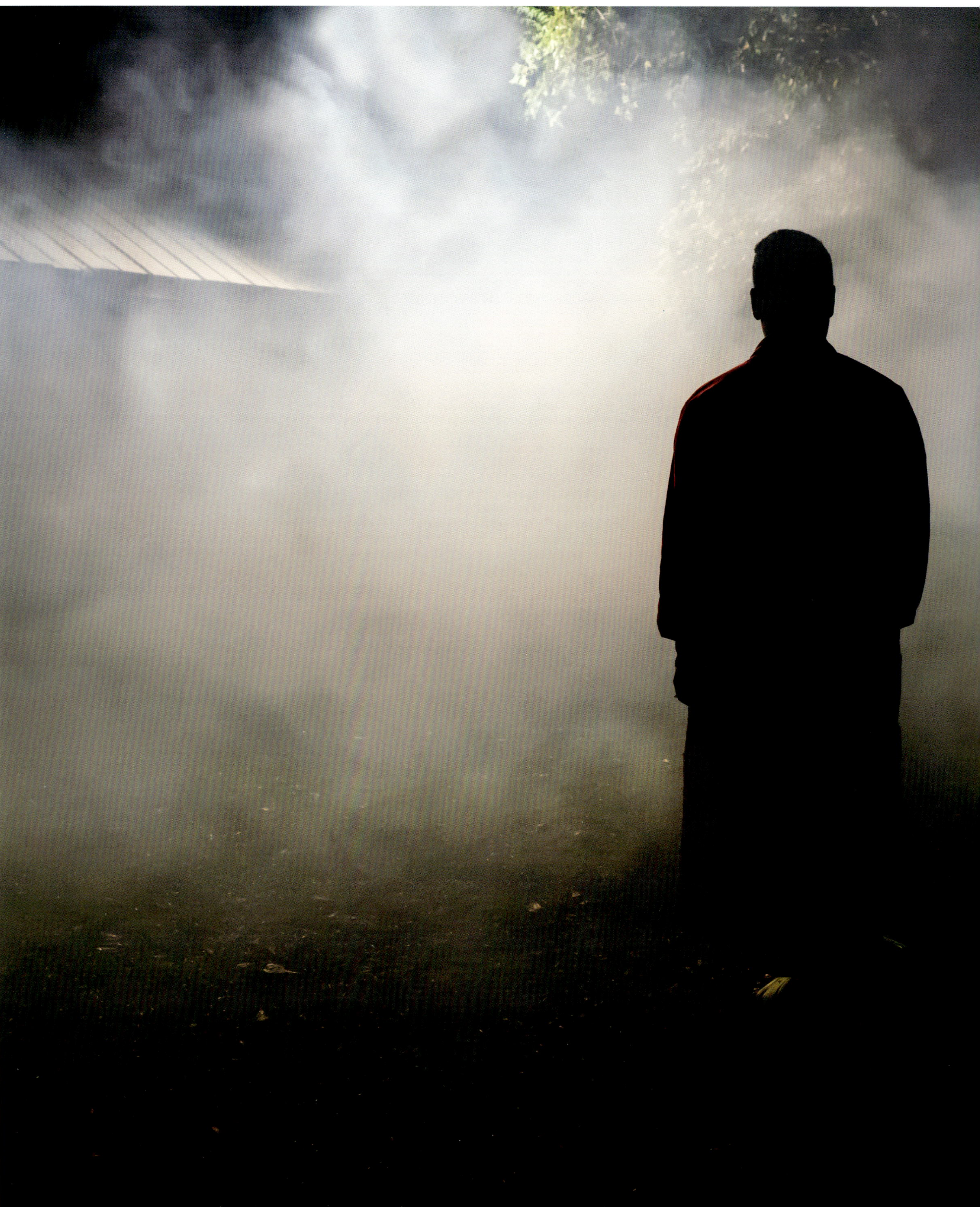

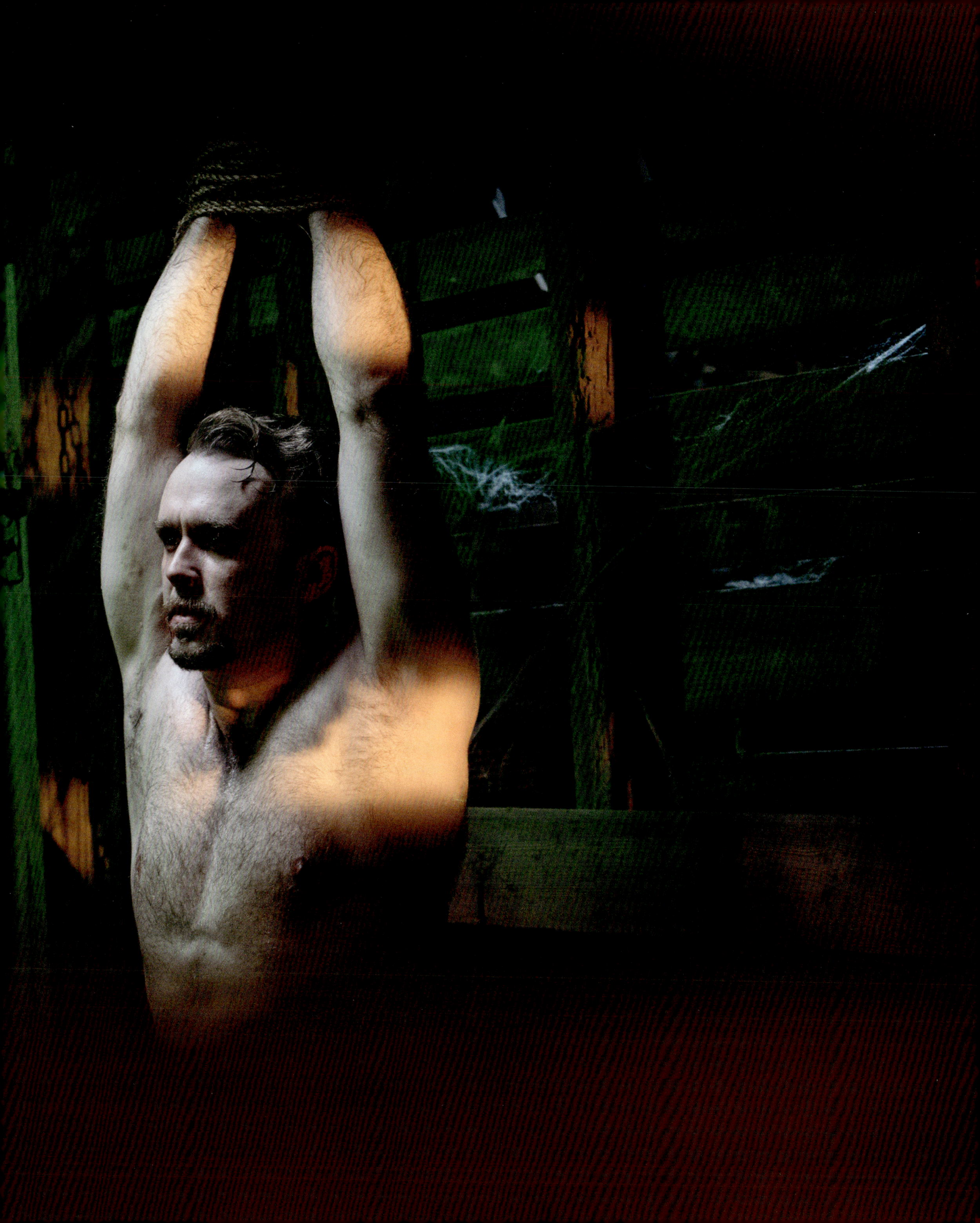

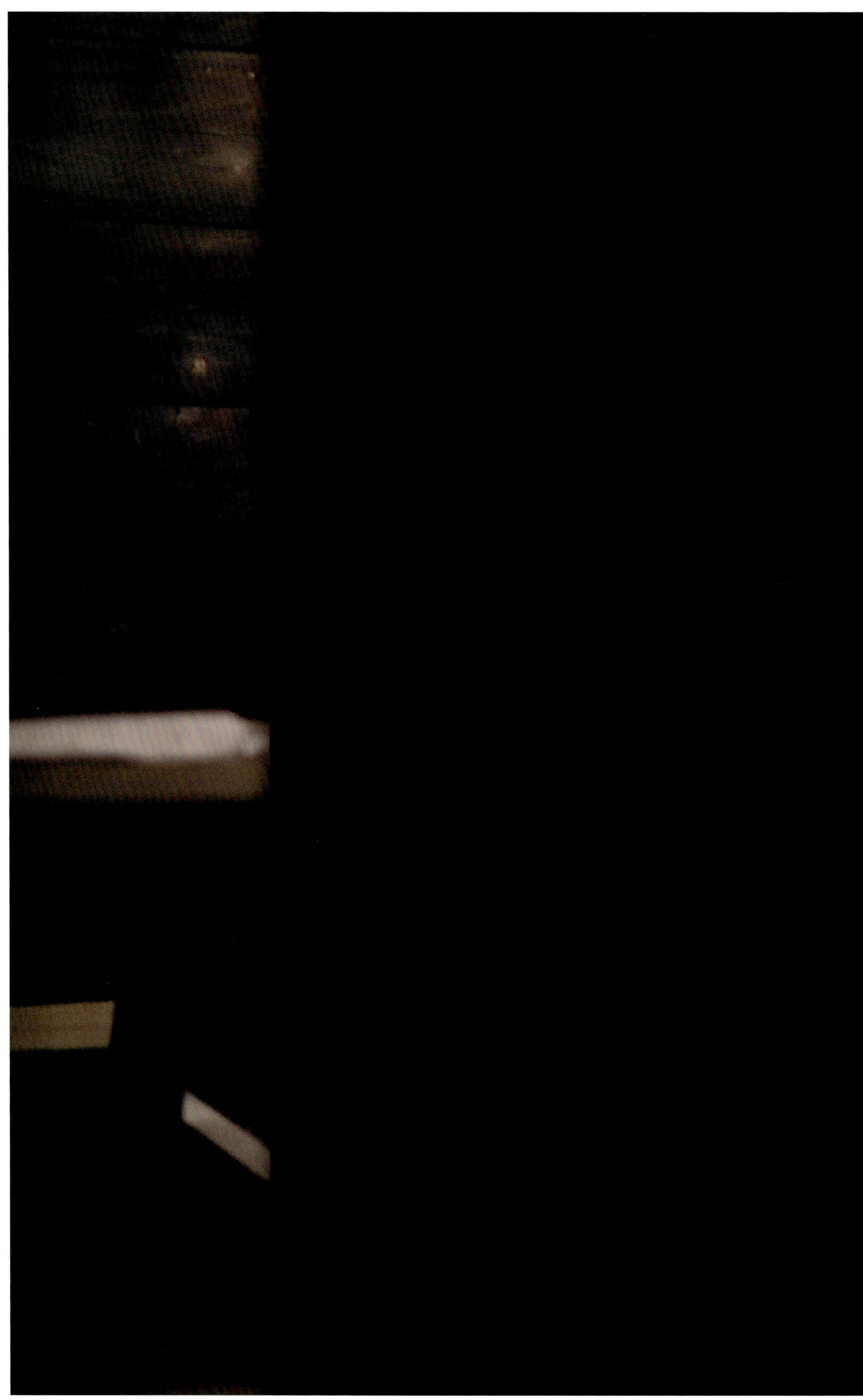

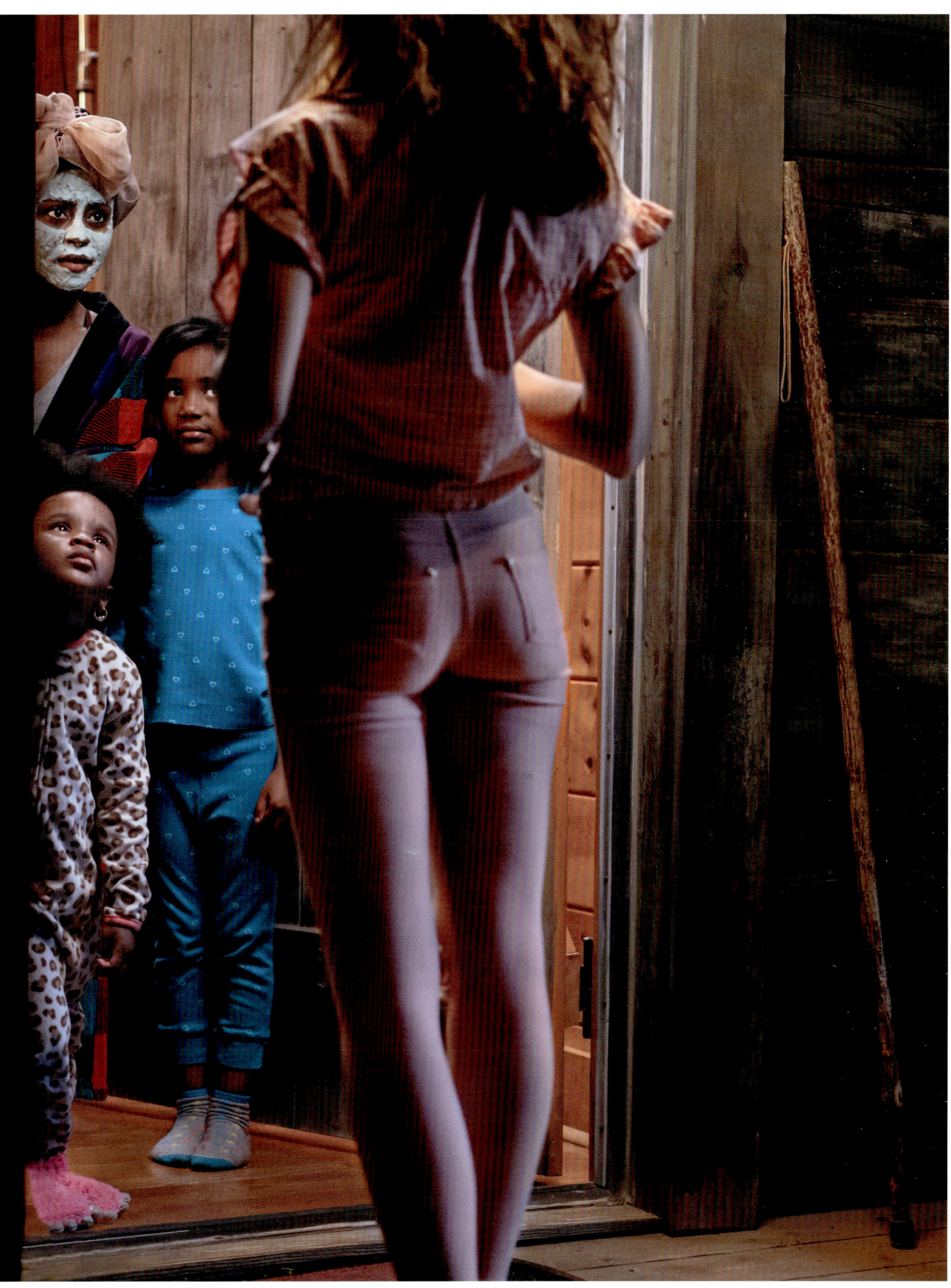

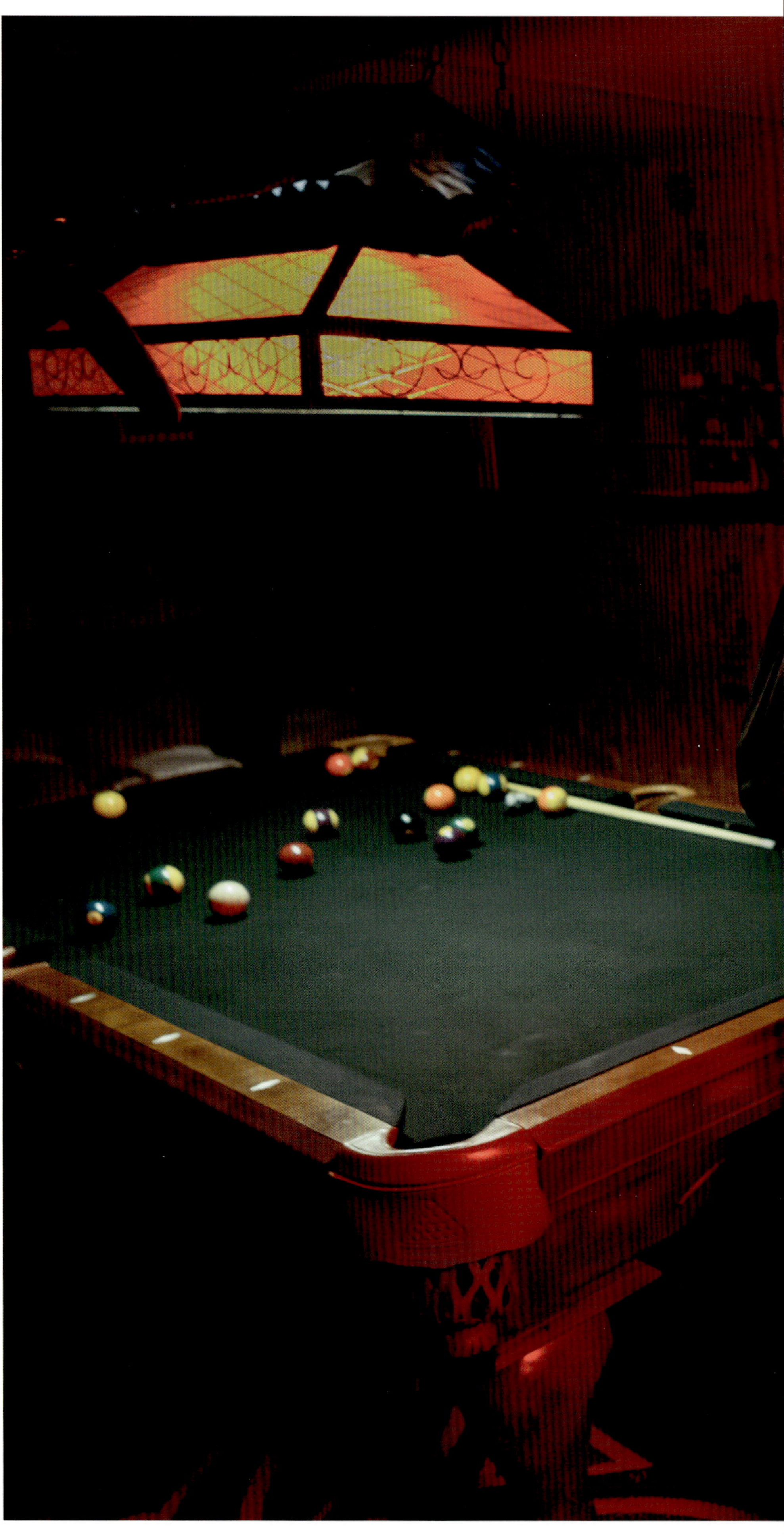

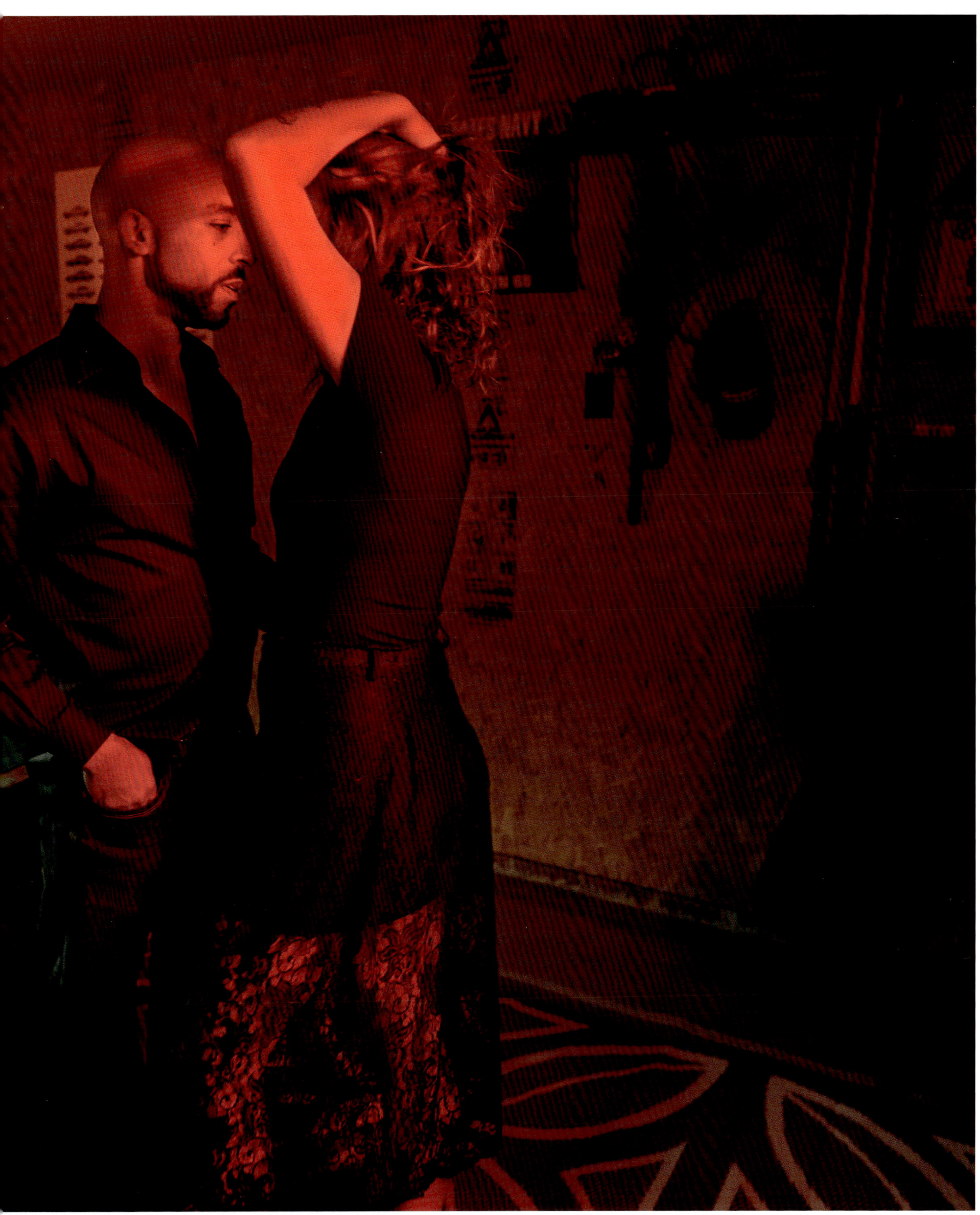

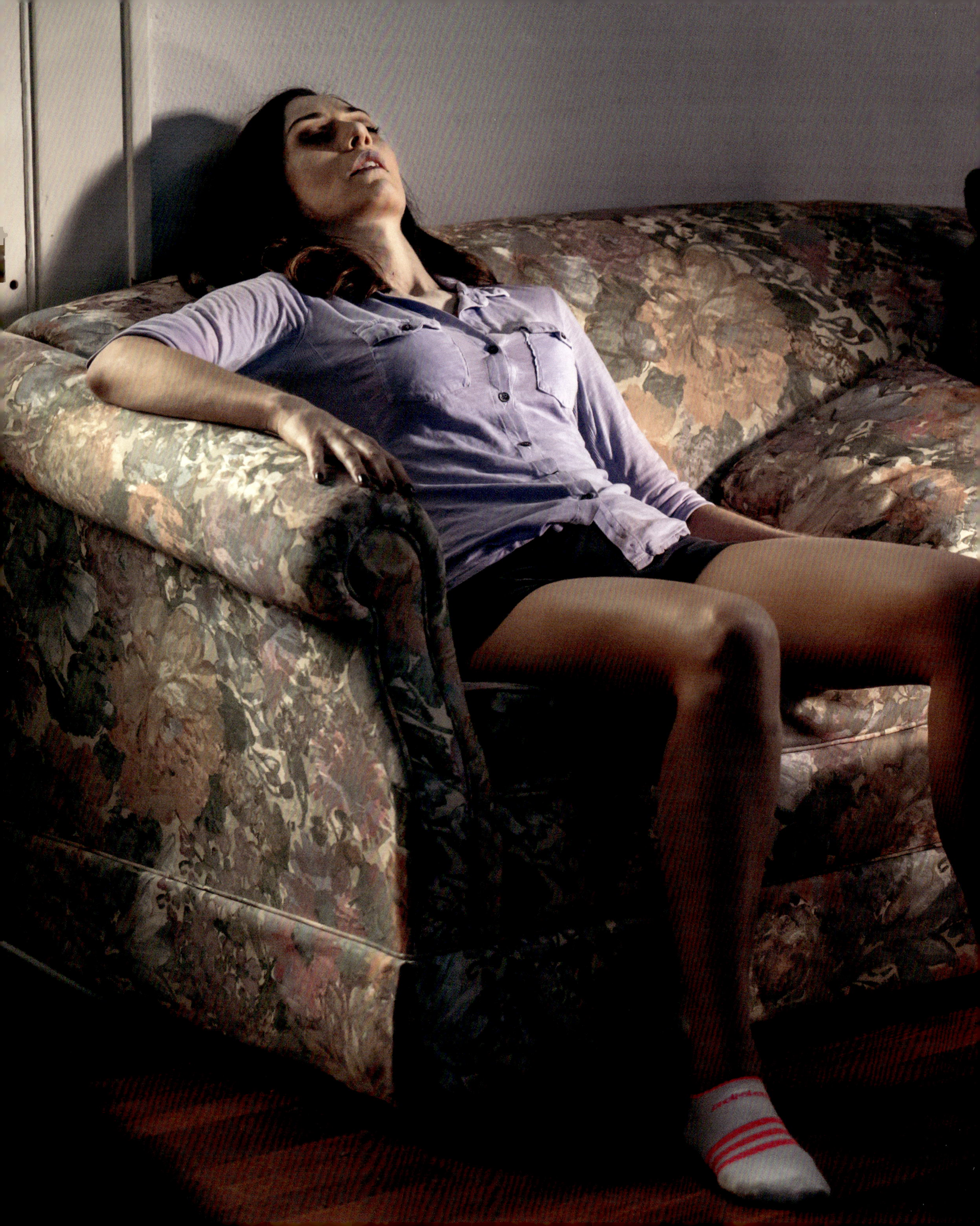

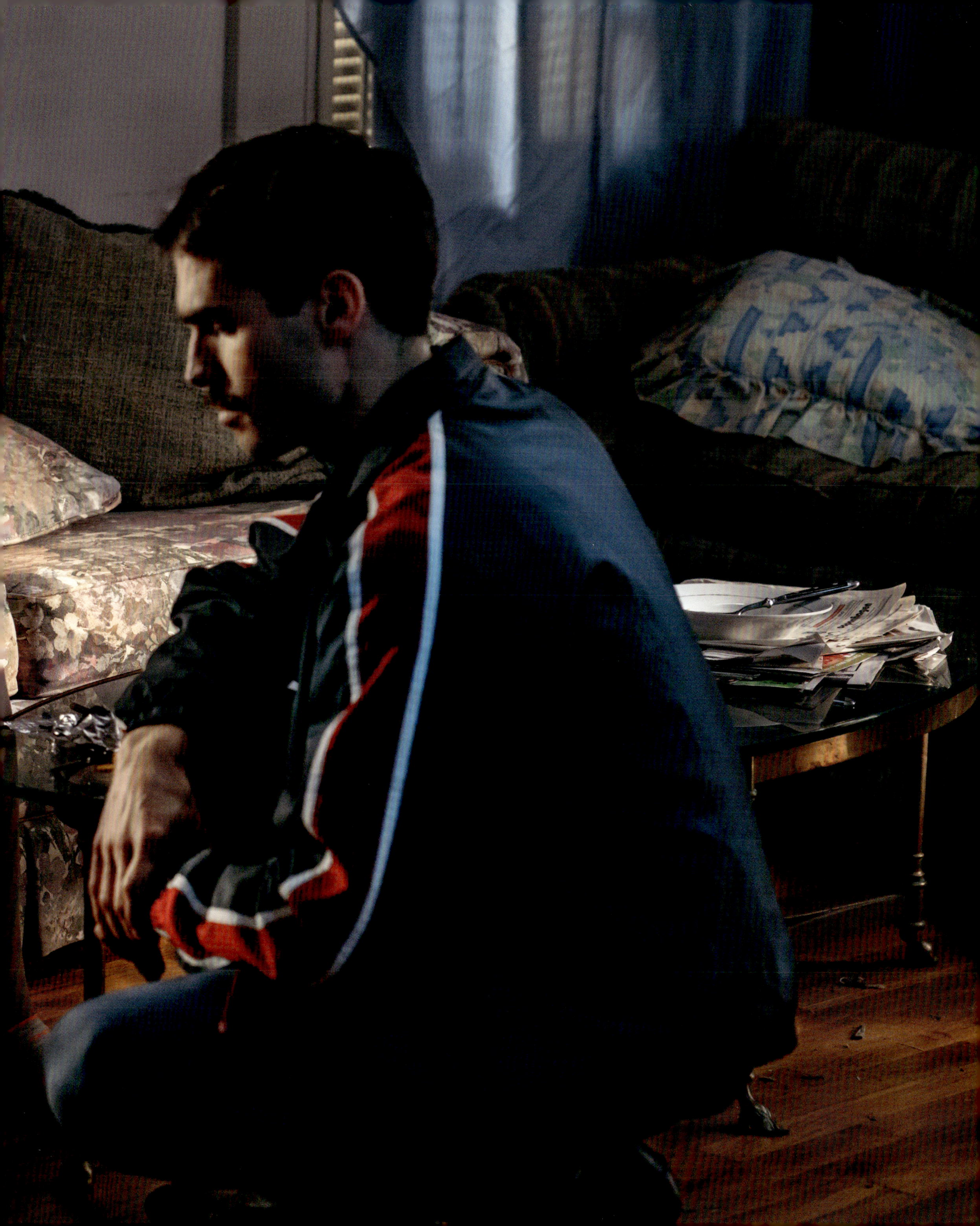

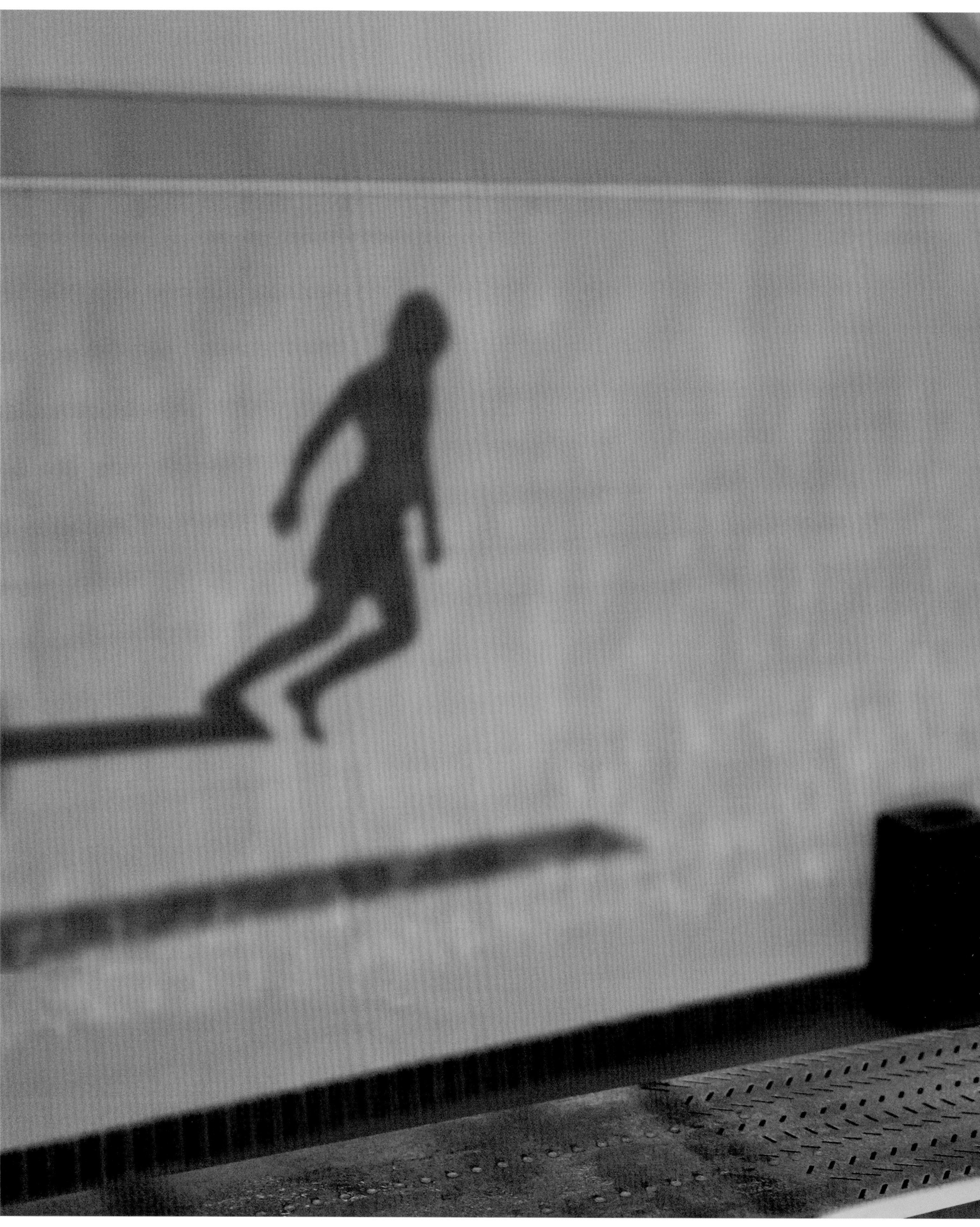

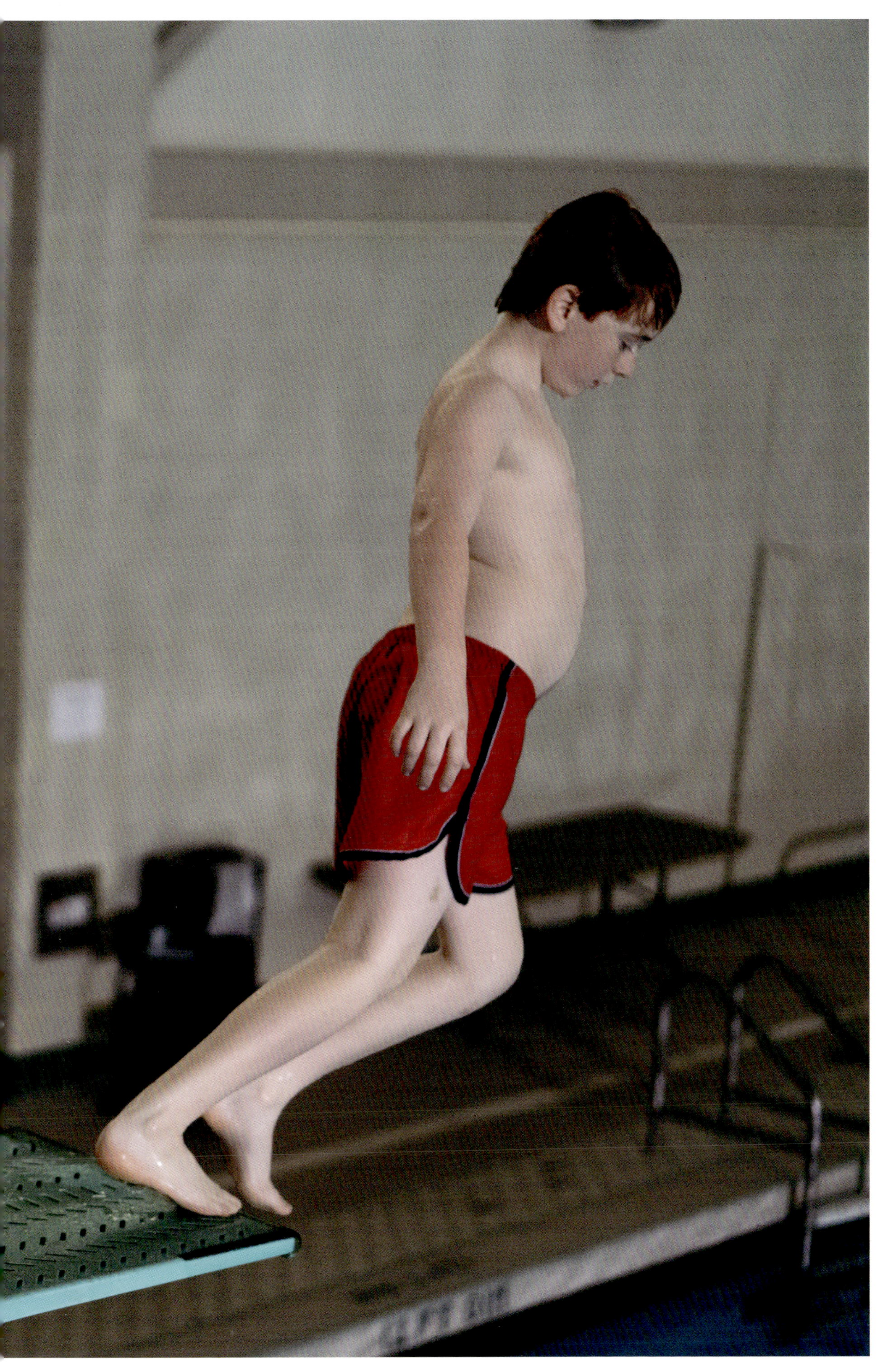

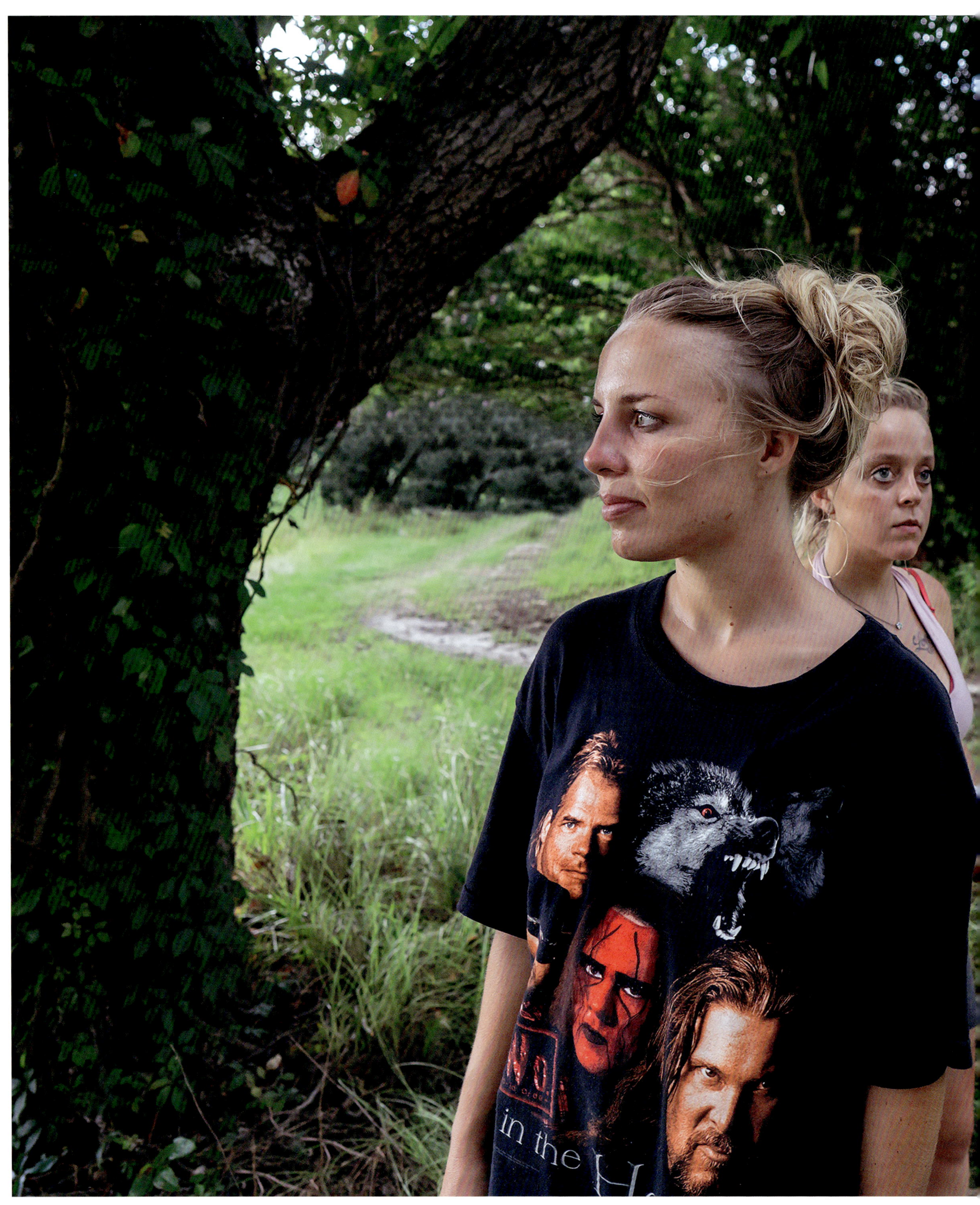

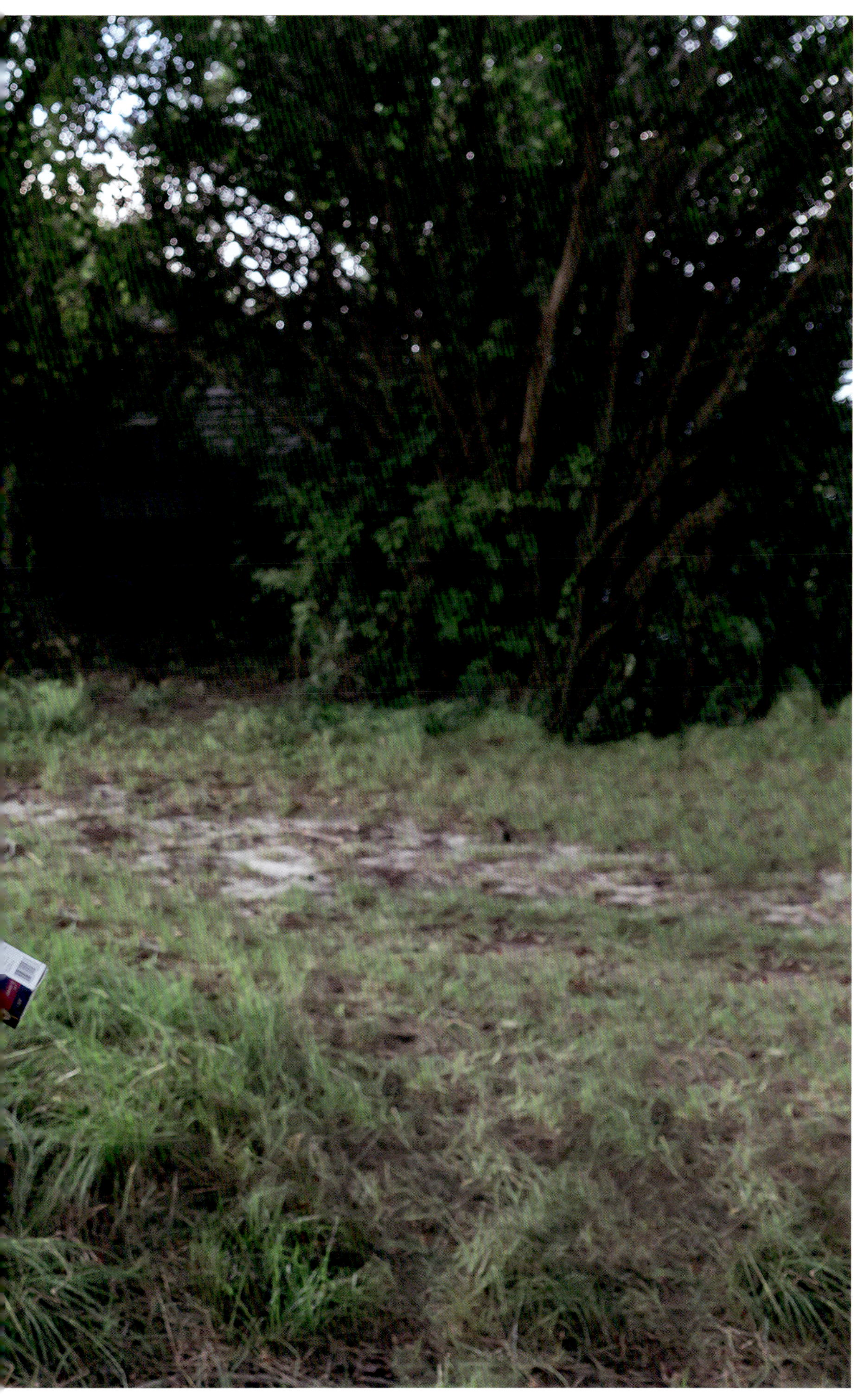

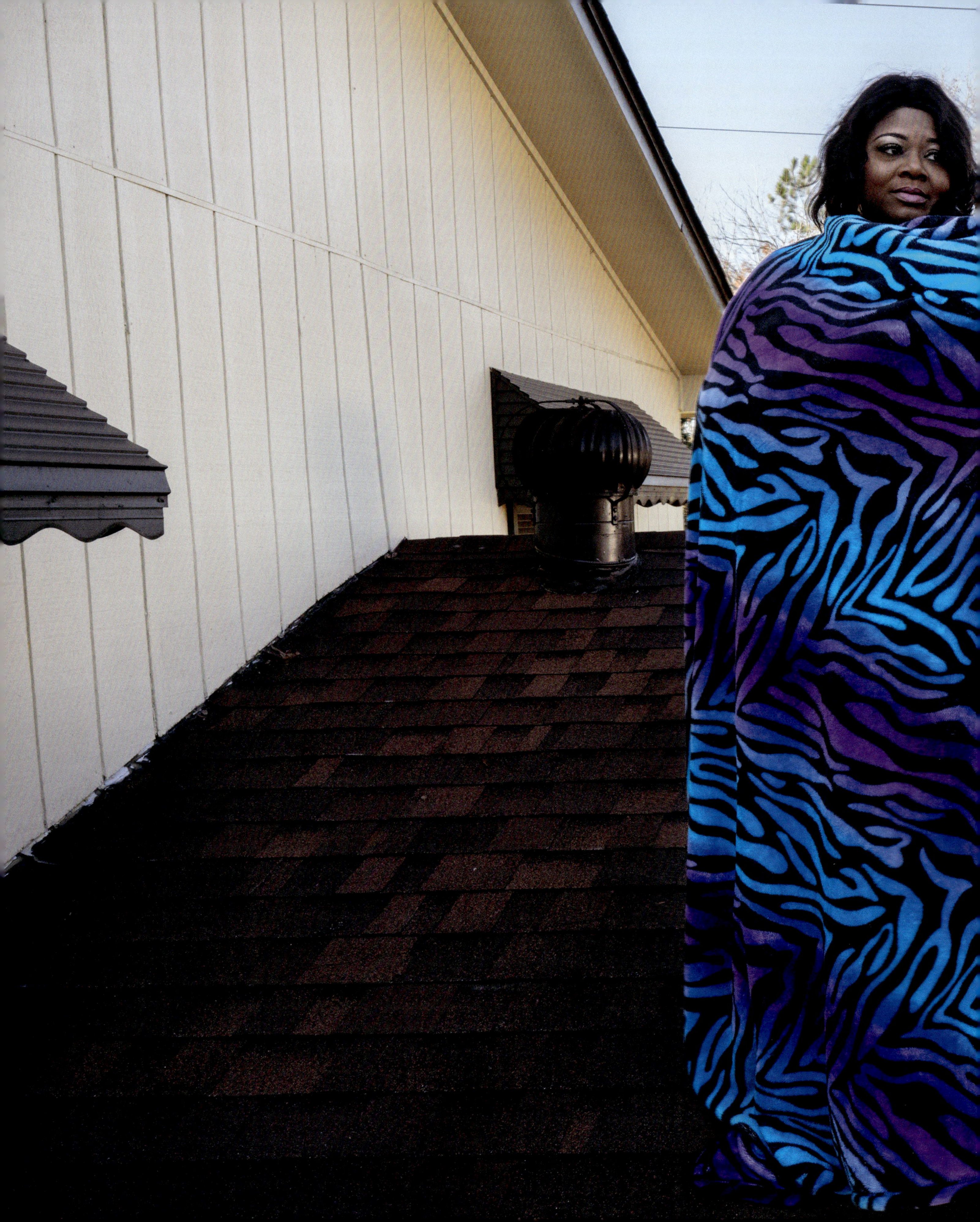

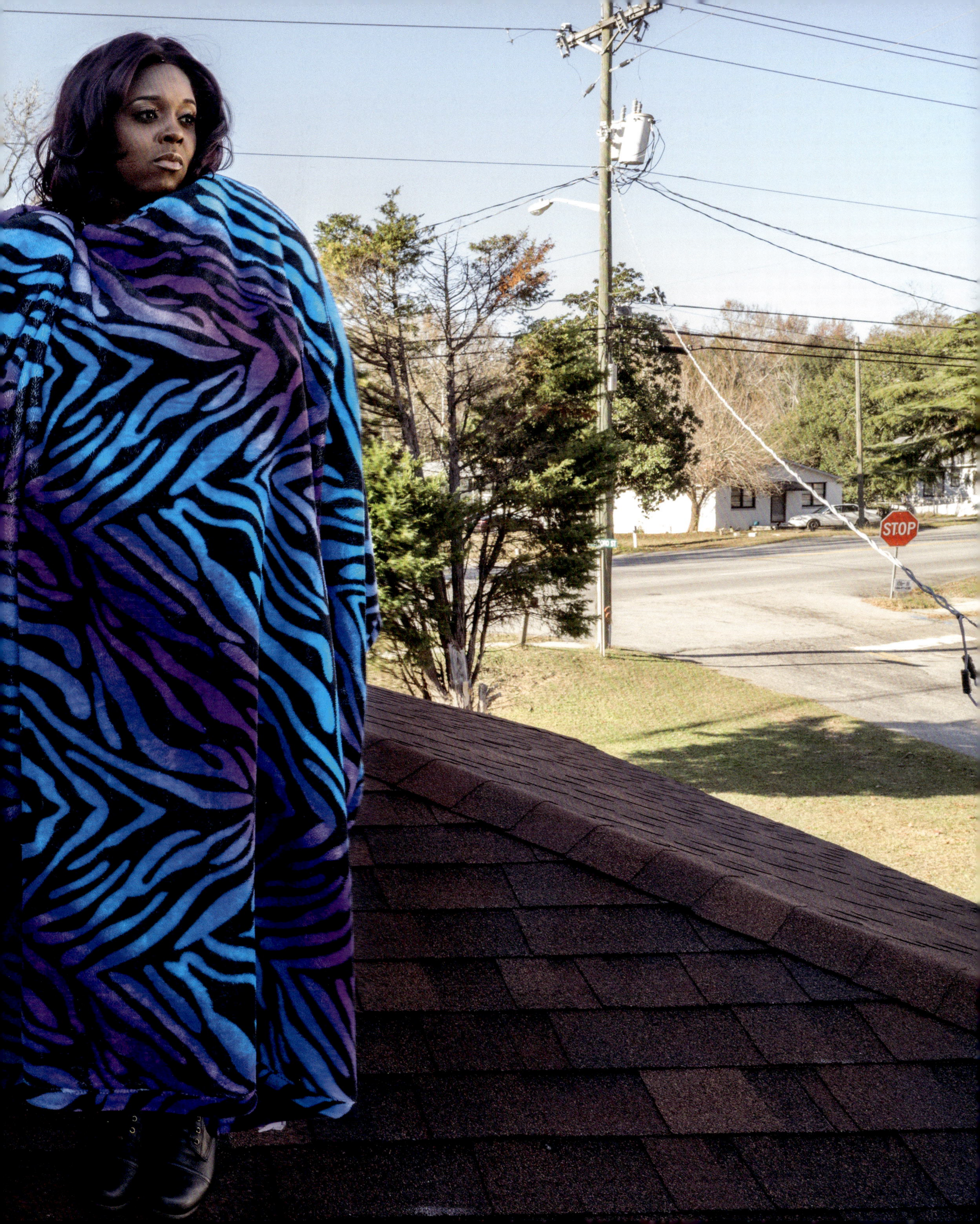

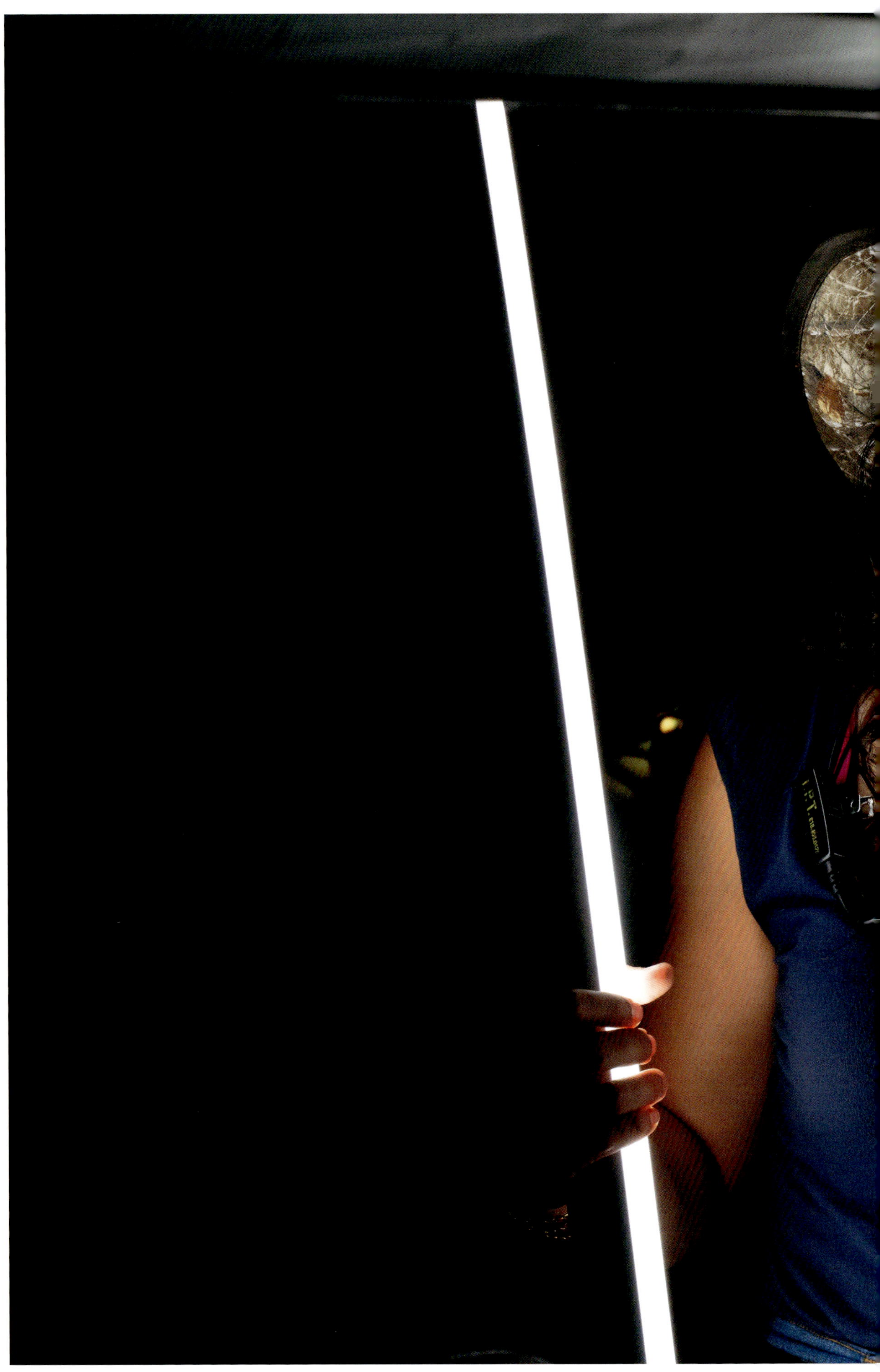

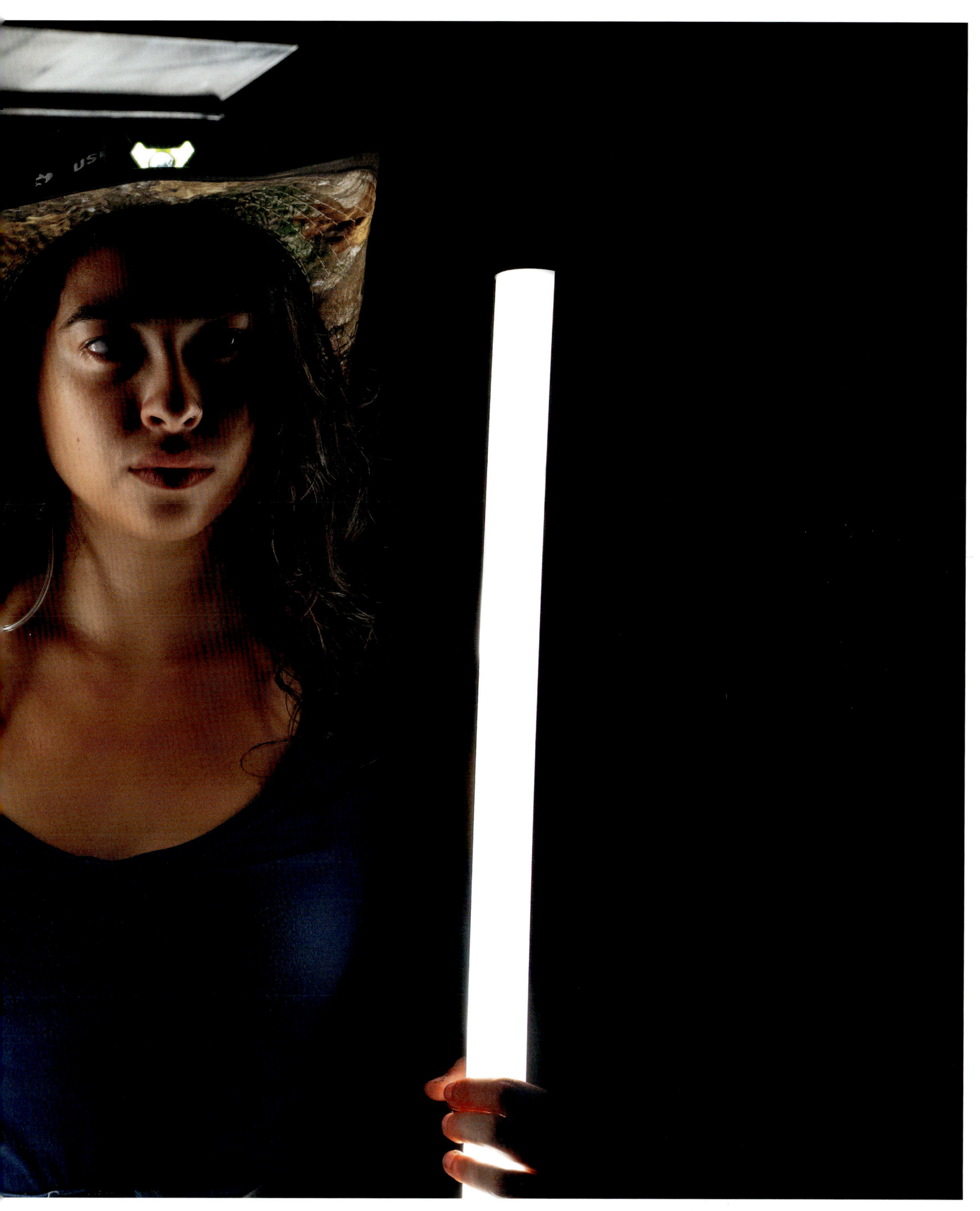

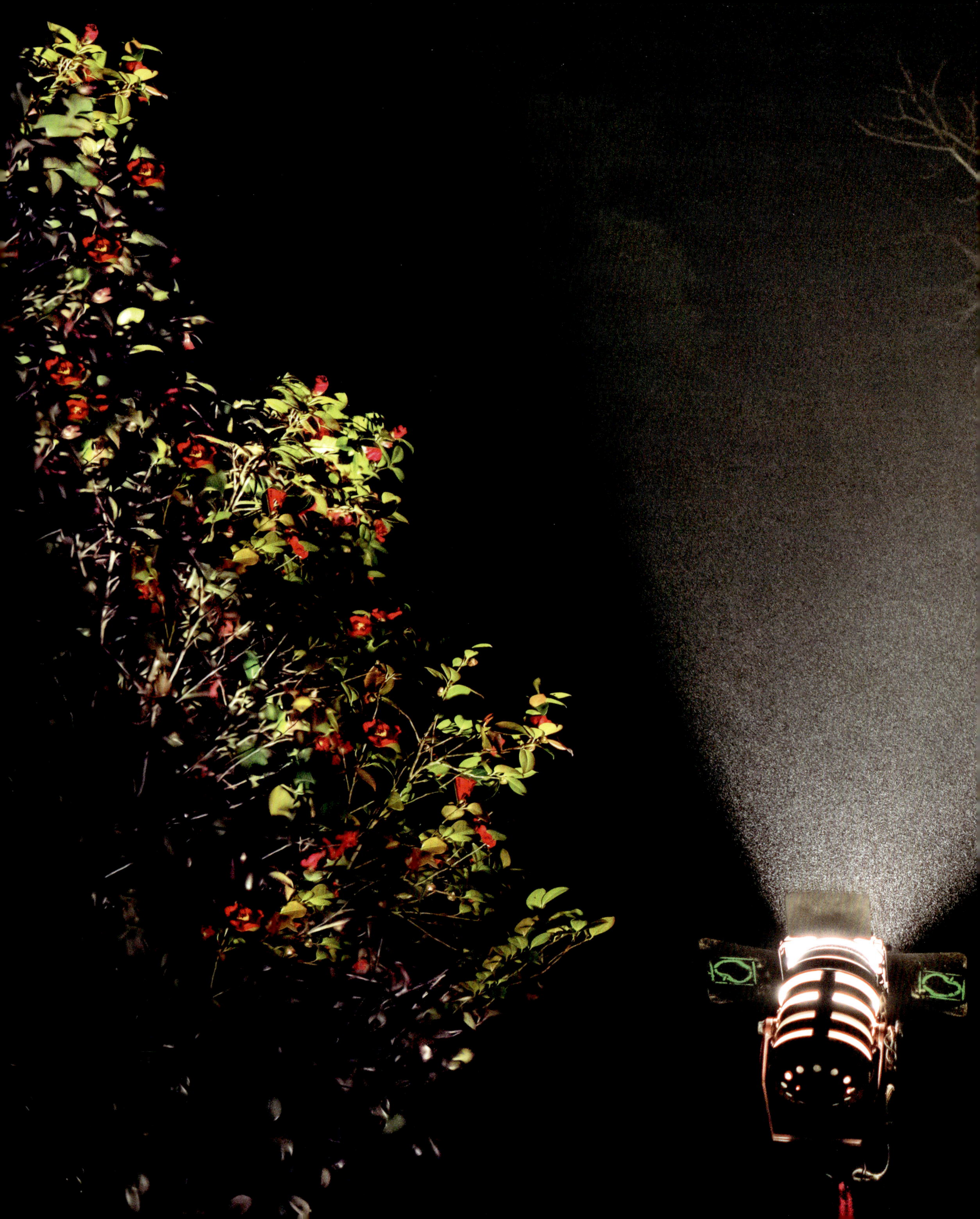

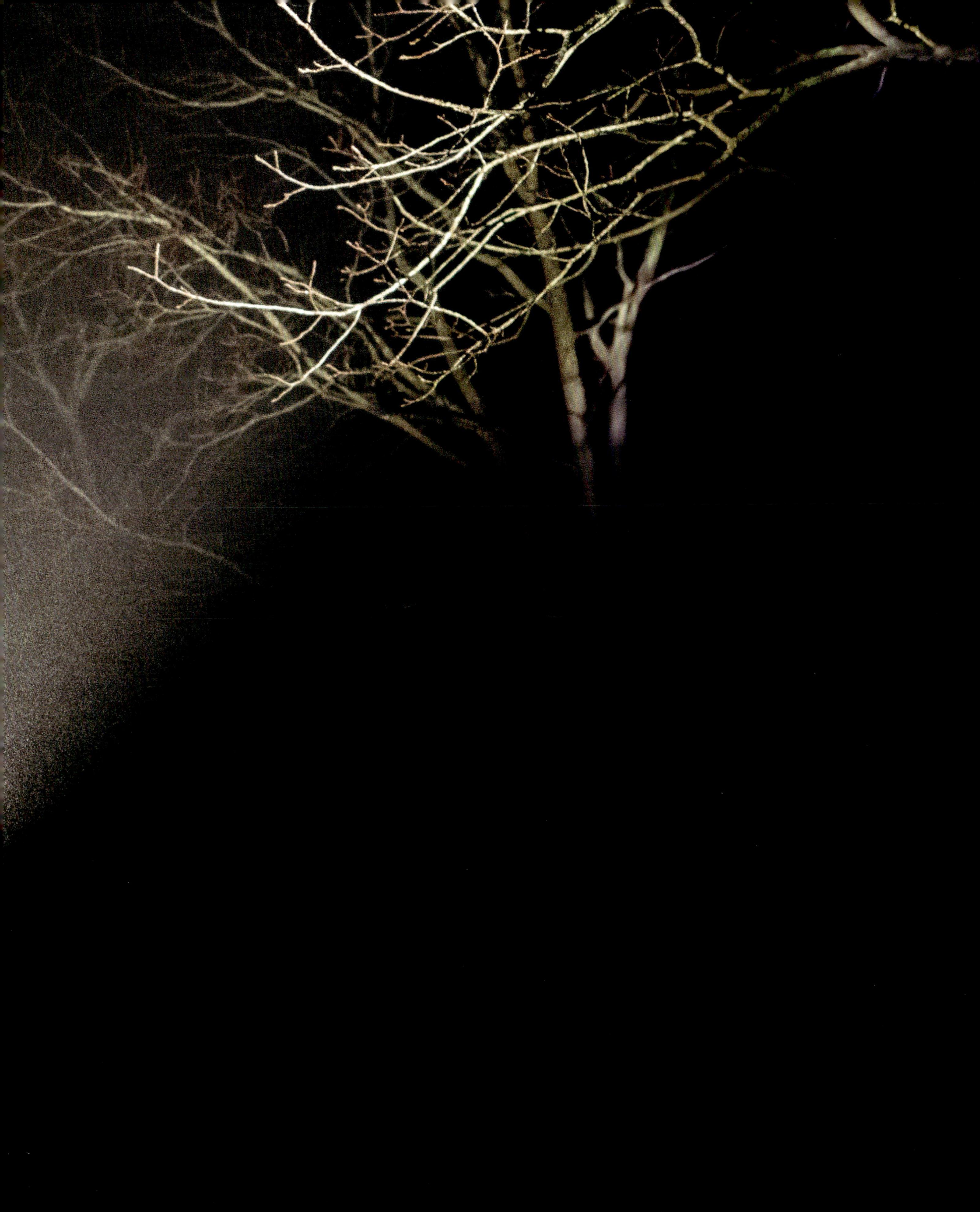

RETROACTIVE DREAMING

by RONI NICOLE HENDERSON-DAY (writer/director of *And the People Could Fly*)

My room was Pepto-Bismol pink with curved plaster walls. It had been this color since my mother lived in that room as a child. Its crank windows had their magic hour in the morning. Every morning in that upstairs room felt like a vivid dream. My Grandfather John, who passed when I was eight, taught me the most essential craft of choosing your dreams. He was a lotto man, so he'd tell me to pull the lever in my mind and call the rolling tiles into a story that I wanted to see, or rather to be. This was the tool he gave me to keep nightmares away, a power to decide how to see things, how to see myself in it all. But mostly, how to see for myself. The choices made could shape your night, wreck your next day, or they could offer insight into how you feel and how to navigate those feelings. They might offer a winning number in the 7 o'clock lottery, if you were lucky. Dreams held weight in my Grandpa John's mind. I guess he knew of the haunts that resided in those upstairs rooms occupied by his children and his children's children. The ways that a family, our family, had fought, frozen, or fled our pain. How children and grandchildren would rotate out and in. Young minds and imaginations who would need a remedy for bad dreams, a plan to follow to stay inspired and hopeful about our own futures.

My love for light and shadow was born there at my grandparents' home. The dazzle of the sun's light dancing on the surface of our teeming little creek. The cylinders of light streaming through holes in the tin siding of my grandmother's gardening shed as she sat atop an upturned bucket, whispering prayers from her heart to God's.

The windows of the two-story brick home had their own way of letting light inside. The afternoon glow that shone through the thick, warbled cube glass window capping the bottom of the stairwell made the air hot and time stand still. That is, until it dropped off abruptly when you reached the 4th-from-the-top step. The crank-to-open windows screened the late summer light as it flooded into shared spaces.

At the largest of these apertures of light in the living room, my grandmother would do her hair. And I'd see her, perfectly framed in that triple set of windows, the thick, gold-flecked, emerald green drapes drawn back against white plaster walls. Her posture was elegant as she leaned in close to her own image, sunlight pouring in on her beautiful honey brown skin. There, in that metal folding chair, my grandmother dressed her brows, removed her headscarf, and unrolled her hair. A cloth-lined wooden basket sat at her feet, filled with the essentials for her grooming rituals: Nature's Blessing grease, rollers with roller paper, a small comb, a rat-tailed brush, and her particular shade of chocolate brown liner for her brow. In the evenings, she'd grease and re-roll her hair, wrap her scarf, and moisturize her supple brown cheeks, eyelids, and forehead with Vaseline. Some evenings, I'd grease her hair for her, and she would bask in the attention, crowned by the evening's fading orange light.

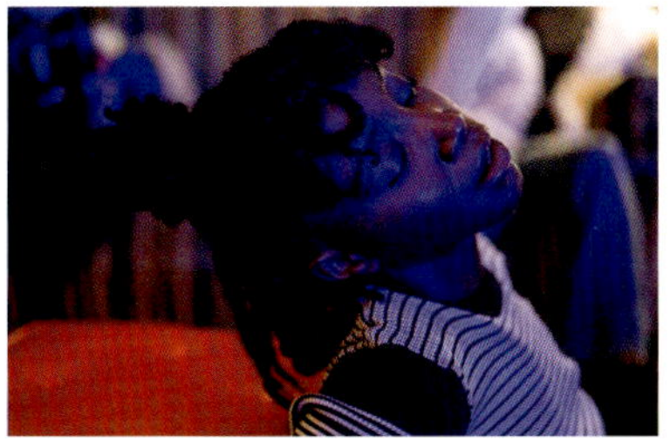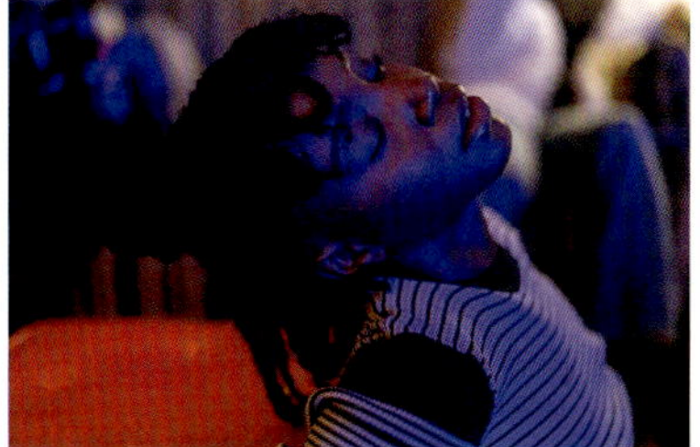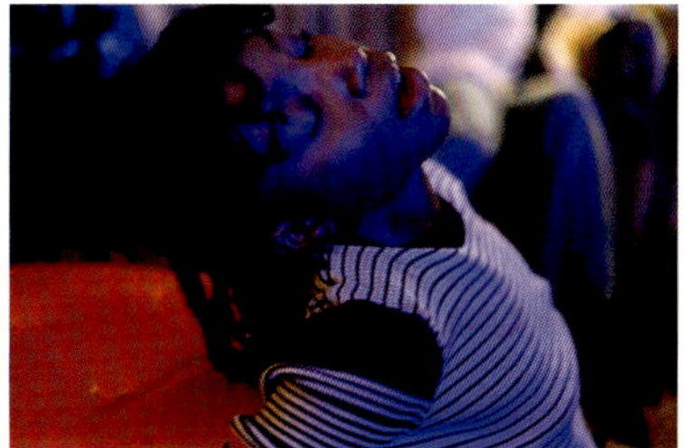

from the set of *And the People Could Fly*

My parents' choices in life allowed me to return often to the refuge of my grandparents' home. Back to church-on-Sundays and dinner-at-six. Lemon cakes and homemade rolls. Stories told over and over, details ripening as we aged. Grandpa John passed away from a heart attack when he was 79. I was eight, and from that time forward, my grandmother took care of us, the last two grandchildren in the line, on her own. My cousin Aaron and I watched her kiss John's picture every morning, the one with her careful script at the bottom: *My Beloved Husband, John A. Sims, the love of my life.* Next she would kiss her parents' photo and then a picture depicting Jesus on All Saints Day.

When my mother passed away years later, her photo joined the morning kissing ritual. Only after my grandmother finished reading and copying her scriptures into a tiny spiral notebook, could you speak to her. She'd carry on, ignoring any and everybody until she had completed her "habit" as she called it. I grew to appreciate this ancestral remembrance as a constant in my life. There was balm for the weary at my grandmother's house. She would rub salve on my back, using slow, circular motions that calmed me, restored me. She reminded me that I was loved, cared for, and, most essentially, not alone.

These childhood memories float in my mind. They drift on light, shadow, and the wandering eye of my youth. Each is a tableau I am compelled to scrutinize, in search of what lies just beneath. But in the tableau of my memory, the shadow isn't a hiding place. It has place and purpose, just as the light does. As in my films, light and shadow are co-conspirators. My grandparents showed me this, how not to overlook the shadow and instead to delve and to watch without judgment. They showed me how to see and celebrate the Black body as Grace embodied. Grace made flesh and come to life because even on heroin, my parents always showed me that they loved me. Each in their own way. Yes, in spite of it All.

And the People Could Fly is about the gravitas of life and about how gravity triples down on a head that hangs low. It is based on a memory of how I once drifted into the home of my mother's favorite dope dealer, an older white woman named Nancy who had plush places for her clients to drift and dream. As a young girl, I wandered into a room of adults who didn't know I was there. In my film, I wanted to revisit this memory but recolor it too. I was a watchful child, and because they, the adults, were in their own respective worlds, I could search the tableau of their escape without consequence. Time moved so sluggishly for them that it barely seemed to move at all. When I grew tired of watching them slip, gather, slip, gather. . . slip. Crash! I rammed my red patent leather Mary Jane into a side table just to jolt them. They startled so slowly. Reaching out in clumsy motions to hide the tools of their trip. I pitied them then. It was years later when I decided that maybe pity didn't serve them, or me, and that if I could do it again, I might choose not to act cruelly, even if it seemed, as a child, justifiable. Maybe, instead, I would remind them of their wings and help them to shake off the weight of a head hanging low.

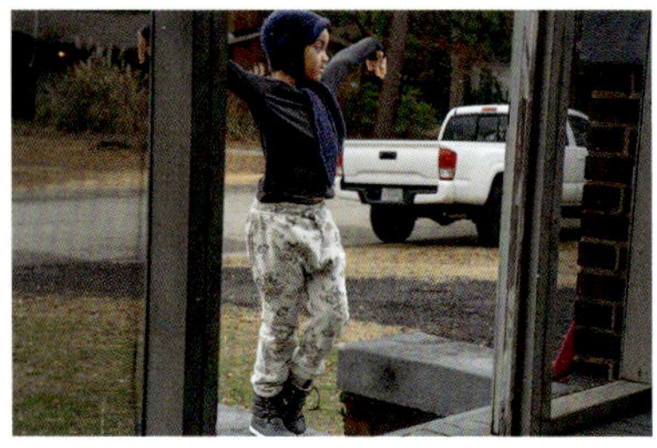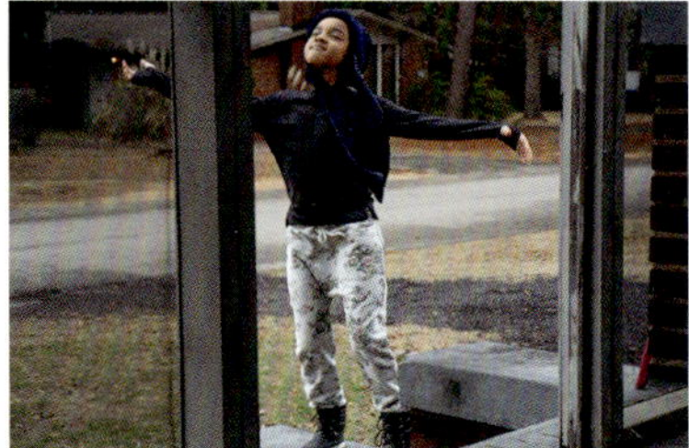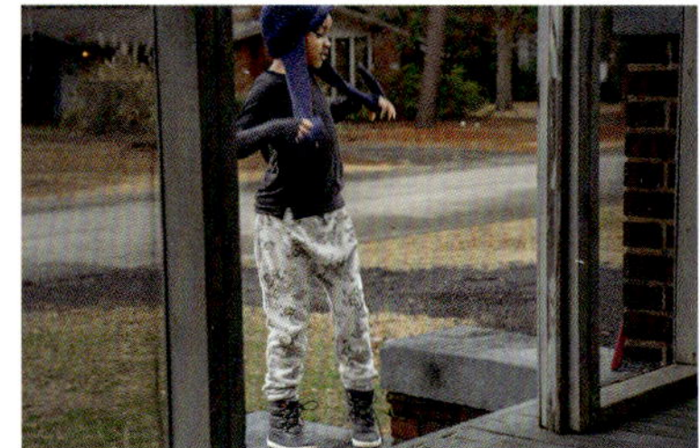

from the set of *And the People Could Fly*

In the recolored memory that is *And the People Could Fly*, my cinematographer, Eric Branco, captures both the gravity that the adults are enduring and the childlike wandering of the young girl at the heart of the story. Conspiring with the camera's choreography is the poignant movement direction by T. Lang and production design by Michaela Pilar Brown. Collaborating with these artists whose work centers healing is an act of healing itself. The rolling tiles of chance have offered me another window through which not only to see my story, but to embrace it, and to grow because of it.

I will be forever in awe of this craft, its opportunities for shared dreaming, for collective work to bring a vision to life. This is why I approach producing a film from a holistic, make-where-you-are standpoint. And while I left the major film cities a long time ago, I have discovered that often, in a smaller town, you find talented folk who, though they haven't been formally trained in film, approach the process with brilliant and fresh ideas. For these artists, our set becomes a training ground, a place to develop film skills that will, hopefully, aid and inspire them as they find their way into their own storytelling.

Call it retroactive dreaming. Producing and making films has allowed me to return to and see my life with the grace I've received from it. I seek to honor my memories with films that empower, forgive, and, ultimately, build communities around telling stories about the human condition in ways that are rooted in unconditional love, humanity, and a deep commitment to healing.

…

AFTERWORD

Alex Harris, 2021

She was talking to herself, listening to music, and dancing. I had just made a short drive to Columbia, South Carolina on the day before the filming of a narrative short called, *And the People Could Fly.* It was a cozy setup, two modest suburban ranch homes across from one another on a quiet street, one for filming and the other for cast and crew. I already knew the producer and was just meeting the director, Roni Nicole Henderson-Day, and members of the cast, when I saw ten-year-old Avye' Luz Garcia through an open doorway. I hadn't expected to photograph that day but picked up my camera and made several pictures. Though I had been told Avye' was an actor, I thought she was just playing, maybe getting rid of nervous energy before her first time on a movie set. But the next day, in a dream-like dance sequence in front of the cinematographer's lens, I saw Avye' use these same gestures to magically animate a group of adults, including the actress playing her own mother.

I know now Henderson-Day created this scene from one of her own childhood memories. It spoke in ways that were profoundly personal to me. This scene was, and remains, like certain scenes from movies I've watched over the years, as real in my imagination as my own true memories, a visual experience I can replay like a film clip unspooling through projector light and developing into a story on the screen of my mind.

…

In 2016, I was awarded a *Picturing the South* commission from the High Museum in Atlanta. The parameters were simple. I could photograph anything I wanted as long as I focused on the South. I admit to getting lost for a year on back roads between Mobile and Bowling Green, and many places in between, before finding my direction. But it was on one of those trips, two hours from my home in North Carolina, as I drove past the exit for the caricature town of South of the Border, South Carolina, that this project idea began to take shape in my mind. Because it was then that I thought back to an experience I had a decade earlier south of the actual U.S. border.

A producer I met in Los Angeles asked me to come to Mexico to photograph on the set of Steven Soderbergh's, *Che.* She admired the photographs I'd made in Cuba and hoped I might capture something of the feeling of the island if she gave me freedom to photograph on set in Campeche, a town in Mexico that resembled Cuban towns of Che's era. I could photograph anything if I didn't get in the way. I imagined my first time on a movie set would be a kind of make-believe experience, and it was. Being on set *made me believe* I was photographing something real. Hundreds of locals from Campeche were playing Cuban townspeople helping Benecio del Toro, as Che, liberate the town of Santa Clara, Cuba. During filming, I watched these Mexicans fight alongside Che's rebels as if their own lives and families were at stake.

It was this border between real and make believe that compelled me between 2017 and 2019 to drive across the American South and photograph on forty-two different independent narrative film sets, limiting myself to films that were about the South or set in the South.

Southerners have a reputation for being storytellers. But Southern storytellers have also stereotyped and romanticized the South. When I began this project, I tried to put aside the images of the South I thought I knew and, instead, to allow my pictures to show me a South I had not previously seen. And I also believed I could discover something surprising by focusing my attention on Southern filmmakers with personal stories they were compelled to tell.

The filmmakers who invited me on their sets were making films during the two years just before Covid-19 was discovered in the United States in March of 2020, a pre-pandemic period when Americans were already living vicariously through the lives of characters on screens, a phenomenon that became hugely more prevalent during Covid. Now these films seem prophetic, evoking so many of the passions and preoccupations of Southern and American society that heated to the boiling point once Covid struck. In my photographs from film sets, we also see lives acted out with an easy physical and emotional closeness that, at the height of the pandemic, already seemed a distant memory – like the Star Trek episode where Captain Kirk thinks he's beamed down to an alien world and asks the first person he sees, "You, what planet is this?" When he is informed he's on earth, Kirk realizes he has travelled not across the Galaxy, but back in time.

I travelled back to my own childhood during the filming of Bonnie Kathleen Ryan's *Graceland*, in Charleston, South Carolina, when I found myself in a sixth-grade classroom she commandeered as her set that morning. The room looked and felt like so many of the elementary school classrooms in Georgia I'd inhabited decades earlier. The history taught to me in those classrooms, like the history my own children were taught much more recently in North Carolina, misrepresented, glossed over, or avoided completely the perspectives of marginalized Southerners in the United States.

This all came back to me in that classroom when I photographed a book on the shelf behind the teacher's desk. On the book's cover was a portrait of girl dressed as we imagine Puritans would have looked in Jamestown, Virginia when these settlers arrived to form the first permanent British Colony on our shores (pp. 30-31). The book was titled, *My America: Our Strange New Land.* That day, *Our Strange New Land* became my title for this book, a phrase I've attempted to turn on its head, to indicate new and different stories of life in the South being told by contemporary filmmakers.

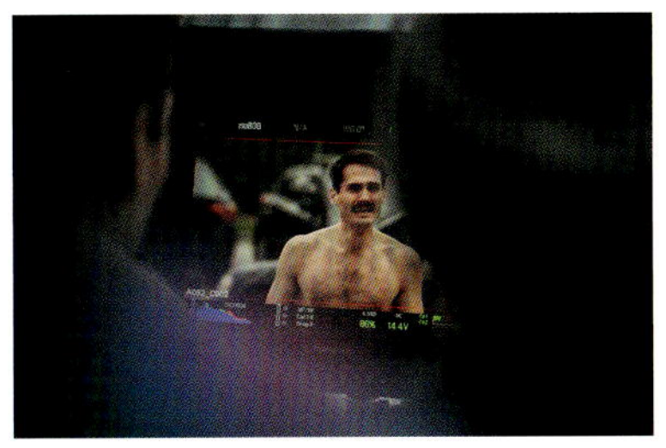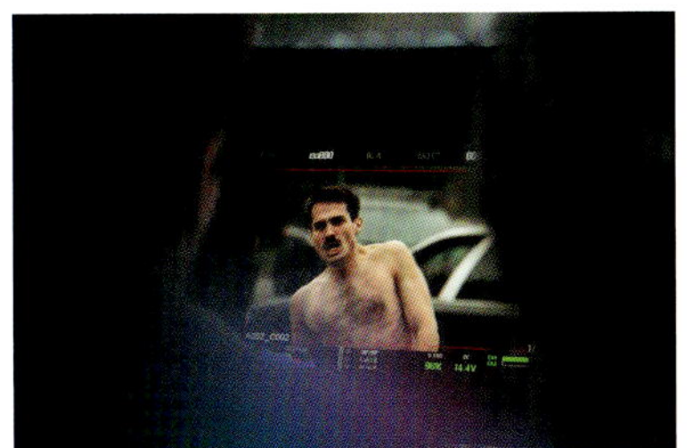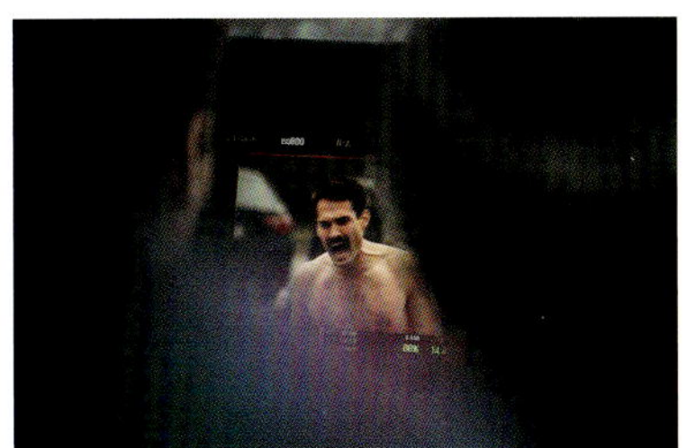

from the set of *Thunder Road*

In filmmaking as in life, perspective is everything. It matters who tells the story. This book is about the imaginations, creativity, and perspectives of a new generation of contemporary narrative filmmakers looking at the American South through a diverse and democratic lens, filmmakers of different social backgrounds, sexual orientations, races, and ethnicities. These filmmakers are evoking a broad range of experiences, coming to terms with presumptions and assumptions that relate not only to the South, but to the whole country.

Like every photographer, I remember, sometimes even mourn, the photographs I missed by not being in the right place at the right time and even the ones I didn't take because the situation seemed too private. On film sets, I had few such regrets. Within minutes of arriving, once introduced to the cast and crew, I was free to photograph unfolding dramatic scenes, sometimes from a very close distance, often the kind of moments and events I would have been unlikely to photograph in the "real" world no matter how much time I spent. Only on one or two occasions was I asked not to photograph a particularly intimate scene. And when I did photograph, usually there were multiple takes, giving me the chance to approach several times from different angles and distances. Photographing on movie sets, I discovered a photographer's dream.

When I began to photograph on film sets, I planned to press my camera's shutter only after the director called "action," to focus solely on actors in front of the cinematographer's lens. In this way, I believed my pictures would create the illusion that these were people in real-life situations rather than scenes in a fiction film. But the more time I spent on set, the more I became fascinated by the actors, sometimes first-time actors like young Avye' Luz Garcia, blurring the lines between their on-set and off-set lives, between their own personalities and the characters they were playing. I started to photograph what was happening behind the scenes, the cast and crew off-camera going about the business of making a film. And because the settings for most of these films were the homes, buildings, and communities where Southerners actually live and work, I also felt free to include people who weren't part of the filming process but were observing the filming.

Looking at photographs in this book, it is often hard to see the difference between my pictures of actors and crew on the film set and moments when I focused on bystanders. I believe now that my photographs speak to an idea that has long been celebrated in literature and philosophy – that is to the ways in which we are all actors in our own lives, practicing our lines, creating our sets, choreographing our movements, essentially (as actors must do) getting into character.

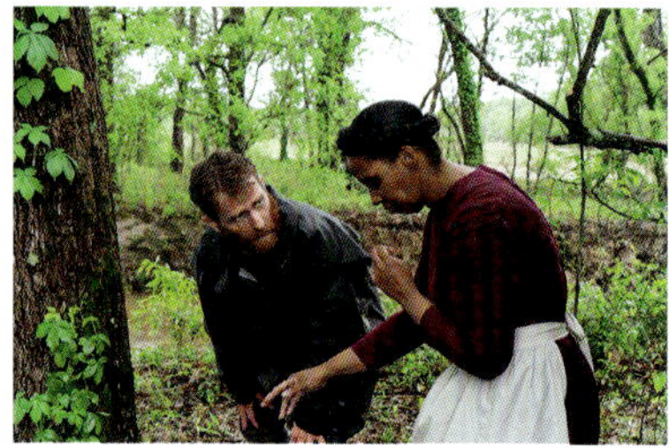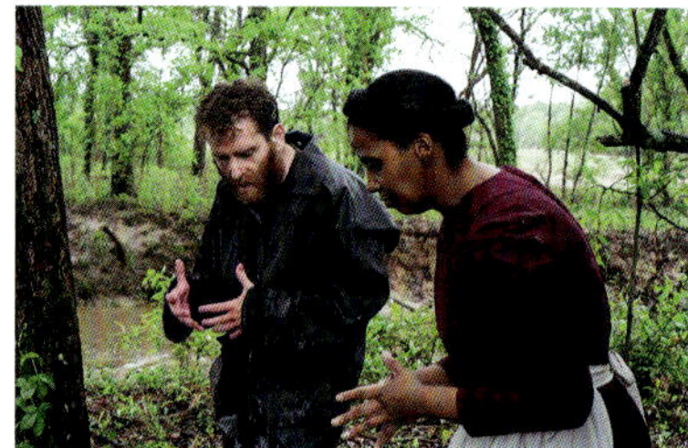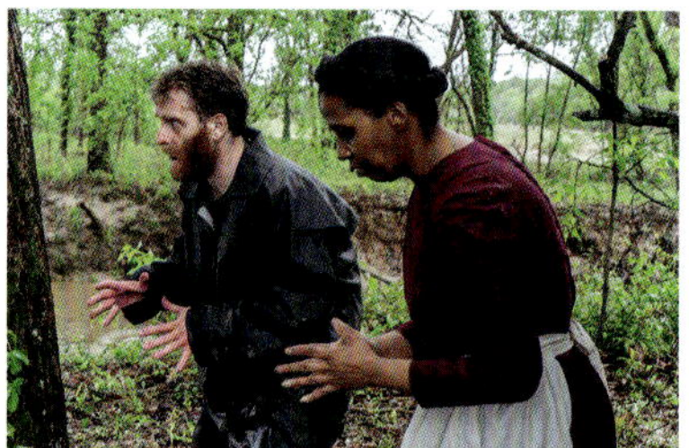

from the set of *Son of a Gun*

Each actor on set seemed to have their own way of inhabiting their movie set character. On my first day on the set of *Thunder Road,* thinking to break the ice with the veteran actor Nican Robinson before filming began, I asked the actor what he had done over the weekend. Nican replied, "I did yoga both mornings, but spent each afternoon writing in the diary I keep for my character." (pp. 26-27). On that same film set, I stood next to the writer, director, and actor Jim Cummings, to photograph him as he prepared to be filmed as a policeman who had just given a eulogy at his mother's funeral, and who was now losing his job and losing control of his emotions (pp. 44-45). Cummings has a special kind of comic genius, but this scene called for him to evoke a deep sadness that would drive his irrational behavior. For a few moments just before 'action' was called, I watched Cummings talk to a photo on his cell phone, his voice rising and cracking. It was a photograph you may have seen, of Prince William standing with Prince Harry at their mother Princess Diana's funeral.

I often saw directors working with actors to display the emotion they were hoping to see. On set in Mississippi for a Civil War era movie called *Son of a Gun*, I photographed writer and director Travis Mills in the midst of recreating skirmish scenes around the siege of Vicksburg with dozens of actors and extras. Mills was whispering into the ear of a first-time actor Nancy Lindsey after several unsuccessful takes in the tumult of a complicated battle scene (pp. 46-47). Lindsey's job was to convey her anguish, to use her voice to compel a battlefield medic to leave the badly injured soldier he was tending, and to accompany her to a home nearby to save a wounded young girl she was caring for. Later, Mills told me what he whispered. "I am about to say some words to you that will be upsetting, so I want you to prepare yourself. But I'm trying to help you…I want you to imagine it's your own daughter who is dying." After that, only one more take was needed (pp. 24-25). If the emotions expressed in my photographs by actors, crew, or bystanders—either on or off set—appear real, it's because they are.

I also witnessed improvisation on set, not just by actors, but by directors, cinematographers, set designers, gaffers, and other crew members. On the second day of shooting his short film, *Handsome* near Hattiesburg, Mississippi, Miles Doleac filmed scenes he'd originally written for broad daylight in torrential rain. Once the cast and crew were assembled, there was no turning back. Miles loaned me an umbrella. In Atlanta, I rode in the back of a truck with co-director and cinematographer Micah Stansell as he filmed three children riding their bikes through a suburban neighborhood for *Let Light Perpetual*, an experimental film he and his wife Whitney were making. Micah, a wonderfully inventive cinematographer, wasn't getting the shots he wanted. He stopped the truck, picked up his electric skateboard from the truck bed, and began skating beside the kids, balancing himself while looking through the viewfinder of his fancy camera.

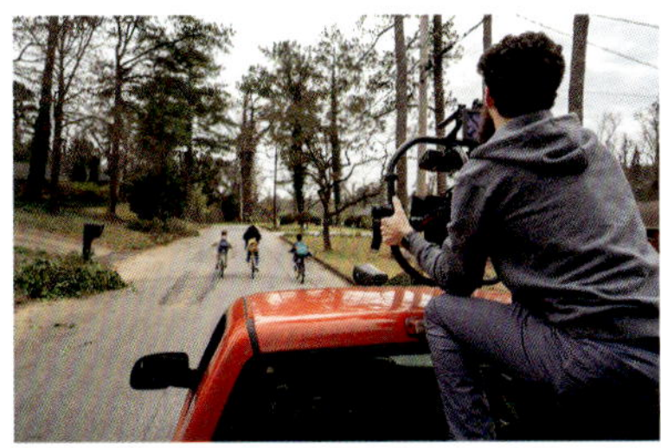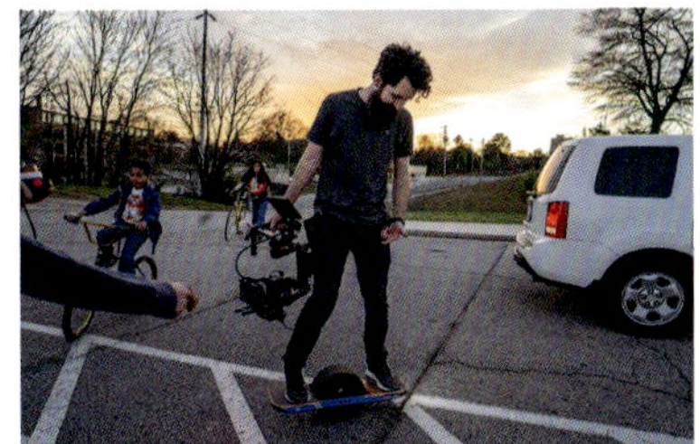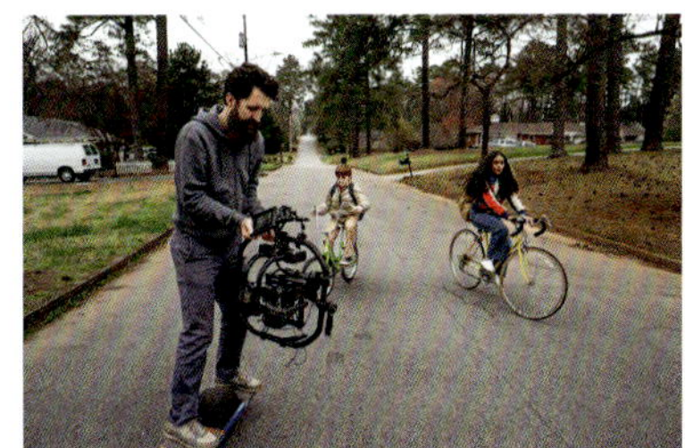

from the set of *Let Light Perpetual*

Roni Nicole Henderson-Day performed her own balancing acts while directing ten-year-old Avye' Luz Garcia in *And the People Could Fly*. Preparing for a scene where Avye', in search of her mother, must enter the living room through a beaded curtain hanging in a doorway, Henderson-Day showed her how to approach the curtain, use both hands to part it in the middle, then with just her head poking through that space, look first to the left, then to the right where she finally sees her mother. Henderson-Day instructed Avye' to move gently, slowly, with the same gradual motion that Eric Branco, the cinematographer, would use to follow her gaze into the room, the same way the adults in the room were themselves moving. After a few minutes Avye' began to play with the curtain, parting it again and again, with one hand and then two, listening to the sounds of the beads as they hit against each other. Henderson-Day stepped away, giving the young actor time to play before shooting her scene.

Still photography, like filmmaking, gains meaning through metaphor. The purpose of a small action can be literal and at the same time hint at something larger. When Avye' started to play with the curtain, I began to photograph her from the other side. I set my shutter speed so the curtain would show movement, but Avye's face would remain still. Later, going through my photographs from that evening, I was struck by one photograph in particular where some beaded strands still obscured parts of her face (pp. 2-3). Avye' is gazing out, but her eyes are unfocused. It's as if she's stressed, worried, lost in thought. I thought of the ways in which Roni Nicole Henderson-Day, like so many of the filmmakers I had the privilege of working with on this project, was herself trying to part a curtain, the way the writer Eudora Welty, writing a text for a book of her early photographs of depression era Mississippi, described her larger purpose as the writer she would become. "My continuing passion is to part a curtain, that invisible veil of indifference that falls between us and that blinds us to each other's presence, each other's wonder, each other's human plight."

…

LIST OF FILMS

A PAINTED SCANDAL, director Sheridan Philipp

ABDUCTED, director Benjamin Joyner, writer Josh Barkey, pp. 50-51, 60-63, 104-105, 132-133

AND THE PEOPLE COULD FLY, writer & director Roni Nicole Henderson-Day, pp. 2-3, 19-20, 54-57, 82-83, 112-113

AT SUNSET, writer & director MaryClare Serio

BEAST BEAST, writer & director Danny Madden, p. 101

BEYOND THE MUSIC: THE SPIES, director Sean Gerowin

BLACK GIRL, MAGIC, writer & director Samantha Beaulieu

BYGONE BILLY, writer & director Shea Sizemore

CALM BEFORE, writer & director Tara Lynn Marcelle, pp. 16-17, 120-121

DOODLE, writer & director A. F. Madison, pp. 28-29

ESCAPE, writer & director Hunter McGregor

FIRE, writer & director John Swider, p. 69

FORGIVENESS, writer & director Idris Pearson, pp. 53, 72-73

FORT MARIA, writers & directors S. Cagney Gentry & Thom Southerland, pp. 40-41

GRACELAND, writer & director Bonnie Kathleen Ryan, co-writer Trevor Munson, pp. 30-31, 52, 98-99

GREENER GRASS, writers & directors Jocelyn DeBoer & Dawn Luebbe, pp. 6-7, 32-33, 106-107, 118-119, 130-131

HALLOWED GROUND, writer & director Miles Doleac, pp. 74-75, 116-117

HANDSOME, director Miles Doleac, writer Travis Mills, pp. 34-35

HAON, writer & director Tanya Fermin, pp. 86-87

HOPE, writer & director Katie Damien

LET LIGHT PERPETUAL, directors Micah & Whitney Stansell, co-writer John Harkey, pp. 84-85, 100, 124-125

LETTERS, director Daniel Smith, writer Ben Trauner

LIBERTY, writer & director Faren Humes, pp. 8-9, 12-13, 64-67, 80-81, 90-95, 110-111

LIGHT FROM LIGHT, writer & director Paul Harrill, pp. 18, 23

LORELEI, writer & director Erika Edwards, pp. 76-77, 126-127

MINER'S MOUNTAIN, writer & director Bennett Pellington, pp. 38-39, 114-115

OH CRAPPY DAY, writer & director Jon Lance Bacon

PARALLEL PARKING, writer & director Aby Rao

PEEK, writer & director Tiffany Albright

PIG FILM, writer & director Josh Gibson

PLAYING GOD, writer & director Scott Brignac, pp. 102-103

SON OF A GUN, writer & director Travis Mills, pp. 21-22, 24-25, 46-47, 78-79

THE ASTRONOMERS, writer & director Anil Dhokai, pp. 48-49

THE FATALIST, writer & director Scott Sullivan

THE FUNERAL BAND, writer & director Nicholas Manuel Pino, pp. 42-43, 70-71

THE PRIVATEERS, writer & director Read W. Ridley

THERE COULD BE NOTHING AFTER THIS, writer & director Andrew Huggins

THUNDER ROAD, writer & director Jim Cummings, pp. 26-27, 44-45, 68, 122-123

UNITED, writer & director Victoria Glover, pp. 58-59, 96-97, 128-129

WAIT FOR IT, writer & director Justin Burkhamer, pp. 36-37

WHAT MATTERS, writer & director Andrew Gajadhar

WHAT THE RIVER KNOWS, writer & director Alicia Inshiradu, pp. 14-15, 88-89, 108-109

ACKNOWLEDGEMENTS

Colin Albea, Tiffany Albright, Jose Angles, John Lance Bacon, Charlie Ball, Henry Bazemore Jr., Flash Bennet, Matthew Bernstein, Jesse C Boyd, Martin Bradford, Emilia Brock, Michaela Pilar Brown, Calvin Bruce, Nancy Buirski, Darby Camp, Lacy Camp, John Cico, Robert Colom, Katie Damien, Danielle Deadwyler, Jocelyn DeBoer, Tracy Deleon, Anil Dhokai, Natalie Dickerson, Nicole Dickerson, Alexa Dilworth, Laura Doggett, Sheri Eakin, Erin Espelie, Shamara Evans, Kendal Farr, Layla Felder, Nicholas Fornwalt, Tanya Fermin, Kate Fisher, Derrick Freeman, Avye' Luz Garcia, Zelmira Gainza, Cagney Gentry, Joshua Gibson, Milagros Gilbert, West Givins, Eva Golson, Andrew Gajadhar, Paul Harrill, Paul Hart, Mike Holmes, Laura Lee Dufresne Houle, Clark Ivers, Alexandra Jackson, Milagros Gilbert, Victoria Glover, Lauren Henschel, Wesley Hogan, Bradley Jackson, Brad Jones, Ben Joyner, Jenna Kanell, Maria Kelly, Gideon Kennedy, Katrina Kinder, EB Landesberg, Nancy Landesberg, T. Lang, Jonah Liam, Dawn Luebbe, Will Madden, Andrew Madison, Tara Marcelle, Anissa Matlock, Mario Mattei, Konnor Megginson, Matt Miller, Diego Najera, Steven Neilson, Virginia Newcomb, Lily Nicole, William Noland, Wesley C. O'Mary, Vanessa Ore, Tatum Osborne, Nick Pilarski, Barbara Pita, Adam Patterson, Idris Pearson, Bennett Pellington, TJ Potts, Karen Price, Christian Ramirez-Coll, Tom Rankin, Daniel Rashid, Jeff Rich, Nican Robinson, Marcus Rosencrater, Fidias Reyes, Anthony Reynolds, Terence Rosemore, Bill Rothschild, Vernon Rudolph, Stephen Ruffin, Bonnie-Kathleen Ryan, Drew Sawyer, Jeremy Sande, Kenny Sands, Shawn Ryan, Danya Sherman, Bobby Siegworth, Shannon Silva, Stephen Shea Sizemore, Lile Sizemore, Jackson Smith, Thomas Southerland, Hunter Stark, Jason Sudak, Lee Thomas, Thomas Torrey, Catherine Trail, Micah Troublefield, Amy Unell, Shawyn Ryan, Erica Vonn, Daniel Voll, Zamarin Wahdat, Diana Ward, Ivan Weiss, Jen West, Lindsay Anne Williams, Creek Wilson, Cotton Yancey, Kristian Zuniga, Greta Zozula

SPECIAL THANKS

Organizations: Atlanta Film Festival, Center for Documentary Studies, Cassilhaus, Cucalorus Film Festival, High Museum of Art, Indie Grants, Indie Grits Film Festival, Longleaf Film Festival, Mobile Film Office, New Orleans Film Festival, North Carolina Film Forum, Richard Powell and the Office of the Dean of Humanities at Duke University, South Carolina Film Commission, Southern Documentary Fund

Individuals: Brett Abbott, MB Abram, Alyssa Armand, Charles Bethea, Paige Blankenship, Sally Bloom, Clint Bowie, Eric Branco, Dan Brawley, Kristy Breneman, Jill and George Brown, Lucinda Bunnen, Tucker Capparell, Ellen Cassilly, Jim Cummings, Marci Tate Davis, Miles Doleac, Channing Duke, Erika Edwards, Christopher Escobar, Felicia Feaster, Emily Forland, Seth Gadsden, Alexander Garcia, Victoria Greene, Deirdre Haj, Danny Madden, Art Harris and Carol Martin, Eliza Harris, Gregory John Harris, Gary Hawkins, Roni Nicole Henderson, Wanda Hopkins, Andrew Huggins, Faren Humes, Alicia Inshiradu, Brad Jayne, Sophie and Alan Joel, Sarah Kennel, Frank Konhaus, Lee Ledbetter and Doug Meffert, Joe Massey, Natalie Metzger, Lowell A. Meyer, Travis Mills, Nicholas Manuel Pino, Aby Rao, Kristi Ray, Dan Rogers, Micah and Whitney Stansell, Randall Suffolk, Claire Tanner, Kevin Tucker, Chris Webster, Benjamin Wiessner, Michael Williams, Caroline Yost, Jennifer Yoffy

Fiscal Sponsors: Lucinda Bunnen, Lubo Fund, Massey Charitable Trust, Southern Documentary Fund, Wanda Hopkins, Chris Webster and family

OUR
STRANGE
NEW
LAND

NARRATIVE MOVIE SETS
IN THE AMERICAN SOUTH

Yoffy Press, Atlanta, GA
yoffypress.com

First Edition
Printed & Bound at SYL, Barcelona, Spain

ISBN: 978-1-949608-20-5

All Photographs ©2021 Alex Harris
Edited by Alex Harris & Margaret Sartor

Essay by Roni Nicole Henderson-Day ©2021
Essay by Alex Harris ©2021

Design & Production by Tucker Capparell

Cover photograph from the set of *Abducted*
Endpaper storyboards ©2021 Danny Madden from his film *Beast Beast*

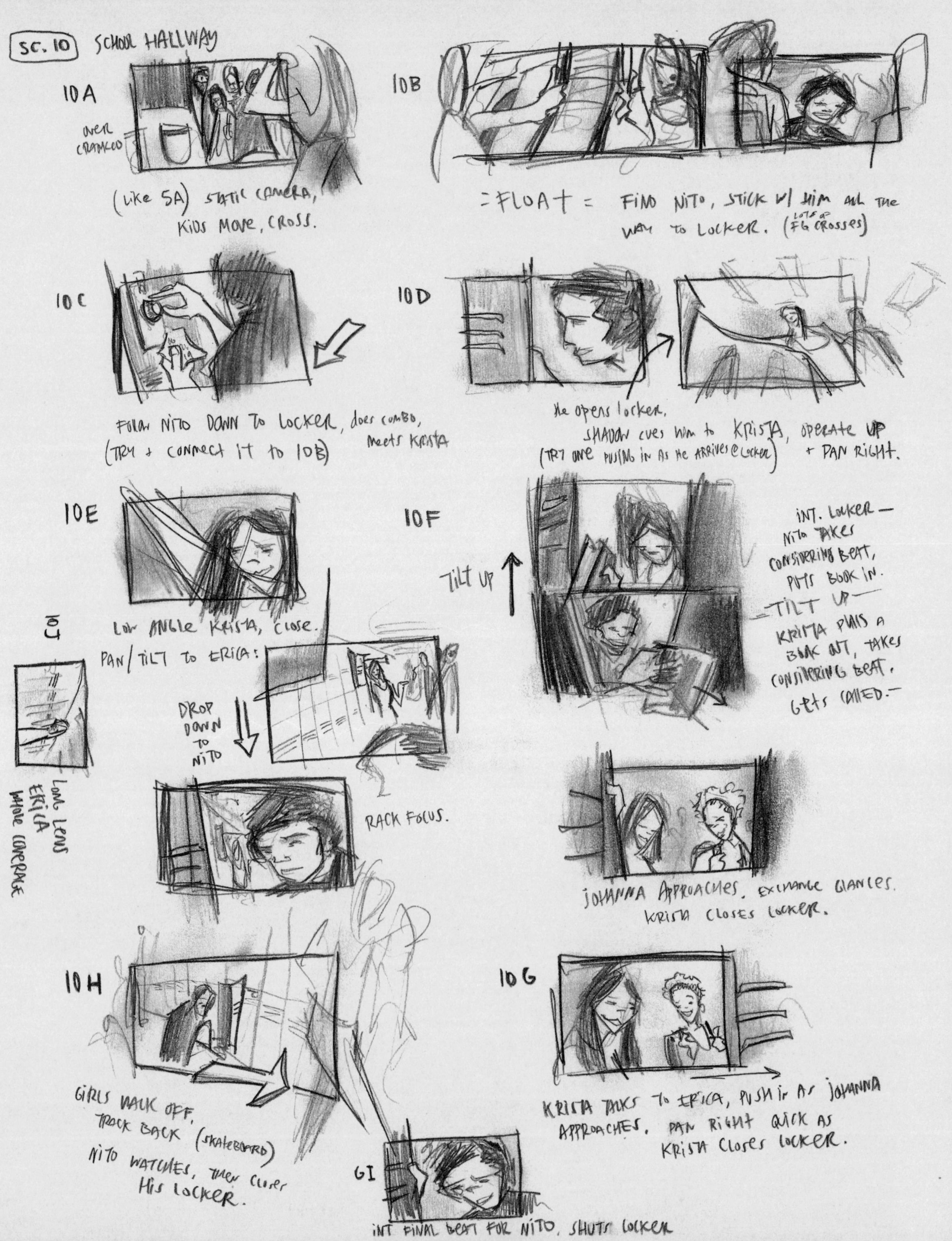

SC. 10   SCHOOL HALLWAY
10A
OVER CRAMCO
(like 5A) STATIC CAMERA, KIDS MOVE, CROSS.
10B
=FLOAT= FIND NITO, STICK W/ HIM ALL THE WAY TO LOCKER. (LOTS OF FG CROSSES)
10C
FOLLOW NITO DOWN TO LOCKER, does combo, meets KRISTA (TRY + CONNECT IT TO 10B)
10D
He opens locker.
SHADOW cues him to KRISTA, OPERATE UP + PAN RIGHT. (TRY ONE PUSHING IN AS HE ARRIVES @ LOCKER)
10E
LOW ANGLE KRISTA, CLOSE. PAN/TILT TO ERICA:
10F
TILT UP
INT. LOCKER— NITO TAKES CONSIDERING BEAT, PUTS BOOK IN. —TILT UP— KRISTA PULLS A BOOK OUT, TAKES CONSIDERING BEAT. GETS CALLED.
10J
LONG LENS ERICA INSERT COVERAGE
DROP DOWN TO NITO
RACK FOCUS.
JOHANNA APPROACHES. EXCHANGE GLANCES. KRISTA CLOSES LOCKER.
10H
GIRLS WALK OFF, TRACK BACK (SKATEBOARD) NITO WATCHES, THEN CLOSES HIS LOCKER.
10G
KRISTA TALKS TO ERICA, PUSH IN AS JOHANNA APPROACHES. PAN RIGHT QUICK AS KRISTA CLOSES LOCKER.
GI
INT FINAL BEAT FOR NITO, SHUTS LOCKER